SHAMANIC WISDOM MEETS
THE WESTERN MIND

BOOKS BY PETER FRITZ WALTER

CREATIVE-C LEARNING: THE INNOVATIVE KINDERGARTEN

TAO TE CHING (ENGLISH AND GERMAN TRANSLATIONS)

DAS DAO DER STAATSFÜHRUNG UND STRATEGIE (GERMAN)

ÉCRITS POÉTIQUES (FRENCH)

ESSAYS ON LAW, POLICY, AND PSYCHIATRY (14 VOLUMES)

EVIDENCE AND BURDEN OF PROOF IN SOVEREIGN IMMUNITY LITIGATION: A PROCEDURAL GUIDE FOR INTERNATIONAL LAWYERS AND GOVERNMENT COUNSEL (DOCTORAL THESIS)

GREAT MINDS SERIES (11 VOLUMES)

INTEGRATE YOUR EMOTIONS: A GUIDE TO EMOTIONAL WHOLENESS

LITIGATION PRACTICE AND BURDEN OF PROOF UNDER THE FOREIGN SOVEREIGN IMMUNITIES ACT, 1976: A PROCEDURAL GUIDE FOR INTERNATIONAL LAWYERS IN THE UNITED STATES AND CANADA

POETIC WRITINGS 1990-2010 (STORIES, PAMPHLETS, POEMS, ESSAYS)

POETISCHE SCHRIFTEN (GERMAN)

SCHOLARLY ARTICLES (21 VOLUMES)

SHAMANIC WISDOM MEETS THE WESTERN MIND

THE 12 ANGULAR POINTS OF SOCIAL JUSTICE AND PEACE

THE BETTER LIFE: TRANSFORMING YOURSELF FROM INSIDE OUT

THE ENERGY NATURE OF HUMAN EMOTIONS AND SEXUAL ATTRACTION: A SYSTEMIC ANALYSIS OF EMOTIONAL IDENTITY IN THE PROCESS OF THE HUMAN SEXUAL RESPONSE

THE LEADERSHIP I CHING: YOUR DAILY COMPANION FOR PRACTICAL GUIDANCE

THE NEW PARADIGM SERIES (BOOK REVIEWS, 3 VOLUMES)

THE VIBRANT NATURE OF LIFE: A SCIENCE-BASED PATHWAY FOR A BETTER, RICHER, AND MORE ABUNDANT LIFE

WALTER'S CAREER AND LEADERSHIP SERIES (3 VOLUMES)

SHAMANIC WISDOM MEETS THE WESTERN MIND

An Inquiry into the Nature of Shamanism

By Peter Fritz Walter

Published by Sirius-C Media Galaxy LLC

3511 Silverside Road, Suite 105, Wilmington, DE 19810, USA

Set in Palatino

Designed by Peter Fritz Walter

ISBN 978–1–150271–28–20

Publishing Categories
Psychology / Ethnopsychology

Publisher Contact Information
publisher@sirius-c-publishing.com
http://sirius-c-publishing.com

Author Contact Information
pfw@peterfritzwalter.com

About Dr. Peter Fritz Walter
http://peterfritzwalter.com

About the Author

Parallel to an international law career in Germany, Switzerland and the United States, Dr. Peter Fritz Walter (Pierre) focused upon fine art, cookery, astrology, musical performance, social sciences and humanities.

He started writing essays as an adolescent and received a high school award for creative writing and editorial work for the school magazine.

After finalizing his law diplomas, he graduated with an LL.M. in European Integration at Saarland University, Germany, in 1982, and with a Doctor of Law title from University of Geneva, Switzerland, in 1987.

He then took courses in psychology at the University of Geneva and interviewed a number of psychotherapists in Lausanne and Geneva, Switzerland. His interest was intensified through a hypnotherapy with an Ericksonian American hypnotherapist in Lausanne. This led him to the recovery and healing of his inner child.

After a second career as a corporate trainer and personal coach, Pierre retired in 2004 as a full-time writer, philosopher and consultant.

His nonfiction books emphasize a systemic, holistic, cross-cultural and interdisciplinary perspective, while his fiction works and short stories focus upon education, philosophy, perennial wisdom, and the poetic formulation of an integrative worldview.

Pierre is a German-French bilingual native speaker and writes English as his 4th language after German, Latin and French. He also reads source literature for his research works in Spanish, Italian, Portuguese, and Dutch. In addition, Pierre has notions of Thai, Khmer, Chinese, Japanese, and Vietnamese.

All of Pierre's books are hand-crafted and self-published, designed by the author. Pierre publishes via his Delaware company, Sirius-C Media Galaxy LLC, and under the imprints of IPUBLICA and SCM (Sirius-C Media).

To Alberto Villoldo and Jon Rasmussen, in deep appreciation of their achievements as western shamans and teachers of the ancient way of healing the luminous energy field, and their additional role as pioneers in facilitating psychosomatic healing that will once be an intrinsic part of modern medicine.

The author's profits from this book are being donated to charity.

Contents

Alberto Villoldo, A Western Shaman

You may be immensely clever, you may have encyclopedic knowledge, but if there is not the vitality of strong and deep feeling, your comprehension is like a flower that has no perfume.

—J. KRISHNAMURTI

Introduction

What is Shamanism?

Why should we learn anything about *shamanism*, the reader may ask, as it's after all an outlandish business, not grown in our culture, and barely affiliated with our traditional scientific method?

Another may argue that it's something laid away for 'wild, primitive peoples,' and still another may come up with: 'That may be normal and even necessary when you live in the forest, but not when you live in a civilized modern society.'

Yet, despite these reservations, not only is the interest in shamanism growing in modern society, but a number of people actually practice shamanic rituals without feeling estranged by their seeming archaic otherworldliness.

Many may have adopted shamanism as a lifestyle that has something *poetic* and soulful about it, speaking in a *metaphorical language* thereby giving soul to even the most ordinary things and behaviors in everyday life.

While shamanism has to be distinguished from *animism* and *paganism*, as we shall see further on, it is true for all natural religions that they affirm the ensouled nature of life, of trees, animals, lakes, planets—and humans.

And further, they see the unity of life rather than, as our science for the last four hundred years, a universe cluttered with unrelated things or objects. What attracts many people to shamanism rather than quantum physics is that our science, while it now acknowledges the existence of a *unified super-string field*, it is way more theoretical—and perhaps even soulless—than the shamanic method that deals with the 'spirits of nature.'

Shamanism researchers such as Terence McKenna or Ralph Metzner have recognized that when natives speak about spirits, they actually denote the unified field, the subtle energy that connects us all, and that pervades all, and which shamans know to use for their purposes.

I have myself done studies both on quantum physics and shamanism and therefore understand either point of view, or scientific point of departure. After several years of immersion in these matters, and having written several papers and books about both shamanism and quantum physics, I may say in public, without intending to offend anybody, that I find shamanism *more coherent, more accessible, more comprehensive, and even more human* than modern science, while I do believe that shamanism and quantum physics deal exactly with the same problems or scientific questions, and give exactly the same answers to them. The difference is the scientific methods that are used, and the different vocabulary to describe and evaluate the observations made.

This is of course but a work hypothesis, and I put it up for mere rhetoric reasons. I believe the reader is entitled to judge if what I am writing here has some common sense to it, or is mere speculation. It needs thorough research and a certain pragmatism to either verify or falsify my hypothesis.

In the present book, I am not going to even attempt doing this, and I might even not be qualified for it. So please take this statement here as an *obiter dictum* and let me proceed with finding out why shamanism is of real interest today for many people in modern international consumer culture.

I have actually talked to quite a few people about this subject and some were giving explanations along the lines of my theory. One person, let us call him Jim, said, for example:

> I am looking since long for an *integrative worldview* after all those philosophies that have only dissected life and have thereby divided people. I have found this unifying worldview with shamanism.

> I know that quantum physics comes essentially today to the same insights, but it formulates them in a bizarre manner, as if coded in a special language that is only accessible to insiders.

> I think shamanism has kept a streak of simplicity that makes it actually more credible, while quantum physics with its overall lack of transparence seems to paint life more complex than it actually is. When the details are complex, that doesn't mean we need to lose sight of the whole.

I found this statement dense and accurate, and it curiously reflects my own inner chatter and intuition over the years. Then I found Ralph Metzner's enlightening reader *Ayahuasca (1999)*, and was fascinated by the fact that Western shamans had received exactly the same insights and messages from the plant teachers, and had had the same kind of visions when taking the brew, as native shamans.

This was actually a very important information in that it disproves the often-voiced assumption that only natives could experience trance states that open the doors of perception, thereby relativizing such experience as 'merely cultural.'

In truth, many Western people have in the meantime had visionary experiences of the same kind or a similar kind; the LSD research done by Albert Hofmann who discovered the consciousness-altering effects of LSD in 1938, and the even more extended research on LSD by the psychiatrist Stanislav Grof showed with clear evidence that the mythological content of the collective unconscious is universal, not person-specific, and not culture-bound.

—See Albert Hofmann, LSD: My Problem Child (1980/2009) as well as Stanislav Grof, LSD: Doorway to the Numinous (2009) and Realms of the Human Unconscious: Observations from LSD Research (1976)

This in turn corroborates Carl Jung's earlier psychoanalytic research on the collective subconscious in an amazing way. Jung namely distinguished between culture-specific and universal content in our collective phantasmagory, but came to the conclusion that the cultural differences are minimal compared to the strength and boldness of the collective message in its universal, unifying character.

Now, here we speak about mythology, but I contend that shamanism is *more than mythology*, more than a poetic, soulful approach life, and the invisible world. It is that, too, certainly, but it is more than that. I contend that shamanism is a true science in that as with any other science, *observation* is its major focus and tool. Had I said 'speculation,' we would have to conclude that it's what we use to call 'philosophy,' and had I said that it's magic, we would have to conclude that it uses suggestions for healing.

Now, don't get me wrong. We all know that shamans also use suggestions for healing, and a whole pandorabox of actions to achieve their goals. But their approach is *not mythological*, and it's not merely art, not merely a technique. It is that also, but at the starting point, shamanism is a science because it observes nature, and this, in very meticulous detail.

Many people in our culture won't accept this *a priori* assumption because they believe science is only valid as a truth-delivering endeavor when it's set within the framework of a technological culture, where all is mechanized, and where science thus uses machines for the observation of nature, or for processing that observation. The best example here is perhaps quantum physics where physicists use gigantic particle accelerators.

One of the next generation electron accelerators will be the 40 km long *International Linear Collider*, planned to be constructed between 2015 and 2020, supposed to start with a collision energy of 500 billion electron volts, and could later be upgraded to 1000 billion electron volts.

The New York Times, February 8, 2007, writes about it with the headline 'Price of Next Big Thing in Physics: $6.7 Billion.' Another just completed particle accelerator is the *Large Hadron Collider* at CERN, outside of Geneva. 'That machine', writes Dennis Overbye, will be the world's most powerful (...), eventually colliding beams of protons with 7 trillion electron volts of energy apiece.'

This kind of research about the quantum field reminds me strangely of *vivisectionist medicine* that was searching the truth of life in the corpses of dead people. And I am wondering about the logic thinking abilities of scientists who are out to find the laws of life in the realm of death, instead of looking at living organisms. We have that behind us, for the most part, and systems research now fills this gap, but we still have the *mechanistic approach* around when it goes to find the truth about the subatomic world. Why do scientists have to demolish matter to find the truth about antimatter?

I am not a physicist so I leave the question open, as I would not be able to give a competent answer. But I do stay with the question and find it valid. It may one day open a door.

My intuition is that what in the subatomic world is called the unified field, super-string field, or Planck scale, is what the natives call the spirit world. The approach of the shaman to this world is both scientific and mythological. The shaman approaches spirits in a true quest of discovery; while this knowledge was traditionally an oral one, transmitted only from master to disciple, it is scientific in the sense that it is empirical and subject to revision. In addition, shamanic experiences, when set and setting are as much as possible identical, can be *duplicated and verified by researchers around the world*. Hence, they are not subjective emanations of the shaman's poetic soul reality, which would namely deprive them of the qualifier 'scientific.'

Terence McKenna wrote in *The Archaic Revival (1992)*:

> The anthropological literature always presents shamans as embedded in a tradition, but once one gets to know them they are always very sophisticated about what they are doing. They are the true phenomenologists of this world; they know plant chemistry, yet they call these energy fields 'spirits.' (Id., 45)

In the following paragraphs, for reasons of clarifications, I shall shortly review what is *not* shamanism.

Shamanism and Animism

It is important to distinguish shamanism from *animism* and *paganism, parapsychology, humanism,* and *theosophy.*

The shamanic quest is different from these conceptions of life, or approaches to life, or scientific methods; it is important to realize this difference, and it is in my view because of the large grey area around these notions that shamanism is often confounded with speculation, superstition, primitivism or worse, a sort of *entertainment.*

It is none of that. It is not related to Zen either or to Taoism; it is not a philosophy. It is, to repeat it, a science.

To begin with, *animism* which is connoted to the old Latin word *anima,* the living spirit, is an intelligent religious attitude that sees all of nature as spirited, alive and intelligent, as well as interconnected by some kind of *overarching soul.* Some use the notion 'ensouled' for the way animists tend to look at the world and life as a whole.

Animists believe that souls or spirits exist in animals, plants and other entities, in addition to humans. Animism may also attribute souls to natural phenomena, geographic features, and even manufactured objects.

However, the difference is that the animist is not a scientific thinker, while the shaman is. Typically, the animist thinker contemplates nature, while the shamans interrogates nature.

In other words, the animist sees nature as existential just like the shaman but stays with this *existential vision,* while the shaman goes beyond and enters into a direct dialogue with nature. When shamans say they have communicated with spirits, what they want to say is that they have been in touch with nature's intelligence, that they have been infused with natural energies, which in most cases are non-human forms of living that have their own vibrational code that comes over in their bioplasmatic irradiation or cell vibration.

The shaman, by letting his own cell vibration enter into resonance with the cell vibration of plants and animals, enters into a nonverbal and cross-species dialogue that can be highly revealing. When shamans do not get access to the energies they try to connect with, they search in a systematic manner for a way to achieve their goal.

The animist thinker does not typically become inventive to that point, and is generally not to that point pragmatically motivated. That is why animism while it's not a religion in the traditional sense, is often taken as a form of 'nature religion,' because it does not generally inquire into the composite nature of creation and the revelatory means that are at the disposition of a shaman.

Shamanism and Paganism

While there are certainly parallels between shamanism and *paganism*, the latter is a term which, from a Western perspective, has connotations to *spiritualistic, animistic, and shamanic* practices or *folk beliefs.* Thus it is a very wide notion, or antithesis to clerical, dogmatic or fundamentalist Christianity.

As such there is nothing even remotely scientific about it. Typical for pagan beliefs is that they are *polytheistic* and worship the spirits of nature. Paganism is typically a ritual and often *nothing but a ritual.* Contrast with that the systematic and pragmatic approach of the shaman, who is a phenomenologist, not a believer in rituals.

In addition, it has to be seen that today neopaganism has become much of a belief system on its own, with its dogma, which is often but an anti-dogma, and there is very little scientific attitude within the neopagan communities as to delivering truth. There is much of worship in paganism, among which goddess worship is perhaps the most well-known. But worship certainly is not a scientific methodological approach to life. The shaman is not a worshipper; he dialogues with spirit entities on an equal level.

It has to be seen also that the term 'pagan' is a Christian adaptation of the *gentile* of Judaism, and as such has an inherent Abrahamic bias, and pejorative connotations among Western monotheists, comparable to *heathen, infidel, mushrik* and *kafir* in Islam.

These negative connotations have precisely to do with the ritualistic and dogmatic stance in paganism, its almost ideological character. It has to be seen that this is a trait completely unknown to shamanism because who is active in shamanic communities is not the group, not the clan, not a herd of worshippers and grass hoppers, but the single shaman in his or her sacred solitude. Shamanism is a solitary experience.

I am particularly conscious of this because before I arrived in Ecuador for my voyage, I have been searching to participate in *Santo Daime* in Brazil which is a uniquely Brazilian spiritualist group ritual where Ayahuasca is ingested during dances, songs and incantations. But as I was not accepted in any one of these esoteric groups, I went, somewhat frustrated, directly to Ecuador, and recounted the experience to Esteban, the shaman, upon my arrival. He quietly and firmly replied to my little report:

—It is good that it did not work for you. I think you were guided. Ayahuasca is not to be ingested in a group setting, but only as a solitary journey. All Shuar shamans agree about this, and there are no exceptions to be made. The journey is a solitary one, the other rituals are mix-ups of various religious rituals, and as such they are *delusional*, not the way to gain real truth!

It is for this reason that ethnologists avoid the term paganism with its uncertain and varied meanings, when they refer to traditional or historic faiths, choosing more precise categories such as *polytheism, shamanism, pantheism* or *animism*. It also should be noted that the fact that neopaganism has its place today within popular culture and is currently gaining in popularity among the young, and with the fashion world, is certainly not conducive to its developing one day a systematic and scientific method toward apprehending reality. This method, however, has been developed by shamanism, as I am going to show in the first chapter.

Further shamanism must not be confounded with *parapsychology, humanism* or *theosophy*. Apart from the fact that shamanism has in common with parapsychology and theosophy that the latter are also scientific in their approach to reality, these sciences have their origin in the Western cultural world and tradition and cannot even remotely be conceived to operate within the shamanic set and setting. Let me explain this in more detail.

Shamanism and Humanism

To begin with, *humanism* is not a science, but an ethical quest, while this quest well affirms using science as a way to find truth.

Humanism is a broad category of ethical philosophies that affirm the dignity and worth of all people, based on the ability to determine right and wrong by appealing to universal human qualities, particularly rationality. It is a component of a variety of more specific philosophical systems and is incorporated into several religious schools of thought.

Humanism can be considered as a process by which truth and morality is sought through human investigation.

Focusing on the human capacity for self-determination, humanism rejects the validity of transcendental justifications, such as a dependence on belief without reason, the 'supernatural,' or texts of allegedly divine origin. Humanists endorse *universal morality* based on the commonality of the human condition, suggesting that solutions to human social and cultural problems cannot be parochial. Humanism rejects deference to supernatural beliefs in resolving human affairs but not necessarily the beliefs themselves.

According to the humanistic agenda, it is up to humans to find truth, as opposed to seeking it through revelation, mysticism, tradition, or anything else that is incompatible with the application of logic to the observable evidence. In demanding that humans avoid to blindly accept beliefs, it supports *scientific skepticism* and the scientific method, rejecting authoritarianism and extreme skepticism, and rendering faith an unacceptable basis for action.

The difference between science and humanism is that humanism is not a science; it only *points to science* as a possible truth-giver, and says that religious dogma, by contrast, is an impossible truth-giver.

As such, humanism is not a method by itself, but an appeal to ethical transparence and consistency. As a result, I conclude that science and shamanism can be compared because both use the scientific method, while they cannot compare with humanism as the latter is but an ethical quest or appeal to reason, not itself a scientific apparatus.

In addition it has to be seen that humanism is a concept that has grown on the soil of modern Western culture, and pretty much as an anti-reaction to Christian fundamentalism. As such it has no place in shamanic culture.

Shamanism and Parapsychology

Among the corner stones of my psychic research over the last twenty years were the extensive studies on spiritism, in general, and ectoplasms, in particular, by Swedenborg, Charles Richet and Baron von Schrenck-Notzing, as well as the meticulous research done at Stanford University on the medium Uri Geller.

While ectoplasm research was never really taken serious before the team Richet-Notzing did meticulous and pedantic research, with all precautions taken against fraud, it is until today a topic that is controversial. The researchers came to the result that the phenomena exhibited are not to be explained with anything known from traditional science. Most of their research was done with the famous medium Eusapia Palladino.

However, the study of energy phenomena in general has given me a clearer picture of what material ectoplasms could be made of. It seems that this substance is a fluid emanation of the bioplasmatic energy that I call *e-force* and that has been called *ch'i, ki, prana, mana, wakonda, shakti, libido, animal magnetism, odic force, universion* or *orgone* over the ages, an energy-information-field that is at the basis of all life and that permeates all, penetrates all and is a major information transmitter in the universe.

—See Peter Fritz Walter, The Vibrant Nature of Life: A Science-Based Pathway to a Better, Richer, and More Abundant Life (2017), The Better Life: Transforming Yourself from Inside Out (2014/2017), and The Energy Nature of Human Emotions and Sexual Attraction: A Systemic Analysis of Emotional Identity in the Process of the Human Sexual Response (2015/2017).

What a group of open-minded researchers such as Eliade, Harner, Schultes, Metzner, Gottlieb and McKenna did for shamanism, one man single-handedly achieved for the recognition of psychic research or parapsychology. This man is Dean Radin. Here is a quote from his book *The Conscious Universe: The Scientific Truth of Psychic Phenomena (1997):*

> When modern science began about three hundred years ago, one of the consequences of separating mind and matter was that science slowly lost its mind. This split became painfully obvious about seventy-five years ago when psychotherapy began to intensely embrace the value of personal experience and behaviorism began to intensely deny the value of personal experience.
>
> Parapsychology fits in this picture by straddling the edge separating the mind-oriented disciplines such as clinical and transpersonal psychology and the matter-oriented disciplines such as neuroscience and cognitive science. Parapsychology explicitly studies the interactions between consciousness and the physical

world. It assumes that downward causation exists in some form, and it assumes that scientific methods can be used to study this middle realm in a rigorous way.

Thus, the persistent controversy over psi can be traced back to the founding assumptions of modern science. These assumptions have led many scientists to believe that the mind is a machine, and as far as we can tell, machines don't have psi. The problem is that most of the classical assumptions that originally spawned the idea of mind-as-a-machine have dissolved in the wake of new discoveries. (Id., 263)

In my own research I soon found that ectoplasms were manifestations of dense bioenergy liberated by mediums in trance. This unique phenomenon, then, is at the root of an array of other research topics in parapsychology such as the materialization of ghosts and psychokinesis.

While psychic research is a very important and revelatory scientific approach to our higher human potential, it is entirely situated within the Western cultural setting and cannot be seriously compared with shamanism. This is so despite the fact that parapsychology also researches shamanism, but the opposite is not true. Shamanism doesn't need parapsychology for evidential backup of its scientific character. To see only that it is thousands of years older than the new science of *parapsychology* that actually only corroborates the perennial science tradition!

Shamanism and Theosophy

This argument is even more true with regard to Theosophy, which is but a *revival of millenary knowledge* that got lost in the last four hundred years of Cartesian reductionist madness.

Theosophy certainly learnt from shamanism. Shamanism has nothing to learn from Theosophy. It's that simple!

Shamanism and Taoism

If there is one teaching that can seriously be considered to have parallels with shamanism, it is Taoism, a philosophical school from ancient China. One of its foremost sources are the *Tao Te Ching*, by Lao-tzu.

—The character Tao 道 means path or way, but in Chinese religion and philosophy it has abstract meanings

Some of the foremost qualities that Taoism values are a non-biased mindset, acceptance of all-that-is, including the world, integration of all of our emotions, magnanimity, as well as patience and tolerance toward the uneducated majority of humans who are caught in innumerable projections due to their refusal to face what-is and their entanglement in possessions, status and time-bound concepts.

Lao-tzu is considered, together with Chuang-Tzu, as the primary representative of Taoism.

Taoism was defeated by violent patriarchy in the same way as its Western homologue, the truly systemic *All-Flows* philosophy if Heraclites, was defeated by the aggressive, polemic and judgmental Platonic and Aristotelian thought that became the basis of the dogmatism of the Christian Church.

I came in touch with Taoism for the first time in 1991, when I was reading the *Tao Te Ching* and the illuminating poetics of Chuang-Tzu, through which I was transformed. The peace and joy that filled me when reading these works of wisdom are not to describe with words—it was sheer bliss, an experience, by the way, that I have never had with reading the bloody stories of the Bible or the bloodless social and sexual policies of the Koran that forever will leave me appalled and depleted of energy.

I will once have to write a larger essay about this transformative experience. So far, I have written an analysis of the *dynamic life patterns* contained in the I Ching that may serve as an entry point for the interested reader.

—See Peter Fritz Walter, The Leadership I Ching: Your Daily Companion for Practical Guidance, 3rd Edition, 2017.

There is one point that I would like to mention here, and where Taoism and Christianity really clash wide apart.

It's the question of judgment, and of judgmentalism or *moralism*. One of the most salient characteristics of the three monolithic and theistic religions, Judaism, Islam and Christianity is that they are *judgmental*, and harshly divide life in black and white, good and bad, high and low, and so on and so forth.

Taoism really does the contrary. It finds unity and fosters growth as the *major overarching pattern of living* where the three major religions dissect, divide, split apart and fragment, and thus repress, regress and kill. It is not in any way judgmental; it simply is beyond any of these dualistic categories. It creates while traditional religions destroy, it is in favor of the young and free expression of emotions, where traditional religions *mutilate the young emotionally* and consider the free expression of emotions as a major sin. Thus, it is truly one with the Divine, while the major religions are truly one with the Devil.

But, to repeat it, Taoism is a philosophy or religion, not a science. Shamanism is.

Shamanism and Zen

Zen emphasizes *dharma practice* and experiential, practical, down-to-earth wisdom, particularly as realized in the form of meditation known as *zazen*, in the attainment of awakening.

As such, it de-emphasizes both theoretical knowledge and the study of religious texts in favor of direct, experiential realization.

The establishment of Chan (Zen) is traditionally credited to the Indian prince turned monk Bodhidharma.

The emergence of Chan as a distinct school of Buddhism was first documented in China in the 7th century.

From China, Chan subsequently spread southwards to Vietnam and eastwards to Korea and Japan. In the late 19th and early 20th centuries, Zen also began to establish a notable presence in North America and Europe.

I began with Zen meditation in 1991, and have done it ever since. In the beginning it was rather painful but down the road I realized that my body improved in many ways through the practice.

Zen is certainly important. It is a philosophy of life, a lifestyle even, a wisdom technique. *But it's not a science.*

We have here a striking similarity with animism, as I have already pointed it out. Both animism and Buddhism are contemplative in nature, that is, their regard upon nature is descriptive, and besides, meditative, in the sense that nature serves the Buddhist as a metaphor for life.

While the Buddhist view of nature is metaphorical, the shaman's view is realistic; it is not contemplative, but inquisitive. This is why it is at its very root scientific, while the Buddhist view is at its very root religious in the sense that contemplating the beauty and perfection of nature helps us to connect with our inner beauty and our inner perfection.

This is what I mean when I say Buddhists see nature as a metaphor. Generally speaking, the spiritual view of life takes nature, and the paradoxical and unfathomable in nature, as a *metaphor for the divine,* for the unspeakable, for the unknown. This is also the Taoist view of nature that is deeply spiritual in the sense that the deepest ground of verity in humans is derived, metaphorically from the complexity that is inherent in nature, and in living systems.

Shamanism's Model Function

What I would term the 'model function' of shamanism is perhaps the most important element in the slow but definite migration of knowledge that roughly since about a century is taking place; it will hopefully result in modern science integrating the millenary wisdom about life that it has formerly ruthlessly discarded out, first through the ecclesiastical, and then through the Cartesian blindfolding of scientific reality.

We always need models, a mold where we can go back to when we lose track, a map that shows the territory, while it's essential to not take the map for the territory.

That we have Western shamans now, men like Michael Harner, Alberto Villoldo or Jon Rasmussen is certainly a good start, but it would probably be hubristic at that point to talk about an *integration of shamanic knowledge* into our own scientific thinking and doing. We are not yet there.

We are at the pioneer level, at best, in the starting holes of a new adventure that may lead us very far, and at the same time far back into *our own perennial science traditions* that were, all of them, holistic, before they were dissected and ostracized, declared heresy, and, later on discarded out from science as 'vitalistic theories' or 'superstitious beliefs.'

Not long ago shamanic science was still taken for a pathology of the senses, 'psychotic delusions,' or a 'schizophrenic perception' of reality.

—See, for example, Mircea Eliade, Shamanism (1964), Piers Vitebsky, Shamanism (2001), Ralph Metzner (Ed.), Ayahuasca (1999), Michael Harner, Ways of the Shaman (1990), Jeremy Narby, The Cosmic Serpent (1999), Richard E. Schultes et al., Plants of the Gods (2002), Terence McKenna, The Invisible Landscape (1994), True Hallucinations (1998), The Archaic Revival (1992), Food of the Gods (1993), Robert Forte (Ed.), Entheogens and the Future of Religion (2000), Luis Eduardo Luna, Pablo Amaringo, Ayahuasca Visions (1999), Adam Gottlieb, Peyote and Other Psychoactive Cacti (1997), Aldous Huxley, The Doors of Perception and Heaven and Hell (1954), Rick Strassman, DMT: The Spirit Molecule (2001), Josep M. Fericla, Al trasluz de la Ayahuasca (2002).

Similarly clear-cut judgments were applied to another human sensory ability that exists within our own culture, but was always considered an *aberration of the senses.* I am speaking of *synesthetic perception,* described by Merleau-Ponty in *Phenomenology of Perception (1945/1995).* Alberto Villoldo considers synesthetic perception as the rule, and was confirmed in his intuition by what he saw and experienced over more than twenty years with the Laika and other native peoples he encountered. He writes in *Shaman, Healer, Sage (2000):*

As the philosopher Maurice Merleau-Ponty wrote in Phenomenology of Perception, 'Synesthetic perception is the rule, and we are unaware of it only because scientific

34

knowledge shifts the center of gravity of experience, so that we have unlearned how to see, hear, and generally speaking, feel, in order to deduce, from our bodily organization, the world as the physicist conceives it, what we are to see, hear and feel.' Synesthesia grows as we bring awareness to touch, taste, sensation, and sound. One of my favorite synesthesia exercises involves 'tasting' your emotions. Become aware of the taste in your mouth. Is it sweet? Sour? Woody? Metallic? Now recall an incident that made you feel sad. Notice if the taste in your mouth changes. Recall a pleasurable situation, and notice again how the taste in your mouth changes. (Id., 116)

While synesthetic perception is known to be a characteristic many genially gifted people possess, to name here only the famous composers *Alexander Scriabin* and *Olivier Messiaen*, where the feat is well-documented, it has never received sufficient attention in our mainstream culture.

Chapter One

The Shamanic Method

Common Assumptions

The first real science humanity has developed, it has developed not under the pulpit of scientists, but of native shamans. This is my proposition.

Of course, when I assume that shamanism is a science, I must be able to show that it uses a method, a scientific methodology, that is, a set of tools that serve to look at nature in a truthful and possibly objective manner. Is that the case with shamanism?

Let us look at the literature first. Most authors' assessment of shamanism coincides with saying that it is a way of apprehending reality, a set of insightful techniques, rituals and patterns, as well as a natural and organic lifestyle centered not at dominating nature or cosmos, but at participating in and understanding nature and the cosmos.

Stanley Krippner and Alberto Villoldo, in their study *Healing States (1984)*, define shamanism as 'an attitude, a discipline, and a state of mind that emphasizes the loving care and concern of oneself, one's family, one's community, and one's environment.' (Id., 85)

Most authors agree with this view, in that the shaman is having a *regulatory function within tribal society,* for bringing inner peace and healing to the clan or the whole of the tribe. But this is not his only function. This quote also does not give flesh to my theory that shamanism is essentially a science, even though this science is used for doing good to people, for healing or for divining future events.

What I am saying is that the shamanic method or technique is not just a fancy ritual, not just an experience of ecstasy, but essentially, a *scientific investigation* into the nature of things, the nature of the cosmos, and the role that the human being plays within this cosmos.

Most authors also agree that the most important to find out about shamanism is its *use of entheogens.*

These are plants that contain psychoactive compounds, such as DMT, which, when taken at appropriate doses, produce a consciousness-altering effect upon our psyche and perception. There are various names for such plants, and the name that is given often reflects the state of mind of the researcher.

Mircea Eliade states in his book *Shamanism: Ancient Techniques of Ecstasy (1972)* that any given shamanic culture was at its decline or caught in decadence when their shamans began to use psychedelics for the shamanic voyage.

However, it has to be noted that today this opinion is clearly contradicted by the large majority of researchers, such as for example Metzner, Harner, Gottlieb, Schultes, Hofmann, Rätsch or McKenna who agree in considering Eliade's bias here as a myopic view and a basic misconception about shamanism. For example, contrasting with this view, Terence McKenna writes in *The Archaic Revival (1992)*:

> While Eliade asserts that the use of narcotic substances as an aid to ecstasy invariably indicates a decadence or vulgarization of the shamanic tradition, there is reason to doubt this. (Id., 15)

The shaman typically is one who stands out because of his unique capability to explore, and travel into different realities and levels of consciousness.

The second point where researchers largely coincide in their opinions is that shamanism cannot be defined under the exclusion of entheogens.

While there are methods to alter consciousness without plants, using esoteric breathing techniques, body postures or ecstatic dance, drumming, prayer, fasting and other techniques, researchers agree that from a point of view of effectiveness there is a large gap between those latter techniques, and the use of entheogenic compounds. Entheogens are *several hundreds of percent more effective* than non-plant based methods.

Several researchers have seriously tackled the question why this is so, and one of the most persisting on this specific point was Terence McKenna. In *Archaic Revival (1992)*, he affirms that entheogenic plants contain the very essential genetic code, the basic information about the evolution of life on earth, and that for this reason the ingestion of the psychoactive compounds they contain leads to an immediate *opening of consciousness*, which was something much broader and more intelligent to experience than mere colorful visions.

Anthropologists who try to understand the phenomenon of shamanism and reduce the entheogenic experience to a mere social game, a distraction or a search for some kind of nirvana are deeply misled. When I say shamanism is a science—actually the first science humanity used for reality assessment—I go even beyond the visionary message of McKenna, and Eliade's assumption that shamanism was merely a set of techniques for achieving ecstasy.

It is therefore not surprising that most anthropologists, and especially those who really do not understand shamanic culture, tend to use expressions such as hallucinogens, narcotic drugs, narcotics or psychedelics when talking about entheogens.

Apart the fact that these plants are not narcotics, because a narcotic drug, such as for example opium, renders somnolent but does not alter consciousness, the important thing to know is that entheogens are not understood, in shamanistic cultures, as leisure drugs, but really are considered as assets of the religious and numinous experience.

That is why the only expression that comes close to the shamanistic mindset is the term *entheogens*, facilitators for getting in touch with the inner god. It has been found that entheogens, apart from their helping us to reach the inner mind, also dissolve habits such as alcoholism, and generally help in a process of social deconditioning. In clear text, entheogens help us lift the veil of the normative behavior code in any given society as they show us options of *different behavior*. They actually show us the *immanent potentiality* in all of nature's setup, and especially in how nature has setup the human being as a basically free creature, who is not a priori bounded by a preset program.

What we can thus learn from taking these plants as a sort of 'social medicine' is to recognize the patterns of *normative behavior* we are caught in and that obstruct our creativity and self-realization.

People who are socially oppressed, racial, ethnic, religious or sexual minorities, may want to inquire into the possible dissolution of rigid behavioral rules and oppressive normative standards in society. They may thus look for the ultimately most intelligent catalyzer that exists to see *all the options reality offers* and, as a result, might want to engage in a consciousness-opening voyage.

The human soul expresses its originality in paradoxes and sometimes in extreme behavior and the very attempt to classify human behavior into rigid 'standards for all' is in itself an ideology, or political program. The more a given society puts up general standards, the more it is alienated from life and its creative roots and the more it is subject to decay and devolution.

This being said, there is agreement among researchers that shamanism is an effective guidepost for revisiting the realm of nature's wisdom and true connectedness with all-that-is.

As far as I can see, people caught in minority groupings and the social fight involved with minority lobbying hardly ever come up with beyond-the-fence solutions such as experiencing entheogens, which makes the extreme poverty of many of those movements, not to say their ultimate system-obedience.

This system-obedience can be seen in many a limitation that social activists impose upon themselves and that are, ultimately, still system-prone. As Krishnamurti said, repeating an old wisdom: the revolt is still within the same frame of mind as the society it revolts against.

The entheogenic quest is therefore an *inner quest*, not necessarily something like a defeatist approach on a social level, but certainly an important add-on to any social activism for any possible social or humanitarian cause.

The Detractors of Shamanism

The detractors of shamanism were the Enlightenment, Cartesianism, Reductionism and Catholicism. Let me point this out in more detail. It is perhaps the most putatively known fact that missionaries had a particular grip on native peoples, and their shamanic rituals, as the Church considered such practices as 'devil's domain.'

It is for this reason not surprising that colonialism together with missionarism was doing harm to shamanism, in many parts of the world. This was direct physical harm, that often resulted in malady or death of the concerned native populations.

That is today standard school knowledge. It is however less known how Cartesian reductionist science, which was a fruit of the rationalistic thoughts of the Enlightenment, was largely prohibiting knowledge about shamanism to percolate into Western society and culture. Here the effect and the harm done was not direct and physical, but indirect. It was something like intellectual or scientific racism.

Ethnology, psychiatry and certain branches of psychoanalysis were initially treating native shamanic wisdom as 'primitive' or 'barbarous' practices. Shamanism was not considered to effect valid healing of disease, but fake healing, or 'magic;' and even less was it considered to be a science.

THE AGE OF ENLIGHTENMENT

The spook of *rationalism* began in the second half of the 17th century, which is not surprisingly also the time when two other large movements started out, industrialization and child protection. This rationalist streak in human philosophy advocated so-called 'Reason' as a means to establishing an authoritative system of aesthetics, ethics, government, and logic that would allow human beings to obtain pretendedly 'objective truth' about the universe.

I simply call it the *Age of Darkness* because it is now firmly established by both quantum physics and systems theory that the values of the Age of Enlightenment were bringing us widespread intellectual and emotional narrow-mindedness, rampant functional disease, spiritual confusion, fragmentation, racism and worldwide ecological destruction. The typical concern for the enlightenment was mechanics; so was its understanding of the world, that is, as a gigantic clockwork.

Most of the intellectual avant-garde today agrees with this critical view, as for example Fritjof Capra, one of the greatest exponents of today's intellectual elite; many further references and other authors are to be found in Capra's books.

> —See, for example, Fritjof Capra, The Tao of Physics (1975), The Turning Point (1987), The Web of Life (1996), The Hidden Connections (2002), Steering Business Toward Sustainability (1995). There are many further references in all of Capra's books.

All that didn't fit in the mindset of those total rationalists was *ruthlessly discarded out* and labeled as 'mysticism,' 'paranoid delusions,' 'freakish daydreaming' or 'charlatanism.'

The sciences that were particularly hit by this myopic paradigm were parapsychology, shamanism and astrology.

It is interesting to see that today adherents of this outdated and judgmental paradigm are to be found in the rings of mechanistic science and skepticism. An example is the fight of Randall James Hamilton Zwinge alias *James Randi* against so-called pseudoscience, and his personal fight against Uri Geller, a medium who was tested by Stanford University and found not to be a fraud.

For James Randi, Goethe's 'school wisdom' theorem literally applies that says that what mustn't be, cannot be.

CARTESIAN SCIENCE

The Cartesian or Newtonian worldview is a life and science philosophy marked by left-brainism, a hypertrophy of deductive and logical thinking to the detriment of the qualities of the right brain such as *associative and imaginative thinking,* and generally fantasy.

It's also a worldview that generally tends to disregard or deny dreams and dreaming, extrasensorial perception and ESP faculties as well as genuine spirituality. The term *Cartesian* has been coined to mark a similarity in reasoning with the reductionist philosophical theories of the French philosopher René Descartes (1596-1650). Historically, and philosophically, it was not Descartes who came up first in world history with this schizoid worldview, but the so-called *Eleatic School*, a philosophical movement in ancient Greece that opposed the holistic and organic worldview represented by Heraclites; but it was through the Cartesian affirmation and pseudo-scientific corroboration of the ancient Eleatic dualism that in the history of Western science, the left-brained reductionist approach to reality, which is actually a fallacy of perception, became the dominant science paradigm. Fritjof Capra, in his bestselling book *The Tao of Physics (1975/2000)*, observes:

> The birth of modern science was preceded and accompanied by a development of philosophical thought which led to an extreme formulation of the spirit/matter dualism. This formulation appeared in the seventeenth century in the philosophy of René Descartes who based his view of nature on a fundamental division into two separate and independent realms: that of mind (res cogitans), and that of matter (res extensa). The 'Cartesian' division allowed scientists to treat matter as dead and completely separate from themselves, and to see the material world as a multitude of different objects assembled into a huge machine. (Id., 8)

Presently, even mainstream science gurus declare Cartesianism to be obsoleted and overruled by the new physics and the emerging holistic science paradigm that is presently breaking through as a preparation for a completely new worldview in the West, while in Eastern culture this organic, holistic worldview was always the prevailing one.

Quantum physics has demolished the classical Newtonian worldview with its strict determinism. As Fritjof Capra concludes, a careful observation of subatomic particles shows that these particles give meaning only when seen not as isolated entities, but when understood as interconnections between the preparation of an experiment and the subsequent measurement.

Quantum physics reveals a basic oneness of the universe at least at a subatomic level of observation, which is exactly what perennial science and mystical traditions of the East and West always have assumed as the main characteristic of reality.

In his second bestselling book, *The Turning Point (1987)*, Fritjof Capra then concludes this insight and extrapolates it beyond the realm of physics:

> In contrast to the mechanistic Cartesian view of the world, the world view emerging from modern physics can be characterized by words like organic, holistic, and ecological, It might also be called a systems view, in the sense of general systems theory. The universe is no longer seen as a machine, made up of a multitude of objects, but has to be pictured as one indivisible dynamic whole whose parts are essentially interrelated and can be understood only as patterns of a cosmic process. (Id., 66)

Thus we can conclude that Cartesianism, which is actually rooted in ancient Greece and became the dominator science paradigm for about four hundred years, was hostile to shamanism, declaring shamans to be either psychotic and delusional, or to be charlatans. It has to be seen that the power of the Church in suppressing and rooting out shamanic cultures all over the world was backed up by science, by natural science, by psychiatry and by 'colonial' ethnology.

To see the holocaust committed against native peoples only as religious fanaticism overlooks the much more important fact that this fanaticism was largely backed by 'rational' science.

REDUCTIONISM

Reductionism is a typical modern-day phenomenon. It is something like a thinking habit that results from a hypertrophy of the left brain. Historically it has taken root with the French philosophers René Descartes (1596-1650) and La Mettrie (1709-1751) who were considering humans as machines and nature as a complex yet entirely mechanical machinery.

Thus, the nature of complex things is reduced to the nature of sums of simpler or more fundamental things.

This can be said of objects, phenomena, explanations, theories, and meanings.

More and more, with a holistic view of the universe as it is emerging from about the 1980s, the mechanical reductionism of Darwinian evolutionary psychology is overcome and science presently changes many of its fundamental paradigms because of this shift in understanding nature, human nature and the cosmos at large.

Let me give a few typical examples for reductionism in scientific texts and popular imaging. For example, it is written by Rupert Sheldrake in his book *A New Science of Life (1995)* that the old idea of a cosmic life energy, life force or vital energy was but a 'vitalistic theory.'

What Sheldrake means is that there is no such cosmic life energy, and he thus was reducing the whole idea of a cosmic energy to the term 'vitalism.'

It has to be seen that often in science and also in political scripts and writings, reductionism is used for belittling, or outright downplaying important concepts and phenomena of life, thereby manipulating public opinion. A reductionist argument against shamanism would be the affirmation that shamanism 'is but a set of wild rituals that put primitive peoples in a state of trance, in which they do all kinds of things they wouldn't do when they are sober.'

Typically, reductionists would deny shamans to be real healers and to have a *scientific approach* to knowledge gathering. They would downplay shamanism as a 'barbarous ritual' that 'may appeal to primitives but is to be rejected by civilized society.'

Catholicism

While Catholicism has ravaged shamanic cultures, especially in South America, and as a result of the *Conquista*, it could have had a better understanding of the shamanic quest because, after all, the esoteric Christian tradition is highly 'shamanic' in the sense that it values the inner experience over the outer ritual.

> —See, for example Thomas Moore, Care of the Soul (1994), Michael Talbot, The Holographic Universe (1992) and Michael Murphy, The Future of the Body (1992), Part 2, (21) and (22), 464-527.

However, just as with Buddhism, this inner quest for enlightenment is not scientific in nature, but contemplative. There are many phenomena that saints produce, for the most part involuntarily, such as stigmata, that cannot be rationally or scientifically explained.

> —See Michael Talbot, The Holographic Universe (1992), Part 2 (5), 119 ff., Michael Murphy, The Future of the Body (1992), Part 2 (21), 464 ff.

It is for this reason lesser a problem of an inner contradiction between the Christian dogma and shamanism, but a general problem of *power*, and power politics, with all organized forms of religion.

The same inner congruence but split on the outside level is to be seen in Islam, between the official dogma and the Sufi tradition. It is important to see that in most shamanic cultures, such as Siberia, or South America, there are religions in place that are neither in contradiction to shamanism, nor are they in any way in alignment with it.

Interestingly, shamans, when questioned if shamanism was a religion, tend to answer that it had nothing to do with organized religion but that the inner quest, the quest for real knowledge was a form of true *religio*, in the sense that it brings us closer to our inner god, and thereby, in a condition of cosmic alignment.

It is in this sense that shamans use *entheogens*, which is why these plants or compounds have been called that way —that is, inner god plants.

—See Piers Vitebsky, The Shaman (1995/2001).

Again, as with the other detractors of shamanism I discussed here, we see that shamanism stands out not because of an inherent conflict between shamanism and religion, but because the shamanic quest is scientific, religious and *teleological* at the same time.

The latter element is important, for it makes exactly the divide with the purely contemplative or existential quest that is at the basis of esoteric religious traditions. If I was to compare shamanism with any other ancient science tradition, I can only think of *alchemy*.

The particularly destructive thrust that Catholicism is to be reproached regarding shamanic cultures, and shamanism in general, is that the Church preached that *non-believers had no soul*, that they were soulless and accordingly, were lacking the essential quality of being human. That was of course a hubristic view that is today largely contradicted even within Church circles. In fact, both the esoteric Christian tradition and the shamanic tradition deal with what they call 'loss of soul.'

—See, for example, Alberto Villoldo, Mending The Past And Healing The Future with Soul Retrieval (2005)

The Shamanic Revival

The shamanic revival may coincide with the publishing of Terence McKenna's book *The Archaic Revival (1992),* but it actually began in the 1970s. To understand the turning of the tide, let us consider the first honest information sources about shamanism that penetrated in the West, and that date back to the 1920s. It was the writings of anthropologist Bronislaw Malinowski (1884-1942), ethnologist Margaret Mead (1901-1978), and the writings of Sigmund Freud (1856-1939) and Carl-Gustav Jung (1875-1961).

Before I come to summarize these early glimpses into shamanic culture and lifestyle, let me give an example for the level of semantic confusion that reigned until very recently in this field of research, since exactly the time that I would qualify as the 'early colonial adaptation of shamanism to the reductionist mindset of Western researchers.'

The example is taken from the article *Lévi-Strauss on Shamanism,* by Jerome Neu, published in Andrei A.

Znamenski's reader *Shamanism: Critical Concepts in Sociology (2004)*. The author observes:

> Lévi-Strauss actually speaks of the sorcerer abreacting for the silent patient (p. 183), which is without sense in psychoanalytic terms. And again, he does not explain why symbolic thoughts should provide a lever for producing physiological changes, except that the thoughts run 'parallel' to the physiology. But do they? If they did, would that *explain* anything? (Id., 314)

This is a striking example of a gigantic misunderstanding. First of all, the author here criticizes Lévi-Strauss for observations he has made, and thus as a mere messenger of a phenomenon neither Strauss nor the author seemed to understand.

Second, it is true that the shaman effects changes in the physiology of the patient by performing acts on himself, or within his own spiritual oversoul, instead of the patient doing anything about them, or taking any remedy against them. This is about the most important fundamental difference between shamanic healing and the healing concepts in larger dominator civilizations. It has been pointed out clearly and with much detail in a study by Sabine Hargous, *Les appeleurs d'âmes (1985)*. In addition, a quote from Terence McKenna's book *Food of the Gods (1993)* leaves no doubt that shamanic healing uses what we today know as the quantum field or quantum interconnectedness for effecting healing:

Usually, if drugs are used, the shaman, not the patient, will take the drug. The motivation is also entirely different. The plants used by the shaman are not intended to stimulate the immune system or the body's other natural defenses against disease. Rather, the shamanic plants allow the healer to journey into an invisible realm in which the causality of the ordinary world is replaced with the rationale of natural magic. In this realm, language, ideas, and meaning have greater power than cause and effect. Sympathies, resonances, intentions, and personal will are linguistically magnified through poetic rhetoric. The imagination is invoked and sometimes its forms are beheld visibly. Within the magical mind-set of the shaman, the ordinary connections of the world and what we call natural laws are deemphasized or ignored. (Id., 6)

It doesn't actually surprise me that the psychoanalytic framework is used to deny shamanism its intrinsic scientific novelty, when compared to traditional physics.

Psychoanalysis at no point in time was a science, but represents a *collection of myths* that ultimately were forged and are upheld for providing a pseudoscientific and ideological roof structure for modern consumer reality.

Terence McKenna has anticipated this scientific novelty while he explains the fact of the co-emergence of healing both in the healer's and the patient's organisms in poetic rather than scientific terms. But his language is accurate in that the unified field is indeed 'an invisible realm in which the causality of the ordinary world is replaced with the rationale of natural magic.' The same is true for the last sentence of this quote, where he says that within the magical mindset of the shaman, 'the ordinary connections of the world and what we call natural laws are deemphasized or ignored.'

The truth is that indeed on the subatomic or quantum level of reality, these natural laws that we know from Newtonian physics are invalid.

Regarding the vocabulary McKenna uses, I can only refer to the old truth that humans consider as 'magic' all they don't really (yet) understand.

Had McKenna anticipated cutting-edge research on the unified field, he would probably have used a scientific instead of a poetic vocabulary to express this truth.

SIGMUND FREUD

I am at pains to qualify Freud's opinions and speculations about tribal cultures in any even remotely positive way. What Freud writes in *Totem and Tabu* (1913) about the 'primitive' Australian aborigines will not lead the interested reader to a comprehensive grasp of shamanism.

In keeping with Freud's personal style, not to say his personal obsession, he uses examples mostly from the Australian Aborigines, gathered and discussed by anthropologist James George Frazer.

In his first essay, entitled 'The Horror of Incest,' Freud points out, with some surprise, that although the

Aborigines do not seem to have any sexual restrictions, they exhibit an elaborate social organization whose sole purpose is to prevent incestuous sexual relations.

In the second essay, 'Taboo and Emotional Ambivalence,' Freud considers the relationship between taboos and totemism, using his concepts of 'projection' and 'ambivalence' developed in his work with neurotic patients, concluding, somewhat precipitously, that 'primitive peoples' feel ambivalent about most people in their lives, but will not admit it to themselves.

In the third essay, 'Animism, Magic and the Omnipotence of Thought,' Freud draws another parallel between primitives and, this time, *early libidinal development.* He asserts there is a belief in magic and sorcery that derives from an overvaluation of psychical acts whereby the structural conditions of mind are transposed onto the world: this overvaluation, he sees in both primitive men and neurotics, concluding that the animistic mode of thinking is governed by an 'omnipotence of thoughts,' a projection of inner mental life onto the external world. This imaginary construction of reality is also discernible in *obsessive thinking, delusional disorders and phobias.* Freud comments that the omnipotence of thoughts has been retained in the magical realm of art.

In the final essay, 'The Return of Totemism in Childhood,' Freud argues that combining one of Charles Darwin's more speculative theories about the arrangements of early human societies, Freud located the beginnings of the Oedipus complex at the origins of human society, and postulated that all religion was in effect an extended and collective form of guilt and ambivalence to cope with the killing of the father figure (which he saw as the true original sin).

It is almost incredible how today anybody can invoke Freud as a cultural or psychiatric innovator, as what he was standing for is simply nihilism and a total ignorance in front of the primacy of spirit over matter that aboriginals do know about since millennia. That neurotics in their confusion sense something true is not surprising, but obviously Freud was not up to match their level of evolution.

He was on a level below 'primitives' and 'neurotics,' ignoring about everything about spiritual laws, stating literal nonsense in most of his books and theories, which, to make it worse, were adopted as eternal truth by subsequent generations of psychoanalysts and even lay people.

More is not needed actually to understand to what point our culture is 'intuitively ignorant' to a point it begins to border ridicule; for otherwise, none of Freud's arrogant assumptions that have no backup even in common sense would never have been adopted as bearing any ontological value.

Bronislaw Malinowski and Margaret Mead

As early as in 1929, Malinowski published his report on the sexual life of the Trobriands in which he draws the reader's attention particularly to the *sexual life of children and adolescents.*

> —See, for example, Susanne Cho, Kindheit und Sexualität im Wandel der Kulturgeschichte (1983); Larry L. & Joan M. Constantine, Treasures of the Island (1976) and Where are the Kids? Children in Alternative Life-Styles (1977) as well as Richard L. Currier, Juvenile Sexuality in Global Perspective, in: Children & Sex: New Findings, New Perspectives (1981) and Floyd Martinson, Sexual Knowledge (1966), Infant and Child Sexuality (1973), The Quality of Adolescent Experiences (1974), The Child and the Family (1980), The Sex Education of Young Children (1981), The Sexual Life of Children (1994) and Children and Sex, Part II: Childhood Sexuality (1994).

Malinowski observed, not without surprise, high sexual permissiveness toward children's free sexual play.

More generally, he noted the total absence of a morality that condemns sexuality in children. Instead, he observed, children engage in free sexual play from early age.

> —Bronislaw Malinowski, The Sexual Life of Savages in North West Melanesia (1929) and Sex and Repression in Savage Society (1927).

Initiatory rites, he found, were absent with the Trobriands since children were initiated from about three years onwards, generally by older children, in all forms of sexual play. This play is completely nonviolent and includes, with the older children, coitus.

The most interesting finding for Malinowski was that in this culture violence was as good as non-existing and that there were equally as good as no sexual dysfunctions.

Trobriands were found to be ideal marriage partners and divorce is a rare exception. Violent crimes are non-existent and incest strongly tabooed and inhibited by social norms.

Other researchers found similar phenomena with the Muria tribe in South India where children stay until their maturity in so-called ghotuls where they live their sexuality freely and in utter promiscuity. Older children initiate younger ones progressively into sexual play.

—V. Elwin, The Muria and their Ghotul (1947), Richard Currier, Juvenile Sexuality in Global Perspective (1981), 9 ff.

These researchers found that after a phase of promiscuity, children, from the age of sexual maturity, form strong bonds and partnerships that are based not on sexual attraction, but on love. They further found that these first steady relationships formed the basis for later marriages that, regularly, last life-long.

This field research conducted by Malinowski and Margaret Mead, while it is certainly of high importance for sexology, cognitive psychology and research on emotions, has not given any information about shamanism.

—Margaret Mead, Sex and Temperament in Three Primitive Societies (1935).

This is simply so and my remark is in no way a value judgment. Their research was not intended to provide information on shamanic culture and lifestyle. But it is quite uncanny to see that before researchers came up with looking at native peoples' spiritual life, they were looking at their sexual life. I guess it says more about the typical obsession of the observers than the subjects observed! And the parallel with Freud's early regard upon aboriginal culture is obvious and not coincidental.

What does this mean?

It means that what quantum physics says is really true, and also on a practical level: the observer is always entangled with the object of observation. When researchers focus on sexuality and physical reality, they will see emerging sexual properties, when they focus on spirituality and metaphysical reality, the will see emerging spiritual or religious properties.

Both Malinowski and Freud were focused on the former, Jung was focused on the latter. All of them were one-sided in a way, considering a partial spectrum of life, not life in its holistic total quality, as shamanism does.

CARL-GUSTAV JUNG

Carl Jung was not a representative of psychoanalysis because he was *different*, so different that I say he was a shaman himself! And I am not the only one who says this.

C. Michael Smith writes in *Jung and Shamanism in Dialogue (2007)* that Jung, during the time of the break with

Freud, his mentor and father figure, became seriously depressed and close to psychosis, which led to as it were his shamanic initiation. The author writes:

> Shamanically speaking, soul loss has traditionally been associated not only with a loss of will, such as we find in depression, or with a loss of vital powers, such as we find in pathological dissociation, but also with a loss of connection to community, to the social sphere. In soul loss, one may be so lost in the 'realm of imagination', in altered states of consciousness, that there is little relatedness to the outer world. In this respect, Jung must have felt very 'lost' indeed.
>
> He heard voices, had visions, dreamt of rivers of blood, talked with spirits as he walked in his garden. He was so absorbed in the altered states of consciousness associated with psychotic, mystic, and shamanic realms that he had to remind himself that he was a doctor, a really existing person with a family, patients, and responsibilities.
>
> During the shamanic initiatory crisis, the initiant has available ritual elders, master shamans to whom he or she can go to guide / and safely contain the transformative process. The wounded healer learns to heal himself or herself partly through the encounter with the spirits, and partly under the necessary structuration and guidance of the ritual elders. Jung had no ritual elder, no analyst to help him sort through and understand the emerging material, and no professional therapeutic containing vessel was available. (Id., 82-83)

From a scientific point of view, it seems daring to call Jung 'a shaman' even though he might have experienced phenomena that are usually reserved for initiants of shamanism and psychic research. The difference between shamanic initiation and Jung's psychic experiences is that Jung lacked a genuine *intention* to become a shaman; his experiences were involuntary for the most part, a result of his extreme psychic tension during these times of trial. He was closer to a psychotic who kind of manages to make senses of his delusions and psychic extravagances.

The difference to shamanism is that the shaman has mastered this initial phase that however, he entered with a firm intention to become a shaman, to enter the shamanic tradition, usually after having received a guiding dream in his adolescent years.

But despite this precaution, I can conclude that Jung's struggle with shamanism was certainly an honest opening to the influence of shamanism upon the modern psychological and psychiatric tradition.

It is documented that Jung left his initiation, though an involuntary one, unharmed, to become a major spokesman for nonordinary states of consciousness and shamanic reality in the our mythopoetic and psychiatric traditions.

> Jung had found the key to his own healing, to his own psychological theory, and to others in his tribe of western society. The Self is the goal of his personal quest and simultaneously the goal of his mature psychological theory. In this insight we have Jung the shaman

becoming healed, and returning with the boon of his tribe: the individuation process is a path towards self-realization. The understanding of the Self and its realization as the goal of the life process, the individuation process, became the program and mission for the second half of his life. From this point on, Jung had a clear sense of his mission (purpose), and a valuable psychology to offer the modern western world. (Id., 96)

Michael Smith asks 'Was Jung a Shaman?' He first says he was not a shaman in the classical sense, as suggested by Eliade, Harner, and others, but that he can safely be called a *wounded healer.* Then he goes on reasoning:

The wounded healer is a fundamental aspect of the shaman. It is through the tended wound that the shaman is able to see, to empathize, and heal. Jung possessed empathic abilities in a high degree, and his abilities increased immeasurably after the resolution of his midlife crisis. Like the traditional shaman, Jung was a loner, an individual who preferred solitude and absorption in the non-ordinary or imaginal dimensions of *what he later came to call the collective unconscious. (Id., 97)*

THE GRAND OPENING

The grand opening, as it were, for shamanism in Western society occurred not before the 1960s. It can quite accurately be seen coincident with the publication of Mircea Eliade's book *Shamanism* in 1964, followed by the books of Michael Harner, Richard Schultes, Ralph Metzner, and Adam Gottlieb.

Newer research eventually recognized that shamanism is the oldest healing practice, a sort of *religious medicine* that originated more than twenty thousand years ago in the Paleolithic hunting cultures of Siberia and Central Asia.

Mircea Eliade observes that the word shaman is derived from the Siberian Tungus word *saman*, which is defined as a technique of ecstasy. The shaman is considered a great master of trance and ecstasy. He is the dominating figure in certain indigenous populations. Most early cultures' healing practices stem from a shamanic tradition. For instance, when visiting the sick, Egyptian magicians often brought a papyrus roll filled with incantations and amulets in order to drive out demons.

It is further recognized today that the shaman is regularly the religious leader or priest of the tribe. He is believed to have magical powers that can heal the sick. The shaman is called upon to mediate between the people of the community and the spirit world to cure disease, exorcize evil spirits, and to promote success in hunting and food production and to keep the tribal community in balance. Traditional shamanic rituals include singing, dancing, chanting, drumming, storytelling, and healing.

The shaman also is a psychologist, or psychoanalyst in tribal society, a sort of specialist in human souls. He is able to see them and know their form and destiny. The shaman controls the spirits. Rather than being possessed by them, he communicates with the dead, demons, and nature spirits. The shaman's work is based on the belief that the soul can forsake the body even while a person is alive and can stray into other cosmic realms where it falls prey to demons and sorcerers. The shaman diagnoses the problem, then goes in search of the wandering soul and makes it return to the body.

Shamanism is still practiced all over the world, although each culture's shamanic tradition has evolved in different ways. Native American medicine men perform soul flights and vision quests to heal. North American Inuit shamans undertake undersea spirit journeys to ensure a plentiful supply of game.

Tibetan shamans use a drum to help them in spirit flight and soul retrieval. Central and South American shamans often use hallucinogenic plants to invoke their shamanic journeys. Australian aborigine shamans believe that crystals can be inserted into the body for power.

Despite the variety of these practices, I stress in this book that the shaman has a methodology, a more or less precise, and 'computable' set of techniques that are orderly, logical and sound, and that are based upon a *scientific* outlook upon reality. This fact is hardly ever mentioned in the admittedly large literature on the subject today.

The Shamanic Method

The shaman is not a theorist, but a scientist, not a theologian, but a pragmatist. He is practical, a solution-finder and his first rule is effectiveness. He is something like a highly effective manager in his universe of natural laws, and he is a communicator; he communicates with the spirit world, the world of the ancestors and the world of the animal and plant spirits.

Now, how did I come to speak of shamans using scientific method to explore the spirit world and learn healing in the trance state? I was studying how shamans learn their 'techniques of ecstasy' and found there is very little ecstatic about this learning process, but that it actually is rather strict, methodologically sound, logical, and empirical.

Shamans observe the living, nature, the human organism, they observe every little detail, and this usually starts when they turn into adolescence. They are rather introvert and often bold and persistent people, men or women, who have in common that they do not accept the common folk wisdom, nor the common lies and superstitions but set out to inquire by themselves. They spend years in solitude, occasionally meeting their tutor, and often have no families in their years of learning. That means that most shamans live rather ascetic lives, that are turned toward their science, toward their discoveries, just like any great Western scientist in his or her younger years of scientific achievement, lab work, experimental studies, and publishing of papers. A shaman receives his basic education from the entheogenic plant teachers, only to a minor degree from another, elder, shaman tutor. Shamans around the world, asked why they knew this and that secret about healing, about certain *hidden connections* or about specific illnesses, answer they learnt it directly from the plant spirits. They tend to affirm that they just humbly asked the plant spirits every time they could not solve a problem or not find a remedy for a certain illness.

And the effectiveness of a shaman, then, is exactly to maximize the response ability he has for all possible problems is is asked to solve, such as sickness, counter-magic, right timing for harvest or even political questions regarding tribe relations, by maximizing his unique communication with the invisible world.

By the same token, shamans around the world, when asked about *reality* tend to affirm that our visible reality, the one most city dwellers think was the only one, is a very minor and rather insignificant form of reality and that the real reality is the hidden one, the one that is unveiled during the entheogenic visionary experience.

If we refuse this bias of a *more-or-less* in terms of reality assessment, we can still enrich our mindset with the option that there might be parallel realities and that all realities, visible or invisible, are equally valid and equally important. Such an opening of science toward parallel universes and acknowledging the option of a multitude of possible realities that are not conflicting each other but may or not be intersecting would be a great advance and evolution of Western science.

I am serious when I allege that an experienced shaman is able, through scientific method of exploration into the unknown, to use the laws of the subatomic world, thereby directly connecting with the unified field for time travel, for rendering himself temporarily invisible, or for traveling with lightning speed to remote places, clothed only in his auric body, while leaving the physical body behind on a bed, while being in trance.

Western society's notion of reality and that of most native populations clash worlds apart. Let me quote from Michael Harner's *The Way of the Shaman (1990)*, which represents a mark stone in shamanism research.

> Shamanism represents a great mental and emotional adventure that implies both the patient and the healer. Through his voyage and his heroic efforts, the shaman helps his patients to transcend their normal, ordinary, definition of reality as well as their self-definition as being sick.

This is a psychological explanation of the healing experience. I can say that a shaman helps his patient to reframe his illness, just as a psychotherapist does; but I can also say that the shaman doesn't really impact upon the perception of the client, but directly upon his quantum field, using the unified field as the connecting agent, and scientific means to regulate the client's energy body.

That is a completely different explanation, because it is *epistemologically different!* When I say that the shaman is a healer, that is one thing. When I say the shaman is a healer using scientific method for healing, that is another thing.

In the second case, there is namely no more difference between a shaman and a physician as both use scientific method for healing. While the scientific tools they use are obviously very different, they both proceed empirically, using observation and verification/falsification of a 'medical theory' for achieving their healing goals.

Now, obviously, my view here is going way beyond the accepted paraphernalia of shamanism research; it is today no more doubted that the shaman impacts upon the perception of the client. I can even say, it's popular knowledge after the movie *What the Bleep Do We Know!?* When the shaman in the movie touched Amanda's third eye or frontal lobe, this was clearly meant as a 'reality changing perception opener.'

But it was hardly meant to denote the shaman as a doctor who proceeds scientifically to heal Amanda's emotional stuckness, sexual neurosis and hysteria that was in part the result of her traumatic marriage experience.

Interestingly, this same statement could be made about hypnotherapy, especially the method applied by Milton H. Erickson (1901-1980) by replacing 'healer' and 'shaman' by hypnotherapist.

In fact, Erickson certainly has learned many of his secrets by studying shamanic theory and practice.

In a way, we can say that our modern psychotherapists are something like Western shamans. They are in fact borderline figures in a worldview that is almost hermetically closed toward recognizing the universal existence of soul values. Or, to remind the saying of Carl Jung, psychotherapy begins with the study of our dreams (individual unconscious) and of our myths and cultural sagas (collective unconscious).

A native would qualify somebody with a narcissism problem as a person who has lost a part or the whole of his soul. A psychotic patient who, in his delirium, says that he's Jesus Christ would be qualified by a native shaman as somebody whose soul is occupied by a spirit who, for whatever reason, speaks through him.

While both worldviews are quite opposite, the fundamental principles of healing, in shamanism, on one hand, and in psychoanalysis, on the other, are not very different.

Where the split opens much farther is where we talk about modern medicine, as it is applied still by a majority of physicians.

The sometimes sharp opposition between physicians and psychoanalysts has its deeper reasons here! The fundamental incompatibility, today, of shamanism and Western society is that the latter lacks almost totally out on acknowledging and integrating the *ecstasy pattern*, which I have identified as one of the *Eight Dynamic Patterns of*

Living. Terence McKenna was asked by Jay Levin to define shamanism. He writes in *The Archaic Revival (1992)*:

> Shamanism is use of the archaic techniques of ecstasy that were developed independent of any religious philosophy – the empirically validated, experientially operable techniques that produce ecstasy. Ecstasy is the contemplation of wholeness. That's why when you experience ecstasy—when you contemplate wholeness— you come down remade in terms of the political and social arena because you have seen the larger picture. (Id., 13)

But what is ecstasy, then? Terence McKenna explains:

> Ecstatic is a word unnecessary to define except operationally: an ecstatic experience is one that one wishes to have over and over again. (Id., 144)

Terence McKenna was probably right in not complicating something that is basically so easy but that most of us have unlearnt through our educational conditioning, while we originally, as small children, possessed the gift to connect with all-that-is.

Most authors in the literature on shamanism emphasize the shaman's role as a manipulator of consciousness, an expert in states of ecstasy, a visionary, a healer, a communicator with the spirit world, and a psychopomp. But I have found only two authors who, like me, are convinced that all this, while it is much already, is not the essential, and that there is more. These authors are

Stanley Krippner and Alberto Villoldo. They relate in *Healing States (1987)*, a book they authored together:

> In other words, shamans represent the world's oldest profession. Their roles probably varied from one society to another, but it is likely that they served a number of functions: artist, healer, magician, priest, psychotherapist, seer, storyteller. In so doing, they assisted the evolution of human consciousness. (…) Shamans were also the world's first scientists. Their discoveries of medicinal and sacred plants were made through observation and trial-and-error, both honored scientific procedures. (…) They provided humankind with the first tangible clues that there was order in the universe, because these observations could be replicated hundreds of times and still yield uniform results. If the shamans did not produce reliable data, their role was endangered and their days of honor were numbered. Thus, humanity owes a massive debt to shamans for their pioneering work in the accumulation of knowledge and the development of human capabilities. (Id., 161-162)

In his later books, Alberto Villoldo stays true to his position and provides many more details for us to see that shamans work in a *methodologically correct* and conscious manner for gathering the data they need for their work.

The specific knowledge they gather for healing has primarily to do with the states and the condition of what Villoldo calls the 'Luminous Energy Field,' which connotes the human energy field that pulsates both within the protoplasm and the surrounding aura.

In truth, Villoldo's books are an invaluable and important source for this knowledge to expand to a greater extent within Western culture.

This knowledge was once hermetic in our ancient traditions, and as long as it was hermetic, that is accessible only to a *chosen few* of sages and natural healers, things were okay. From the moment however that first alchemists and later natural scientists tried to vulgarize this knowledge, problems arose. It was not a minor confrontation, as a number of scientists lost their lives, Giordano Bruno perhaps the most prominent on the list. This knowledge taboo persisted even in the 20th century, and we need only to think of how Wilhelm Reich ended his days to be reminded of how fierce, blind and brutal the opposition was.

The Western tradition that was for more than a millennium under the knowledge denial of the Church, was not ready to receive this knowledge; things got even worse with the Cartesian science tradition, that is roughly during the last four hundred years, while this science was declaring itself separate from religion and agnostic. This science paradigm completely rejected the *concept of the ether*, the human energy field and the very existence of a creator energy that is the origin of all life.

It was the emergence of quantum physics, especially its two proven base assumptions, *uncertainty* and *nonlocality*, that made for a wide opening where formerly there were only barriers and fears. Actually, the impact of quantum physics upon the Western scientific paradigm was so dramatic that scientists felt the ground had moved away from under their feet. But it was exactly this dramatic shift in consciousness, and the insight that the observer is inevitably entangled with the object of observation that made for novelty and new ways of scientific thinking.

Within the last two decades, then, and given the unwavering and almost tumultuous progress of quantum physics beyond the borders of what Krishnamurti called 'the known,' there was something like a grand opening not only in science but also in society, in the whole of our consumer culture, for this millenary knowledge to be eventually accepted and integrated.

What actually changed in this tremendous paradigm shift was not so much science itself, but the way we are perceiving reality; as a result of this shift in perception, our scientific processes and methodology changed accordingly. It is important to see this difference, for it is the very way of thinking of native peoples that *our perception conditions reality* and all we do and achieve within this reality.

Once I look at the world in a different way, I will do a different kind of science. Once I see that my old science was destroying the planet, I will be able, from my new holistic perspective, to conceive and design a new science that is sustainable, and that respects and integrates spiritual values.

It is on this fertile ground that Villoldo's books could take root in our culture while just some decades before the knowledge they bring would perhaps have been violently rejected. Now, things look quite different; there has not been a time in our culture that was more vibrantly interested and motivated to learn the most possible amount of knowledge that was formerly rejected and banned, as part of the forbidden tree of knowledge. A first breakthrough was happening with the books of Carlos Castaneda in the 70s and 80s, then, at around the same time, with the books of Terence McKenna.

But it must be seen that at that time, the idea of a shaman being a scientist was still so daring and outlandish that even a popular author such as Terence McKenna carefully guards against possible attacks when he states in the *Archaic Revival (1992)* that he was 'not a scientist, but an explorer.'

To reduce shamanism to being a catalyzing method for bringing about ecstasy, while this is certainly true, is not giving justice to the science of shamanism. It would be as if saying that medical science is to bring about painless operations, and generally, was a methodology not for healing people, but for effective painkilling. (That medicine actually used to have this reductionist approach to healing, I won't discuss here as it's off-topic, and also because things are quite dramatically changing now).

While I admit that it was daring to state shamanism is a science, just two decades ago, now such a view cannot be dismissed as groundless or speculative. Why?

Because there is evidence, a lot of evidence to corroborate my theory. Villoldo's books are a *good starting point,* and they contain much of the knowledge I have found in other recent publications about shamanism, but explain matters in more detail, and in a way that is *comprehensive* not for a few select field researchers only, but for many people.

To begin with, the shamanic medical system and methodology differs in several ways from the our medical science model. The first fundamental difference, I have mentioned already earlier on; it is the fact that the shaman impacts first of all *upon his own neuronal and bioenergetic network* for effecting changes upon the neuronal and bioenergetic network of his client. This means the shaman uses *quantum interconnectedness* for bringing about any beneficial changes in the complete organism of the client.

The second important difference is that the shaman doesn't directly impact upon the physical body; he impacts upon the subtle, auric body, the luminous energy field; this is systemically sound as any changes effected in the quantum field automatically will trigger changes in the physical body. This is actually very smart as a healing methodology because the spirit body creates and maintains the denser physical body; as a result, changes in the physical body are always preceded by changes in the subtle energy body.

Now, the interesting thing is that shamanic medical science in this point fully resonates with the insights and practices of intuitive and clairvoyant healers within our own culture. I have found important references in the writings of Paracelsus, Franz Anton Mesmer, Carl Reichenbach, Wilhelm Reich, Charles W. Leadbeater, Shafica Karagulla and Dora van Gelder Kunz, to name only these, that actually show in minute detail that shamanic healing wisdom exactly coincides with their Western esoteric correlates.

—See Peter Fritz Walter, The Vibrational Nature of Life (2014)

It is important to note that both the shamanic and the traditional healing systems of large civilizations are very old, much older namely than our modern medical science.

Another parallel, I have found in the oldest healing tradition of India, Ayurveda, and both Chinese and Tibetan medicine. These traditional healing practices equally know about the luminous energy field and effect healing primarily by manipulating anomalies in the field.

Science and Ecstasy

Now, how can the experience of ecstasy go together with a scientific attitude? On first sight, the two experiences or attitudes toward life seem to be contradictory. But our Western scientist also returns home from the lab and has dinner, and perhaps watches television and goes to a party to have some fun, and we would not for that reason deny to him that his basic approach to life is *scientific*. And the shaman amuses himself with ecstatic dances, right?

He is stamping and hopping like a fool, to show that he can relax and let go, right? No. This comparison is an entire non-sense. The shaman uses ecstasy for sharpening his perception, as a scientific tool, for accessing perception channels hidden to us in the normal waking state. So science and ecstasy are by no means contradictory experiences, attitudes or methods. They are complimentary!

They go hand in hand when it goes to register a most-possible slice of the cake of life, and of experience, means, first of all, of nonsensory or extrasensory experience.

Ecstasy is one of the *Eight Dynamic Patterns of Living*, one of the basic ingredients of life with all native populations around the world. Contrary to common belief, ecstasy is not to be confounded with overindulgence or debauchery, or any form of 'bloody ritual' you may think of spontaneously when encountering the notion for the first time. To repeat what McKenna once said, ecstasy is the 'contemplation of wholeness,' thus in other words it's an individual and a collective form of meditation.

When I contemplate wholeness, I am in a state of bliss, or blissful awareness. *Now I can't see why this heightened state of awareness should clash with scientific observation?* I assume the two ways of approaching the world are valid, and are non-conflicting, even complimentary. They sustain each other.

When Albert Einstein was working on relativity theory, he had a dream vision in which he saw the whole theory written down in precise mathematical equations, accomplished once forever. And he would accomplish it later in exactly the way he had seen it in that vision. Another well-known example is the discovery of the benzole ring. After benzene had been the subject of many studies, inter alia by Michael Faraday and Linus Pauling, it was still unknown which molecular structure the molecule had while the empirical formula for benzene was long known.

In 1865, the German chemist Friedrich August Kekulé published a paper suggesting that the structure contained a six-membered ring of carbon atoms with alternating single and double bonds.

Only in 1890, during a honorific event organized to his honor by the German Chemical Society, Kekulé spoke of the creation of the theory. He said that he had discovered the ring shape of the benzene molecule after having a reverie or day-dream of a snake seizing its own tail (this is a common symbol in many ancient cultures known as the Ouroboros). This vision, he said, came to him after years of studying the nature of carbon-carbon bonds.

These inner visions that are reported by scientists and inventors all over the world, are moments of contemplation where the mind meets itself, and contemplates the wholeness, the hologram of a specific creation. Typically, those visions are preceding the accomplishment of the theory or invention, and thus they can be said to be *premonitory*.

There are many other examples that show that ecstasy is not bounded within tribal cultures but a phenomenon of the human mind in its greatest dimension that goes beyond space and time, and is connected with the creator force. Seen from this perspective, it was never questioned that science and ecstasy could not go together, or that a scientist might be non-scientific when he has such kind of visions. Experience shows that the contrary is true, it is the greatest, most reputed and most honored scientists who have these holistic experiences.

If this is true for our highly intellectual culture, then I think it's so much the more true for shamanic culture. Compared to our cultural setup, within shamanic cultures, values like intuition, nonsensory experience and nonordinary states of consciousness encounter less of stigma and are more easily accepted. In shamanic culture, one would not even think that ecstatic experience could probably interfere with logical, scientific scrutiny..

Let me explain this with two examples, the relationship between science and divination and why thinking in terms of a Gestalt is scientific thinking.

Science and Divination

When I talk about *divination*, I include all possible devices, methods and traditions that are used for getting a glimpse of truth for decision-making, or potential outcome of specific events around a chosen developmental theme.

Thus, divination can mean *astrology*, it can mean *Tarot* and it can mean *geomancy*, and it definitely also can mean using the *I Ching*.

Before the advent of quantum physics, science never cared about explaining divination and why it works, while archetypal and transformational psychology, especially the Jungian branch of it, has been a pioneering and thought-provoking pathway for opening the depth of the psyche and its divinatory potential to the modern researcher or psychologist. One of the leading publications in this context is Sallie Nichols' *Jung and Tarot (1986)*.

Here, shamanic traditions surely have been showing the way, when our own science paradigm was still stuck in denial and prejudice about the alleged 'psychotic character' of native shamans, and the practice of divination as 'a god-forbidden devil's play.'

It is important in this context to realize that divination is not deterministic in the sense that 'the future is predetermined,' while this assumption often appears to be repeated in vulgarized publications on esoteric sciences. The truth is that no diviner can ever predict 'the future,' as the future is simply an extrapolation of present thought content, and subconscious thought patterns, as well as emotional patterns.

What the diviner does in fact is to scan the content of our unconscious and project this content into some or the other cognitive system that renders it visible and intellectually graspable.

Hence, what divination explains is but the status quo of the asker, the person who comes to the diviner with a particular question or project. While it is true there is a certain probability that the present of consciousness perpetuates itself into the future, by extrapolation of its content on a timeline of events, this is no 'prediction' of the future, simply because the asker can change their content of consciousness *hic et nunc.*

This is why I developed, years ago, the idea of combining astrology and other forms of divination with what I came to call *Creative Prayer* as part of my *Life Authoring* self-coaching technique. The prayer technique is used as an add-on to the astrological consultation in the sense that it helps changing the present content of consciousness, after it has been rendered cognizable by the projective system of astrology. I learnt the technique basically from three books by Dr. Joseph Murphy, *The Power of Your Subconscious Mind (1963), The Miracle of Mind Dynamics (1964)* and *Think Yourself Rich (2001).*

The solution to the riddle of how divination works is contained in one single phrase of this book. Here it is:

> Remember that because your future is the result of your habitual thinking, it is already in your mind unless you change it through prayer.

—Joseph Murphy, The Power of Your Subconscious Mind (1963/2000), 165.

What divination does, to repeat is, is to read our habitual and repetitive thought patterns, and extrapolate them on a virtual time line into the future. This is, then, what is colloquially called 'predicting the future.' When you know what it's really about and how it is done, you see that it doesn't make sense, but can be understood as an oversimplification of the truth.

After all, if the future was predestined, as for example Calvinism assumed, Murphy and many other new thought authors would not have written their books; and they would not lecture as ministers and spiritual guides. They do it because they have realized that wrong beliefs about life and living are destructive and make for much of the misery we encounter in human lives, and in the world at large. Our mind is fragile in the sense that it can easily be manipulated by the mass media; worse, when fortune tellers, astrologers and diviners come along to pretend they are 'predicting the future,' the outcome may even be dangerous as their assumptions may act on naive souls like hypnotic spells that then may gain the power to realize as *self-fulfilling prophecies*.

The reader may imagine where this can lead, and how much strife and turmoil this may produce in the lives of humans around the world.

Murphy has seen it all around himself, and even in his own family, how people fall ill and even die, without having to die, because of the suggestions they receive from others in the form of hypnotic spells wrapped in various forms, and also, unfortunately, in professional divination, when done by unspiritual, greedy and dishonest people.

And it's a fact, only to look at the Internet, what masses of scam artists are around in all those fields called esoteric, new age, mindpower and all the rest of it. When such *accumulated power of irresponsible manipulative greed* meets the fragile and ignorant mind of the 'man in the street,' we can virtually predict disasters to happen.

This messy situation with people being mislead by both their own beliefs and predictions received from others was one of the reasons that motivated Murphy and before him, Ernest Holmes, to write their books. The science that I have in mind when I put up the dichotomy science vs. divination is the *Science of Mind*, also called *Religious Science*, as it was founded by Ernest Holmes in 1927, and expanded and commercialized in the 1960s by Dr. Joseph Murphy and Catherine Ponder, and others.

I studied the *Science of Mind* thoroughly over the last fifteen years; it emphasizes the priority of mind over matter—spiritual monism—and also the priority of the present over the past and any form of predestination.

It is not known to many that the Bible is against both astrology and fortune telling. For example, Deuteronomy 18: 9-12 affirms:

> 9 When thou art come into the land which the LORD thy God giveth thee, thou shalt not learn to do after the abominations of those nations.
> 10 There shall not be found among you any one that maketh his son or his daughter to pass through the fire, or that useth divination, or an observer of times, or an enchanter, or a witch.
> 11 Or a charmer, or a consulter with familiar spirits, or a wizard, or a necromancer.
> 12 For all that do these things are an abomination unto the LORD: and because of these abominations the LORD thy God doth drive them out from before thee.

When I came across these Bible quotes in 1991, I was first revolted! I found the Bible forwarded here a form of Christian fundamentalism that was completely against my convictions and spirituality. Yet I wanted to understand what the Bible meant here, what the deeper meaning was behind these admonitions.

Thus I was asking 'how does the Bible relate to divining?' And why does it exhort us to be careful with it? To begin with, let me quote an example from Murphy's book *The Power of Your Subconscious Mind*.

> *How Suggestion Killed a Man*
> A distant relative of mine went to a celebrated crystal gazer in India and asked the woman to read his future.

The seer told him that he had a bad heart. She predicted that he would die at the next new moon.

My relative was aghast. He called up everyone in his family and told them about the prediction. He met with his lawyer to make sure his will was up-to-date. When I tried to talk him out of his conviction, he told me that the crystal gazer was known to have amazing occult powers. She could do great good or harm to those she dealt with. He was convinced of the truth of this.

As the new moon approached, he became more and more withdrawn. A month before this man had been happy, healthy, vigorous, and robust. Now he was an invalid. On the / predicted date, he suffered a fatal heart attack. He died not knowing he was the cause of his own death.

How many of us have heard similar stories and shivered a little at the thought that the world is full of mysterious uncontrollable forces? Yes, the world is full of forces, but they are neither mysterious nor uncontrollable. My relative killed himself, by allowing a powerful suggestion to enter into his subconscious mind. He believed in the crystal gazer's powers, so he accepted her prediction completely.

Let us take another look at what happened, knowing what we do about the way the subconscious mind works. Whatever the conscious, reasoning mind of a person believes, the subconscious mind will accept and act upon. My relative was in a suggestible state when he went to see the fortune teller. She gave him a negative suggestion, and he accepted it. He became terrified. He constantly ruminated on his conviction that he was going to die at the next new moon. He told everyone about it, and he prepared for his end. It was his own fear and expectation of the end, accepted as true by his subconscious mind, that brought about his death.

The woman who predicted his death had no more power than the stones and sticks in the field. Her suggestion in itself had no power to create or bring about the end she suggested. If he had known the laws of his mind, he would have completely rejected the negative suggestion and refused to give her words any attention. He could have gone about the business of living with the secure knowledge that he was governed and controlled by his own thoughts and feelings. The prophecy of the seer would have been like a rubber ball thrown at an armored tank. He could have easily neutralized and dissipated her suggestion with no harm to himself. Instead, through lack of awareness and knowledge, he allowed it to kill him./

In themselves, the suggestions of others have no power over you. Whatever power they have, they gain because you give it to them through your own thoughts. You have to give your mental consent. You have to entertain and accept the thought. At that point it becomes your own thought, and your subconscious works to bring it into experience.

Remember, you have the capacity to choose. Choose life! Choose love! Choose health! (Id., 29-30).

There is a difference between *foolishly accepting* a 'prediction' by an astrologer or fortune teller, or to use, for example, the I Ching, for decision making. The same is true regarding serious astrology; it is a question of *professional ethics* to avoid being suggestive in any way. This is equally true for a serious Feng Shui consultant,

Tarot expert, and even for paranormals who practice their profession within the rules of the unwritten ethical code set in Antiquity for all *Hermetic Sciences*.

From the side of the client, a certain level of emotional maturity is equally required! How many people die because they receive 'death sentences' from their physicians, taking for granted that the gods in white coats determine their destiny, and for the most part ignorant about the pitfalls, limitations and outright ignorance of medical science!

There is a responsibility linked to every new piece of knowledge you learn and digest. This responsibility requires you to use the knowledge not with a foolish, immature mindset that takes everything for granted when it comes from a so-called 'authority.'

Science and Gestalt

As I have shown in my reviews of some of the lesser known books by Wilhelm Reich, this scientist's conceptual framework had firmly embodied the *Gestalt*. Reich's genius as a scientist was his gift of observation, and his particular talent to see not single elements of a process, but the *whole* of the process.

Reich was in this respect really different from the main bunch of his mechanistic professional colleagues. In our days, Reich would probably be considered as one of the leading-edge scientists. Generally speaking, when we observe living processes, we can either put our focus on single elements, or the substance, or we can focus on the *process*, and the *form*. Both form and substance are present in living systems.

Our culture has created the line as a symbol for evolution. However, the line is an artificial construct, inexistent in nature, a purely mental achievement, while evolution is cyclic. It allows the line only in combination with the circle, so as to say, resulting in the *spiral*.

Merriam-Webster's Dictionary defines the spiral as *relating to the advancement to higher levels through a series of cyclical movements.* The curving movement of the spiral is what it has in common with the circle; the increase or decrease in size of the spiral is a function of its moving upward or downward.

Interestingly enough, the spiral is by far the dominating form to be found in nature, and in all natural processes. It is a symbol or Gestalt for evolution in general. Life is coded in the spiraled double-helix of the DNA molecule. The spiral is the expression of the periodic, systemic and cyclic development that is in accordance with the laws of life.

The progression of the spiral shows that it always carries its root, however transporting it through every cycle onto a higher level or dimension; whereas the line leaves its root forever. All towers of Babel are manifestations of the line; they are linear and are created by linear thought structures.

True growth is always cyclic and spiraled, and nonlinear.

On the subject of bringing in Gestalt thinking in the logic of healing, Manly P. Hall, in his book *The Secret Teachings of All Ages (1928/2003)* writes about Paracelsus:

> Paracelsus discovered that in many cases plants revealed by their shape the particular organs of the human body which they served most effectively. The medical system of Paracelsus was based on the theory that by removing the diseased etheric mumia from the organism of the patient and causing it to be accepted into the nature of some distant and disinterested thing of comparatively little value, it was possible to divert from the patient the flow of the archaeus which had been continually revitalizing and nourishing the malady. Its vehicle of expression being transplanted, the archaeus necessarily accompanied its mumia, and the patient recovered. (Id., 347)

It was Gestalt considerations and the insight that nature is basically an assemblage of patterns, and not of matter that led researchers recently to eventually corroborate the age-old assumption that our universe is *holographic,* and thus programmed in holographic patterns that are all mutually interconnected. Ervin Laszlo writes in his remarkable study *Science and the Akashic Field (2004):*

> In a holographic recording – created by the interference pattern of two light beams – there is no one-to-one correspondence between points on the surface of the object that is recorded and points in the recording itself.

Holograms carry information in a distributed form, so all the information that makes up a hologram is present in every part of it. The points that make up the recording of the object's surface are present throughout the interference patterns recorded on the photographic plate: in a way, the image of the object is enfolded throughout the plate. As a result, when any small piece of the plate is illuminated, the full image of the object appears, though it may be fuzzier than the image resulting from illuminating the entire plate. (Id., 55)

Before I come back to the role of the shaman as a scientist within shamanic culture, which is the main part of this study, I shall explain why shamans make ample use of entheogens to get connected with their inner god or the unified field, and what some of the most powerful entheogens are.

Further, I am going to provide a real life example, report of a *shamanic voyage* I made back in 2004, with a Shuar shaman in Ecuador, when ingesting the traditional Ayahuasca brew for the first time in my life. It namely becomes clear through my report that one can well maintain one's scientific approach and mental clarity when being in a state of ecstasy.

I would even say that my cognitive abilities were widened and enhanced by the brew, and nothing interfered with my clear observation.

While my experience with Ayahuasca was not really a positive one as I was unable to move further down the rabbit hole, it was a very important learning experience for me, and I was able to derive considerable conclusions from it. I was namely able to see that the common mechanistic theory that says the trance state is triggered by nothing by the DMT contained in the brew is at least incomplete, if it's not completely wrong. What triggers the trance state and the whole of the experience is the psychic power, and *intention* of the shaman when he prepares the brew and during the ceremony itself; it is the power of this intention that as it were regulates the whole of the experience.

Chapter Two

Consciousness and Shamanism

Introduction

When looking for evidence that shamanism is a *science*, I came early in life to realize that it is far from obvious what science really is, or what science *naturally* is—when we look at it from a point of view that is not conditioned by our own cultural bias. In fact, as a boy already, when building a small radio and experimenting with electronic circuits, I became aware of the *primal scientific method*, which is trial and error, and acute observation, and then the inductive logical work of comparing the outcome, changing the settings, and comparing again, and so forth.

While I did later not become a scientist, nor, as I had planned, a recording and television technician, I kept a basic intention to look at life not from a magical and purely artistic perspective, but from one that is based upon information, knowledge, observation and methodology.

Since leaving high school and during my extensive law studies, I was deepening my knowledge in psychoanalysis and medical hypnosis as well as perennial sciences both from the West and the East. My law studies and work as a legal researcher taught me that so-called *scientific knowledge* is often a mere formula for manipulating opinion by invoking *established research* or *scientific authorities.*

This is unscientific because it means to measure the knew with the parameters of the old. Only much later, and *inter alia* through the writings of Edward de Bono and J. Krishnamurti became I aware that this form of reductionism is inherent in the functioning of the brain and the way perception works.

> —See, for example, Edward de Bono, The Use of Lateral Thinking (1967), The Mechanism of Mind (1969), Sur/Petition (1993), Tactics (1993), Serious Creativity (1996) as well as J. Krishnamurti, Freedom from the Known (1969), Education and the Significance of Life (1978) and Beyond Violence (1985).

This brought me to the conviction that *exact science* is a myth because all science is relative to the observer's own set of beliefs. Meanwhile, my insights about science philosophy are widely confirmed by quantum physics and *recent consciousness research,* but when I first uttered them, more than twenty years ago, I was encountering but suspicion and estrangement. What I learnt from this is that instead of accumulating knowledge, we should always check if new knowledge we acquire *resonates within ourselves* and thus confirms our own intuition and sense of truth. For only then it is useful and reinforces our own higher intelligence. There is no knowledge outside of this source and all knowledge is thus *individual* in the sense that not all truth is valid for all.

The present chapter will show that there is no split in the *cognitive assessment of natural healing* practiced within shamanism and by shamans when looked at through the eyes not of mainstream science, but using the millenary cognitive tools of *alternative science*, and particularly our insights into the functioning of hypnosis.

In addition, let me address an important argument people often come up with: they repeat that 'drugs will render you addicted.' While this argument is true for alcohol, for coffee, for tobacco, for most tranquilizers, for some medical drugs, for some of the hard core drugs such as heroin, it is probably not true for Cannabis or Hemp, and it is certainly not true for entheogens. Reputed shamanism researchers such as Michael Harner, Adam Gottlieb, Richard Schultes, Ralph Metzner or the McKenna brothers have repeated it over and over in their publications.

Regarding a synthetic entheogen, LSD, which was was used in psychotherapy, the literature has clearly defended the view that it renders in any way addictive. The discoverer of the substance, the Swiss chemist Albert Hofmann from Sandoz Laboratories, testified for LSD being non-addictive.

—Albert Hofmann, LSD: My Problem Child (1979/2009), 15, 57.

Why the substance ultimately was put on the index of forbidden drugs has nothing to do with addictiveness but has purely political reasons. Terence McKenna notes in *Archaic Revival (1992)*:

> The solution of much of modern malaise, including chemical dependencies and repressed psychoses and neuroses, is direct exposure to the authentic dimensions of risk represented by the experience of psychedelic plants. The pro-psychedelic plant position is clearly an antidrug position. Drug dependencies are the result of habitual, unexamined, and obsessive behavior; these are precisely the tendencies in our psychological makeup that the psychedelics mitigate. The plant hallucinogens dissolve habits and hold motivations up to inspection by a wider, less egocentric, and more grounded point of view within the individual. (Id., 219)

What is Ayahuasca?

Ayahuasca, already mentioned as a favorite entheogen brew among shamans, is intended to bring about a trance for self-discovery, healing, contacting spirits or exploring consciousness.

The brew contains *Banisteriopsis Caapi*, also called Ayahuasca liana, and the Chacruna shrub *(Psychotria viridis)*, a Mono Amine Oxidase or MAO inhibitor.

—See, for more details, Richard Evans Schultes, et al., Plants of the Gods (1992), 124 ff.

There are many other entheogens used for religious purposes, and they form an integral part of shamanism.

Entheogens are plants that contain psychoactive compounds, such as DMT, and others, and that, when taken at appropriate doses, produce a consciousness-altering effect upon our psyche and perception. It has been equally affirmed that entheogens, apart from their helping us to reach the inner mind, also dissolve nasty and somehow destructive habits such as alcoholism or heroin addiction, and generally help in a process of social deconditioning.

Entheogens help us to see behind the veil of the normative behavior code in any given society as they show us options of *different* behavior. What we can thus learn from taking these plants as a sort of *social medicine* is to recognize the pattern of normative behavior we are caught in and that obstructs our creativity and self-realization.

I shall now first report my Ayahuasca journey, and then evaluate it in a hopefully objective manner, using scientific methodology to evaluate it.

An Ayahuasca Experience

I had two options to experience Ayahuasca on my trip to South America in June 2004. It was either the *Santo Daime* ritual in Brazil, which is a mixup of psychedelic experience and a modified Christian liturgy, or encounter the wistful plant teacher as part of a shamanic ritual in Ecuador. I chose the second, not only because I got the contact with this shaman already before, but also because I felt that none of these churches in Brazil were really welcoming me as a participating visitor. In Ecuador, then, Esteban, the shaman, told me that the original ritual was a pure and solitary experience of encountering the plant teacher, and not a group event. This confirmed my intuition and I was glad to have chosen the more original initiation instead of indulging in a vulgarized and sectarian mix of perhaps incongruent elements.

The morning after my arrival in Misahualli, I met Esteban, the shaman, who was a young man with little shamanic experience. He was a short, strong and healthy native in his thirties who had a rather *pragmatic* approach to life. Esteban did not hide that he was not a grown shaman, but just a beginner in shamanism and I got an intuition that he might not be able to help me with my fear problem. In addition, the two seemed to be caught in a negative pattern regarding Jimela's husband, a Polish businessman, the person who had invited me.

From what they said, he seemed to be a strongly authoritarian character who had not understood their culture and had reacted several times in a rather displeasing way during the Ayahuasca experience.

After breakfast, I went out with Esteban to collect the plants. Close to Esteban's own wooden house, we found a very nice and about 15-year old Ayahuasca liana that Esteban called *la madre*. It was a strong liana of about fifteen centimeters diameter at the bottom and becoming finer and finer higher up. It was spiraling around its host tree and at its top end firmly rooted in the branches of the tree. Esteban first decided not to take this plant but a *daughter* of the mother, but looking around we found only very small and thin ones that Esteban, after careful examination, rejected as not being fit for the brew. So we went back to the mother liana and Esteban climbed up the tree, asked me to hand him the knife, climbed higher, put the knife in a fork of two branches, and balanced it exactly so that it didn't fall down, climbed still higher and cut a medium-sized liana of about two meters that fell down next to my feet.

I was praying to the plant to allow us taking it, as this is a holy custom of the natives. Not far from the place we found the liana, we also found the second plant for the brew, which is a Mono Amine Oxidase inhibitor, that is called *Chacruna* or *Psychotria viridis*. Esteban used for it another name in Spanish that I did not retain. He put the liana and the leaves carefully in a little bag that he carried on our way back to the hotel.

When we were arriving back, the sun was getting out a bit and immediately the air became hot and sticky and I had a heavy headache that lasted until the afternoon when I could eventually get some sleep. As I am not used to this climate, the two hours walk had exhausted me.

However, after sleeping I felt alert and fine when, at about eight in the evening they called me for the ceremony.

Esteban, his wife, and Jimela were sitting around a fireplace, in a the little hut of the hotel that looks over the river and where the floor was covered with a thick layer of beach sand. It was strange that, following my intuition, I went to this place while I did not know that they were there.

Jimela had knocked at my room door and left and I did not know where she had gone. Some intuition told me they might be in a hut behind the restaurant that previously I had seen during lunch and that I thought was the private apartment of the hotel owner. Still more alien was the fact that when I got there, I saw three people, two women and one man, sitting in arm chairs, and in the dusk I did *not* recognize them. This never happened to me in my life before, that I saw people I know and did not recognize them. I was looking at them a moment and they did not say anything. Finally I said:

—Can you tell me where I can find Jimela and Esteban?

And Jimela got up and greeted me, and I went to the chair she advised me, and I was very confused. The hotel owner, this slim aloof French, was stitching in the fireplace with a fork, trying to light the fire, in vain. He had no regard for me. At the end, he was not even able to light the fire. Only on my angered remark about the misplaced amateurism of that guy, Jimela went there to light the fire again, and that time successfully.

I wonder why all this happened as it happened?

It wasn't dark yet, all was well visible, but in that moment upon entering the spacious hut that is open all around and well lit, I had not recognized them. Had I been in a state of hypnosis already?

By the way, I experienced hypnosis already when I encountered a magic healer from the Philippines in the cabinet of a natural healer in Frankfurt, Germany. He put the audience in a state of hypnosis, suggesting that he was opening the belly of the patient, taking out the intestines, cleaning them and putting them back. I had seen all this with the other participants, the open belly, the blood, the strange sound like a wobbling noise when he put his hands deep into the intestines of the person in order to find strange objects that he threw out on the floor and that looked like small black stones.

The woman who had been treated before me, and who was sitting next to me, complained about strong pain in her belly after the treatment, while I went through the experience unhurt. Whatever the rationale is of magic healing, one thing is sure: this kind of group hypnosis works perfectly well and suggests a scenario to our minds that is more real than reality. You can't but affirm that you have *seen* it while you know of course that no belly was open and no blood was flowing and no black stones were to be found on the floor. And indeed, the first spot I was gazing at when we went back to normal perception was where one of those black stones were formerly to be seen, and even heard, on the floor. Needless to say that there was nothing.

I complimented them about the choice of the place that I found ideally suited. They said it was the first time they did it here, actually for my convenience, and that formerly they had done it in a little hut outside of the hotel. The advantage here was that I could any time go to my room, relax, or go to the toilet if I needed to. And that had been a wise precaution indeed as I would find out later...

Esteban was looking handsome in his traditional dress and I found set and setting really appropriate. I was in a positive mood when drinking the cup and was surprised about the good natural taste of it. In all the books was written that the taste was horrible and that some people even vomited only because of the *appalling taste*. Nothing of that. It was a plant taste, bitter, but agreeable.

During this half hour of waiting for the DMT to be absorbed by the blood so that the trance could start, I made up in my mind a hypothesis that I have not found in any book, and it seems that no researcher has hitherto come up with it. My strange experience when entering the hut was giving me the idea: *And what if nothing in that plant really produced the effect, but if all was a hypnotic trance induced by the shaman himself?*

While I knew that it was a daring hypothesis because we cannot deny the Ayahuasca brew containing a considerable amount of DMT, and knowing from much laboratory research how DMT is affecting human consciousness, it is, I think, something that needs to be addressed.

When we are scientific, we actually *must* address this possibility because it is scientific method to scrutinize *all the causative factors* of a result produced in an experiment. And when we do that, we cannot per se exclude from the start the hypnosis explanation I am forwarding here. While I find it little probable myself in view of the fact that Esteban was a rather young and hardly experienced shaman, I think we would have to disprove the hypnosis scenario in order to more firmly establish the plant teacher theory. And this, nobody has done it yet.

The experience started about half an hour later. I was feeling the trance actually from the fingers up, in the lower arms, then climbing into the whole body. I felt very clearly how my arm muscles gradually relaxed and this experience reminded me of the medical hypnosis I experienced as part of the hypnotherapy I did about ten years ago.

Only that, with Ayahuasca, the trance was getting much stronger. It was a unique experience. I immediately was aware that the whole thing was not an automatism, but a *directed* voyage. It was directed by an intelligence. This intelligence communicated with me in a subtle way. It was very gentle, loving and caring, and the trance was very gradual, actually as if it had been especially adapted for me and my needs. With my eyes closed, I saw some faint colored forms, like arrangements of flowers or ornamental drawings and thought they were not as colored as in the books, but rather a physical phenomenon of the retina of the eye that was stimulated by the drug. My logical intelligence—that was at no moment veiled or dysfunctional during the whole experience—suggested me that these visions had no meaning in itself and that the experience was something much beyond the mere visual effects.

It then came to my mind that most reports about the Ayahuasca experience only focused upon these visions, and in my view people have taken the symbol for the truth or the finger for the moon. The young French couple who manages the hotel had told me at lunch about their own Ayahuasca experience: *Just visions ..., you know, very nice!*

There was a noise developing that I found very interesting. I was clear enough in my mind to detect within this noise the river's sound, the cricket's sounds, the frog's sounds, and yet I found that noise being of another quality than just a mix of all those natural sounds. And it was gradually raising, and after some time, I clearly understood that this sound was something like the *pulsation* of the universe, of life, and that creation was a result of *sound*, that life intrinsically was vibration, was sound.

Then I got clear telepathic messages that I should go beyond that first phase and intuitively knew that there was three or five depth levels of the trance and that I was just in the first. Then the intelligence gave me signals. It was like a gentle knocking at my doors of perception. It was a flickering of about five red squares at the left upper corner of my vision, when my eyes were closed.

I intuitively knew that this was the signal to go deeper, and yet I could not. Every time it happened, the fear came up and blocked me to go beyond. I then remembered that it was this fear, from childhood, that had prevented me from realizing myself, that it was this fear that was blocking me to experience hypnosis really deeply and not only slightly, that it was this fear that blocked me to really give my best when I played piano in front of an audience or did anything I really love to do.

The rest of the experience is without importance. It was a terrible struggle between the *call* that I received to go beyond the fear and the fear block itself. I began to vomit and had to call Esteban two times for help. To make it worse, I could not remember Esteban's name, and thus formulated in my mind a cry for help, and that, to put this cry in language, needed some really hard effort:

—*Chamán, ayudame por favor!*

Esteban then got up from his chair, put his hand on my head, blew cigarette smoke in my face and treated my aura with a special device made from dried leaves, a sort of rattle that is used like a feather to give passes from top to feet, similar to what is done in hypnosis. This treatment helped me wonderfully, but only as long as it lasted.

Actually, I opened my eyes several times just to see if the others were still there.

Interestingly, the communication with the intelligence stopped *at once* when I opened my eyes, and in that condition, I felt swindle. Only when closing my eyes again, the communication would gently be taken up by the plant intelligence. Sadly, I felt isolated from the other humans or any other humans, as if I was totally alone on earth, as if there was no soul connection between them and me, while intellectually I since long affirm this connection to be true and part of all life. But emotionally I could not feel it, I could not understand it. *I felt I was locked in my body, cut off from all other life, and cold.*

I saw the two women sleeping in their chairs and Esteban, on my right, was looking strange. The trance view of him was not the normal view of him. When he was talking to me, his face appeared diabolic and grinning and it made me still more afraid. His mouth was not in the middle of his face, but shifted to the right side, and very large, as if it was open, and white inside.

Now I must recall a similar experience. It was when I got a Bach plants treatment from a very experienced natural healer in Germany. This woman had studied with Filipino healers and was using hypnotic trance for healing. Holding one flacon after the other of the Bach essences in her left hand, she let me put my left hand into her right hand in order to establish the *flow of the current.* In that moment, I had experienced the same what happened with the Filipino healer and during the Ayahuasca experience.

I relaxed and my consciousness shifted. When I looked at her face, I saw that she had *three eyes*, one very large third eye on her front, at exactly the location where there is our *third eye chakra*, only that in this state of trance, I saw a real eye there, a large one, much larger than a human eye. I was not afraid to see her and telepathically knew that she was spiritually a developed soul with true healing capabilities.

The strange difference between her and her aura and Esteban and his aura is that this woman's aura had a calming, luminous and beneficial effect on my soul while the aura of Esteban had a frightening and confusing effect.

After each treatment Esteban gave me and despite the fact I vomited out all the contents of my stomach, there was obviously still enough DMT in my blood to continue the experience. Well, in hindsight, this would actually favor the hypnosis theory again because from what I read in books, with most other people, once they had vomited out the contents of their stomach, the trance was broken, while in my case it was not. The intelligence called me still, so gently, so lovingly, so calmly, and I could not get over the block. But it might also be that the DMT was still in the blood while the actual substance, the Ayahuasca brew, was already evacuated from the stomach.

The most important experience was that this intelligence questions everything. Every thought I had was immediately returned to its contrary and every phrase that

I pronounced in my mind was reduced to some more general insight. For example I heard myself thinking:

—I love life …

And it was immediately reduced to:

—I *love* …

Or I heard myself thinking:

—I feel to be alive …

And it was reduced to:

—I *feel* …

And the intelligence seemed to tell me telepathically that I was *locked* in language, that all my experiencing of life was conditioned upon language, and that I hardly ever perceived life *directly*, spontaneously, as an immediate connection.

I knew that this intelligence was connected to all, was connecting all and was all. It simply *was*, and it gently invited me to enter this connection, this wonderful all-encompassing love that it irradiated. Several times, when I wanted to communicate some of the experience to Esteban, the intelligence seemed to hold me back. Once I wanted to say something regarding the intelligence, and I was stopped in the midst of the sentence:

—*Esta inteligencia* …, was all that I could say.

The intelligence seemed to wanting to free me from the conditioning I had received in early childhood through language, and through using language for describing reality. It might be that my fear is in some way connected to language and my fear block a hypertrophy of language or of my left brain. This is how I can try to explain it while all what I write here and can express in words never can come close to the actual experience.

I was constantly communicating to the intelligence as well. I had prayed already before the experience to reveal my life's mission to me and to free me from fear, and I kept addressing Ayahuasca in respectful terms during the experience to assist me in my quest for truth. And as if it was a final test that this intelligence really understood me, I said this, when I felt I wanted to go back to my room and sleep:

> —Dear Ayahuasca Spirit, thank you so much for all the insights, please stop calling me now. I was not able to get over my fear block now, and I hope I can find the courage to continue because I know you will reveal me so much more when I get deeper in the trance. But for now I have decided to stop. It is enough.

And immediately the *calling* stopped, the flickering lights did not appear any more and the *alien* noise was calming down and stopped as well. This alien noise, I understood then, was the *language* of that intelligence. It was something like many people, in some distance, speaking all at the same time, and as if many conversations converged to a chaotic no-sense that was but the secret code or pattern of a deeper, much more unified language of the universe, and of which our human language is only a tiny and almost insignificant part.

Esteban suggested to guide me back to my room and I stumbled back, with his support, because I was hardly able to walk and felt swindle. In my room I spent at least two hours of dreadful vomiting and diarrhea. It was *la purga* as it is described in many personal reports about the Ayahuasca experience.

Eventually I became very quiet and full of gratitude and I said this in my thought, in German:

—*Ich möchte Liebe!* (I want love)

And immediately the response was:

—*Ich möchte lieben …* (I want to love)

And with all my heart and my soul I understood this subtle difference and it was clear to me that in this difference of language was *all the difference*. It was the secret to happiness. I had taken love as a commodity that can be received, instead of understanding that love was not something to receive, but something to build, something like an attitude, and this attitude, it seemed to me then, simply was total openness. And I think this insight transformed something in me.

Shortly after that I fell easily asleep and slept wonderfully, without dreams, until around eight in the morning, and woke up like newborn, feeling light and alert. While usually, after the many strange dreams I normally have, I wake up fearful, anxious and powerless and have to do a whole program of prayer, meditation and exercises every morning, I now felt completely free of any fear and of any past. It was the most exhilarating morning in my life, and perhaps, in some way, the start of a new life.

Hypothesis

My hypothesis is that the consciousness-transforming cognitive experience subsequent to ingesting the ritual *Ayahuasca* brew is not, as it is often suggested, the direct result of plant chemistry, but of the shaman's consciousness reaching the experiencer's consciousness *through the medium of plant chemistry as a thought and energy transmitter.* This view is not to be understood in a reductionist way. I do not say that all is to be *reduced* to one single root cause, but propose to consider *one more option* in our scientific investigation of paranormal phenomena.

There are several facts and events around my Ayahuasca experience that are explainable soundly when applying my own hypothesis instead of trying to match it with the theory that psychedelic experiences are caused, as a *linear effect*, by a plant-contained chloride named DMT.

To anticipate a little on my conclusions, my hypothesis provides a *nonlinear* explanation of the psychedelic experience. My hypothesis does not deny the existence of the chloride and its possible effects on the human psyche. But I contend that the mind-opening effects noticed by the novice after ingesting the brew are a result of the shaman's consciousness impacting upon a *passive perception matrix* that is part of the plant realm and that the shaman uses as a transmitter platform.

I repeat that I do not discuss away any possible other explanation, so much the more as I myself, after the trance began to grip on me, had the impression there was an intelligence in touch with me, an intelligence that was *alien* in a way, and that I attributed to the plant realm. My point is not to invalidate any of the current hypotheses about psychedelic plant substances, but to help finding a valid theory that shows what it is that effectively opens, modifies or expands human consciousness during the Ayahuasca experience.

—See, for example, Mircea Eliade, Shamanism (1972), Piers Vitebsky, Shamanism (2001), Ralph Metzner (Ed.) Ayahuasca (1999), Michael Harner, Ways of the Shaman (1990), Jeremy Narby, The Cosmic Serpent (1999), Richard Evans Schultes et al, Plants of the Gods (2002), Terence McKenna, The Invisible Landscape (1994), True Hallucinations (1998), The Archaic Revival (1992), Food of the Gods (1993), Robert Forte (Ed.), Entheogens and the Future of Religion (2000), Luis Eduardo Luna & Pablo Amaringo, Ayahuasca Visions (1999), Adam Gottlieb, Peyote and Other Psychoactive Cacti (1997), Rick Strassman, DMT (2001).

Before I am going to give some flesh and bones to my assumption, let me report that I found till now at least a couple of references that seem to confirm my point. As the result of a general research on shamanism and entheogens, and particularly Ayahuasca, that I undertook over several years, I must conclude that most of the researchers seem to defend a rather *mechanistic causation theory* that sees the source of all paranormal phenomena in the chemical plant substances. For example Terence McKenna, under the spell of his large knowledge on ethnopharmacology, and his brother Dennis McKenna, an ethnobotanist, never left a doubt in all their writings on the subject of psychedelics that causation of altered states of consciousness is due to psychoactive compounds in plants called *entheogens*.

The question what exactly the role is that the shaman plays in opening greater pathways of consciousness is left open or remains subject to speculation.

Dr. Rick Strassman, a researcher on DMT, has quite the same linear idea about causation and sees plant chemistry as the activating force, and the title of the book is a typical American euphemism. The book's approach is all but revolutionary, it is hardcore mechanistic and linear, with very little holistic insight.

—Rick Strassman, DMT: The Spirit Molecule (2001).

I have found so far only two researchers who express a view that really makes sense. Their research seems to corroborate my own findings. Jeremy Narby, in his book *The Cosmic Serpent (2003)*, puts up the daring hypothesis that causation is due to biophoton emission, not plant chemistry. He observes that initially his approach to psychedelics research was a valid branch of research that however from the middle of the 1970s onward disappeared from the scientific literature. What is seen in psychedelic visions, according to Narby's research, are photons emitted by the DNA. Narby writes in *The Cosmic Serpent (2003)*:

> Researchers working in this new field mainly consider biophoton emission as a cellular language or a form of nonsubstantial biocommunication between cells and organisms. Over the last fifteen years, they have conducted enough reproducible experiments to believe that cells use these waves to direct their own internal reactions as well as to communicate among themselves and even between organisms. For instance, photon emission provides a communication mechanism that could explain how billions of individual plankton organisms cooperate in swarms, behaving like super organisms. (Id., 127-128)

Now, succinctly speaking, what Narby wants to show is that what the shamans perceive as *spirits* are in reality biophotons emitted by the cells of the human body:

> What if these spirits were none other than the biophotons emitted by all the cells of the world and were picked up, amplified, and transmitted by shamans' quartz crystals, Gurvich's quartz screens, and the quartz containers of biophoton researchers? This would mean that spirits are beings of pure light – as has always been claimed. (Id., 129)

In fact, Narby's theory does not exclude that causation might also be due to plant chemistry, but he surely concludes that what is seen, what is perceived, is not parallel reality but the reality contained in our own DNA and the superconscious memory surface that is connected to it. A perhaps more convincing evidence of causation being an effect of the shaman's own superconscious powers, and not of plant chemistry, is brought forward, or at least hypothesized by the American medical anthropologist, shaman and psychologist Alberto Villoldo.

In his book *Shaman, Healer, Sage (2000)*, Dr. Villoldo introduces the third chapter entitled *The Luminous Energy Field* with an entry from his journals. Don Eduardo was one of the powerful Inca shamans Villoldo studied with for many years:

> I've found that the San Pedro potion does nothing other than make me sick. (…) I'm convinced that the altered state I'm in is created by Don Eduardo's singing. And then there is the energy that he claims enters the ceremonial space when he summons the spirits of serpent, jaguar, hummingbird, and condor. (…) What I can't explain is the fact that I'm seeing energy. It only happens when I sit next to Don Eduardo. When I go more than a few feet away from him I sense nothing. It's like he is surrounded by an electric space, where the air actually tingles. When I'm inside his space I see everything he sees. (Id., 41)

The perhaps most convincing corroboration of my research comes from theosophy and the pulpit of Charles W. Leadbeater. If clairvoyant research is or is not considered as valid scientific research under the present reductionist science paradigm is not *my* problem. From a point of view of science as methodically sound, holistic, mentally sane and intelligently conveyed observation of nature, clairvoyance *is* science. As a little excursion, let me quote what a clairvoyant herself has to say about this extraordinary faculty of perception that is clairvoyance. Dora van Gelder writes in her book *The Real World of Fairies (1999)*:

> The fact is that there is a real physical basis for clairvoyance, and the faculty is not especially mysterious. The power centers in that tiny organ in the brain called the *pituitary gland*. The kind of vibrations involved are so subtle that no physical opening in the skin is needed to convey them to the pituitary body, but there is a special spot of sensitiveness just between the eyes above the root of the nose which acts as the external opening for the gland within. (Id., 4)

In his book, *The Astral Plane (1894)*, Leadbeater very much stresses the fact that we can hardly judge a human being by their acts only; in fact, as thoughts are much more important as an influence upon the world than most of us know, when we praise somebody for his achievements and judge him or her 'a good person,' we may be completely wrong, because that person may have exerted a ravaging influence on others and the world by their self-talk, by their way of thinking about others, and by their way of judging others harshly over years and years, in their mind.

What self-talk namely creates are *elementals* or thought-forms and these thought forms are more or less permanent, and gain permanence over time and depending on the emotional energy we invest in these thoughts.

I think it's good that Leadbeater addresses this point so clearly because most people in our culture are completely ignorant about the impact of thought on the world, on others and on their own karma. Leadbeater writes:

> The fact that we are so readily able to influence the elemental kingdoms at once shows us that we have a responsibility towards them for the manner in which we use that influence; indeed, when we consider the conditions under which they exist, it is obvious that the effect produced upon them by the thoughts and desires of all intelligent creatures inhabiting the same world with them must have been calculated upon in the scheme of our system as a factor in their evolution. In spite of the consistent teaching of all the great religions, the mass of mankind is still utterly regardless of its responsibility on the thought-plane; if a man can flatter himself that his words and deeds have been harmless to others, he believes that he has done all that can be required of him, quite oblivious of the fact that he may / for years have been exercising a narrowing and debasing influence on the minds of those about him, and filling surrounding space with the unlovely creations of a sordid mind. (Id., 54-55)

Now, regarding the elementals that are created through thought and intent, and the gestation that is brought about by the repeated fostering of a well-defined thought pattern, Leadbeater explains that these elementals are not autonomous in the sense that they can begin to act on their own and trigger changes; they must be pushed to do so:

> But the 'elemental' must never be thought of as itself a prime mover; it is simply a latent force, which needs an external power to set it in motion. It may be noted that although all classes of the essence have the power of reflecting images from the astral light as described above, there are varieties which receive certain impressions much more readily than others - which have, as it were, favourite forms of their own into which upon disturbance they would naturally flow unless absolutely forced into / some other, and such shapes tend to be a trifle less evanescent than usual. (Id., 55-56)

The spirits of nature, as rediscovered by inter alia Dr. Evans-Wentz in his study *The Fairy Faith in Celtic Countries (1911)*, and observed by clairvoyant Dora van Gelder in her book *The Real World of Fairies (1999)*, have certain well-defined characteristics and they are quite distinct of human beings. Leadbeater explains:

> We might almost look upon the nature-spirits as a kind of astral humanity, but for the fact that none of them— not even the highest—possess a permanent reincarnating individuality. Apparently therefore, one point in which their line of evolution differs from ours is that a much greater proportion of intelligence is developed before permanent individualization takes place; but of the stages through which they have passed, and those through which they have yet to pass, we can know little. The life-periods of the different subdivisions

vary greatly, some being quite short, others much longer than our human lifetime. We stand so entirely outside such a life as theirs that it is impossible for us to understand much about its conditions; but it appears on / the whole to be a simple, joyous, irresponsible kind of existence, much such as a party of happy children might lead among exceptionally favourable physical surroundings. Though tricky and mischievous, they are rarely malicious unless provoked by some unwarrantable intrusion or annoyance; but as a body they also partake to some extent of the universal feeling of distrust for man, and they generally seem inclined to resent somewhat the first appearances of a neophyte on the astral plane, so that he usually makes their freaks, they soon accept him as a necessary evil and take no further notice of him, while some among them may even after a time become friendly and manifest pleasure on meeting him. (Id., 61)

What this means is that by *impacting upon reality* by thought and intent, and through emotional focus, we actually create *elementals*, which are thought-forms that are somehow embodied and individualized. Now, what I conclude from this insight, extrapolating the research of clairvoyant Charles W. Leadbeater to shamanism, is that the shaman, when concocting the traditional Ayahuasca brew, and when focusing on it, actually builds *elementals* by his intent and the thought-forms resulting from this focus. These elementals then, are absorbed by the plant matrix, or the psychoactive compounds in entheogenic plants, and are transmitted to the adept who desires to be initiated by the shaman, through ingesting the traditional Ayahuasca brew.

There is another recent research that also seems to corroborate my hypothesis, and also Leadbeater's clairvoyant observations. It has this time nothing to do with shamanism but comes from a core physics research.

It is William A. Tiller's highly innovating research on the power of intent involved in the transformation of matter. In his book *Conscious Acts of Creation*, and the DVD with the same title, Dr. Tiller, Stanford University Professor Emeritus, claims that there is ample evidence for the fact that conscious and condensed thought, and intent impact upon matter, and actually change matter.

> Based upon years of detailed research, Dr. Tiller has amassed convincing experimental data showing that in seemingly the same cognitive space, basic chemical reactions and basic material properties can be strongly altered by human intentions. Essentially, he says, we are all capable of performing what we typically think of as miracles. (DVD Cover Text)

If our intent projected on time and space creates what Leadbeater and others call *elementals* or if it creates *thought-forms* or if it creates a collapsing of the wave function, to use an expression of quantum physics, really does not matter. We might as well call it magic thought power or telepathy. What imports is that we see that there is no magic other than the impact of spirit upon visible and tangible reality. When I extrapolate this research, I must conclude that shamanic power is more than the mechanistic ingestion of plant chemistry 'to make things happen.' Then I will see that it's the preparation of the concoction much more than its chemical ingredients that make for the outcome of the experience, and that's ultimately *intent projected into the subtle matrix of plant consciousness* that is the trigger here.

The Consciousness Theory

I shall discuss the theory that I bring forward in this paper using my own experience with Ayahuasca as a point of reference. There are eight arguments for supporting my hypothesis that I will bring forward and illustrate with examples. These arguments are:

1. Preparation of the brew;
2. Trance lasting hours after extensive purge;
3. Effect of the shaman's use of cigarette smoke;
4. The shaman's *focusing his thoughts* on the client;
5. The *strange* reception;
6. The *hypnotic view* of the shaman's face;
7. Similarity with hypnosis used in natural healing;
8. Similarity with hypnosis used in psychiatry.

Let me now discuss each of these points.

1) THE AYAHUASCA PREPARATION

Upon my question about the details of the preparation of the brew, it is highly interesting what the shaman conveyed to me the morning after my arrival in Misahualli, Ecuador. We had been discussing the religious nature of the Ayahuasca experience and Jimela, his assistant, was talking about her husband *Rafal*, a Polish businessman who, from what they said, appeared to be a prototype of a skeptic. For him, the plant simply contained a chemical that brings about certain psychedelic effects in the human brain, and it was all a matter of ingesting that chloride so as to experience the consciousness-altering effects.

Interestingly, from what I was told, things worked out in a way to firmly contradict his positivistic worldview. After several attempts to convince Rafal of proper *set and setting*, and the necessity of careful preparation of the religious experience, Esteban and Jimela said they had given up on him and let him prepare the brew by himself.

The occasion soon was given through the reception of several business friends from Poland that Rafal wished to initiate in the Ayahuasca experience. To everybody's surprise the ceremony ended with a total failure. Rafal complained later to Esteban that his friends *did not feel anything*. And Rafal himself, while having gone through the experience several times successfully when the brew was prepared, with all due care, by Esteban's mother, could not understand that the effect was practically zero this time, plus headache for several hours.

I was intrigued.

—How can that be? I asked Esteban.

—Well, he replied, you see it's not just a matter of cooking that stuff and reducing a large pot of the brew to a tiny cup that you later drink. It's not just concentrating that substance. It's much more.

—What more? I insisted.

—It's *respect*, basically. This respect must be shown in many ways. The tradition for example says that a woman who has her days must not be in the house, and the couple must not engage in intercourse during the time the brew is on the stove; the children must not make noise and preferably remain playing outside. And then, there is one more element. During the whole three to four hours the Ayahuasca is on the stove, the shaman must focus on the pot. His entire psychic energy must be *focused* upon the brew all along it's on the stove. He should not engage in any other thought, he should not leave the house, he should not have any leisure time and he should by all means not touch a woman. He must give his entire respect to the Ayahuasca until the moment it is ready.

—What does this imply practically? I asked.

—It implies that he concentrates his thought energy on the event. He is mentally preparing the event in the sense that he prays to the serpent, the *Boa Constrictor* which is the spirit of the Ayahuasca, to please provide a meaningful experience to the ones drinking the brew so that they may be guided on the right way. That means he will not quit the room where the stove is burning and he will kind of *court the brew* with his whole attention, caring for the fire, the right level of heat, and so on. He may smoke, but his mind must remain focused upon a positive outcome of the later experience. He also must feel a sort of *reverence* toward the Ayahuasca spirit. It means that he really is pure in his intentions, and not doing it for money, for example, but with the intention to help people, either for their spiritual advancement, or for healing, depending which branch of shamanism he is personally adhering to.

While I found that some of the precepts Esteban mentioned were simply destined to assure that the tradition not be spoilt by the ignoramus using it as a showcase kind of thing, I listened very carefully when he spoke about the *focus* the shaman had to give to the brew, about the mantras he had to recite over the brew, about the prayers he had to say and over the energetic input he had to give to the brew in form of *total attention* and a stringent concentration of his thought energy upon the outcome of the experience.

2) THE LASTING TRANCE

The second interesting point in the experience is that after having vomited out completely the contents of my stomach, and rather violently so, the effects of the trance lasted for several more hours.

I already felt sick after the first thirty minutes passed agreeably, went on my knees and experienced a rather painful purge because my chest and back muscles began to hurt intensely. It took at least half an hour until I was back in my chair. And even then, the vomiting reflex persisted while nothing was coming out any more, except small quantities of stomach saliva.

And every time I closed my eyes, all would restart as a meticulously working computer program. Closing my eyes was like a code contained in that software. When I closed my eyes, and not before, the intelligence namely asked me telepathically if I wished to restart; affirming silently, I was at once experiencing the *slight visual effects* again and the trance began to get hold of my body once more.

Unfortunately every time instead of being able to let myself get deeper and deeper into that agreeable state of numbness and comfort, something in me terribly resisted and built an annoying level of anxiety that I was absolutely unable to get rid of. The anxiety, then, in turn triggered the vomiting reflex. I was mentally very clear about it all and how it was setup altogether, and told Esteban several times that I understood my resistance to the brew as a psychological defense against self-abandonment; and yet I was unable to cope with that dreadful anxiety.

Esteban however had no advice for me except suggesting me to go back to my room and sleep, and I felt helpless, then, and kind of *guilty*. Why was I resisting?

This went on for several turns. Each turn I would call him for help and he would slowly get up from his chair, put one of his hands on my head, blow cigarette smoke in my face and give strokes to my luminous body with the feather, and this felt *great*. Interestingly, when he blew smoke in my face, the trance immediately vanished, even if I left my eyes closed. How could that be, as the DMT was all the time in my blood?

These few moments filled me with delight, with confidence, with positive feelings and a sense of well-being.

Then I would thank him, he would go back to his chair and sink in his own trance, and all would get back to the former desperate condition, and the vomiting would restart.

And eventually I asked to be guided back to my room and even there, about one to two hours after I had vomited out the brew, the process would restart in just the same way as before, just upon closing my eyes as the signal to restart.

Sleeping was only possible in the early morning hours, after more than two hours of a virulent duplex reaction of my body: I got diarrhea and vomiting at the same time. I was once really laughing about it, while I felt so much pain and misery, because I was getting into a *rocking* movement between the toilet and the sink that were luckily quite close to each other. That was my Ayahuasca rock!

Only when I was *completely empty and pure*, I felt I was ready for sleep. And then it was really wonderful, like being in heaven, a wonderful dreamless sleep and a very happy *light* feeling when waking up in the early morning.

3) THE SHAMANIC TREATMENTS

How can it be that the treatments I received from the shaman could completely change my condition for the time they lasted? As I said, they consisted of several elements some of which I have not yet mentioned:

- ‣ Putting his hand on top of my head for a moment;

- ‣ Gently blowing cigarette smoke into my face;

- ‣ Giving me *magnetic strokes* with a feather-like device;

- ‣ Chanting an *ikaro*, a magic chant.

There was a moment when I became aware that my terrible anxiety had to do with my early childhood, that I had been abandoned as a small baby several times, a fact that my mother, when I was already adult, more or less hesitantly told me once when she was drunk.

I felt a great sense of comfort from the care I got from the shaman and it seemed to me that this care contained the same *love* that a mother bestows on her baby and I was just absorbing that love as if I was a small helpless baby.

But scientifically speaking, if the hypothesis is true that the trance is induced by DMT, how can the effects of the trance completely stop, while the DMT is still in the blood, under the influence of a kind of *psychosomatic energy treatment?* If the trance was *only* induced by the DMT, as a linear kind of causation, there is hardly any even remotely logical reply to find to this question. However, from the perspective of my hypothesis that the plant is only a *passive matrix* absorbing and remitting, and perhaps amplifying as well, the *thought energy* received from the shaman, then what I am saying begins to make sense.

Truly, *all* the effects of the DMT ceased, including the disagreeable swindle that set in every time when I opened my eyes, and I left them open every time I got the treatment as I found it pacifying and nice, and liked to see the shaman in his traditional dress and his serious and caring allure when gently blowing me cigarette smoke in my face.

There was a tenderness in his simple silent movements that greatly contributed to comforting me and alleviate my anxiety. But logically, if the shaman was the *agent* of the trance and not the DMT, or if it was both, if he was the *primary* agent of the trance using plant consciousness as a transmitter of his thought forms, it is clear that he could stop it at will and re-trigger it at any moment in time!

4) FOCUS AND INTENT

In our initial talk about the Ayahuasca experience at the morning upon my arrival, Esteban had addressed the issue of *focus and care* in dealing with his clients. I think he wanted to come over as a serious practitioner of the shamanic science as there are today many charlatans, especially in the tourism-plagued areas in Peru and Ecuador. And explaining me more about his work and attitude, he said he would very intensely focus upon the client when beginning the trance. I was intrigued and asked:

—Do you drink the Ayahuasca brew as well, or only the client?

He replied that it depended *on the wish of the client*, and if I wished him to drink the brew together with me, that was okay with him. I affirmed that I wished him to do that and asked him why he focused or concentrated upon the client after the latter had ingested the brew? He replied he focused his mind on the client in order to help him better access the *boa spirit*, the mother spirit of the Ayahuasca, as he himself had been in touch with this spirit from the start, and that this was after all the precondition to being a shaman.

Thus, consciously remembering this conversation with Esteban, I tightly observed him when we started the ceremony, and indeed, after we had drunk the brew from the beautifully carved traditional silver cups, he was sitting down not like me in the beach chair, stretched out and relaxed, but in a fetal forward position that suggested to me he was *concentrating on something*. And he remained in that position for a long time, actually as long as the preparation lasted, the time before the DMT begins to being absorbed by the body and deploy its effect—which is about thirty to forty minutes.

Then, when I felt the trance began, he was stretching out in the chair in a more relaxed position. And I think that even for a third observer this connection of events, this

Gestalt as it were would suggest the hypothesis that it's the shaman who is the *primary trigger of the experience,* and not just some chlorides in a plant concoction.

5) THE STRANGE RECEPTION

Upon entering the hut, I saw three human figures in beach chairs and did not recognize them. I was *unable* to recognize who they were, as if my thoughts were seized by an unknown power, or as if there was an overlay over my thinking process. I felt I was floating.

Please note that at that moment I had just come from my room, refreshed after some sleep, and yet suddenly, upon entering the place where the ritual was going to take place, dominated by an alien force.

I have never had memory lapses or anything even remotely close to a lack of memory for human faces. I have a very good memory for human faces, even after long years to have known a person, and meeting her again. But here, there is no valid reason to be found why I did not recognize the three persons sitting there.

Something like that never happened to me before. I felt as if *under the influence* of something that rendered me incapable of assessing the reality of the simple scene I was facing. It was just after sunset, and it was not yet dark, around eight in the evening. The distance between them and me was not more than five or six meters, not more and perhaps less. The strangeness or queerness of the moment was the fact that I did not *feel* their presence. It was as if there were humans present but that these humans were strangely *disconnected* from me. And they did not invite me to come closer and just remained silent, and I felt like an idiot, not knowing what to do, not knowing what to say. Eventually, feeling really *embarrassed*, I asked if they knew where *Jimela and Esteban* were? And only then the female got up from her chair and approached me and I saw it was Jimela.

When I apologized for not having recognized them upon entering the hut, they said it did not matter, *but to me it mattered a lot*. How could something like that happen? It remains a mystery to me until this day. I namely evaluate this event as an overlay of consciousness. Already at that moment the shaman tried to get into my consciousness interface, and he did this by what he said he always did when preparing for accompanying a client on an Ayahuasca trip: he *focused* on the client's consciousness. This *focusing on the client* simply was a native variation of what in Western medical science we call hypnosis. He had *hypnotized* me, even before I had taken in a drop of the Ayahuasca brew.

And this is essentially the core of my hypothesis. And as I am not a newcomer to hypnosis, because otherwise I would probably not have discovered this intriguing explanation of how shamanism works, I erect this now as a theory and ask scientists for evaluating it by either corroborating or falsifying it.

I will honestly relate in this paper my earlier experiences with hypnosis both in the setting of natural healing and in the medical hypnosis setting.

6) THE HYPNOTIC VIEW

Strangely, when I was in the trance, I saw the shaman's face differently. I guess the experience would frighten anyone with lesser paranormal knowledge and experience.

His face seemed distorted, ugly and diabolic. His mouth was shifted to the right, open and white inside. And this *strange mouth* did not move while I heard Esteban talking, and even talking quite fast, so fast that I wanted to tell him to talk more slowly because my understanding of Spanish, while normally good, was reduced in trance, but finally I did not get a word out and just remained silent.

I remembered my experiences with hypnosis and especially the one I went through with the quite extraordinary female German healer that I will report further down.

Needless to add that this *strangeness* about Esteban's face resulted only in increasing my anxiety and discomfort about the whole of the Ayahuasca experience.

7) HYPNOSIS AND NATURAL HEALING

It is important to retain here that hypnosis itself was not at all something strange or alien to me because I have had quite extensive experience with it in the past, and I think it is important that I relate this experience shortly.

To repeat it, without this experience, I do not think I would have come up with the present hypothesis; I would probably have accepted my Ayahuasca experience as a *queer* one and forgotten about it.

Now, let me be very precise what I am talking about. I am talking here about *medical hypnosis*, not about *stage hypnosis*. There is almost a world of difference between both forms of hypnosis. Medical hypnosis is a form of auto-hypnosis in the sense that it builds upon the full consent of the patient and his active participation in the progression of the trance, while in stage hypnosis the willpower of the individual or the entire audience that is hypnotized is as good as put to zero. Let me illustrate this a little further. It is recognized in the meantime that, for example, the acrobatic trick of *sawing the woman* can be done in two different ways. The traditional way was to hypnotize the entire audience and *suggest* to them what they were going to see, as for example the woman cut in two, who yet afterwards leaves the box unhurt.

As stage hypnosis has been *discredited as a form of abuse* and also because the art of stage hypnosis was an orally transmitted knowledge and got more and more lost with the disappearance of the *circus* as an institution, today, in almost all cabaret's, when you see the *sawing the woman* trick, it's a simple trickster effect you are succumbing to. And yet still today a famous popular figure such as *David Copperfield* admits that part of his magic is hypnosis, and not only tricking the audience out with visual and sensory effects, immense speed of action, and uncanny ways to act.

Thus, the two experiences of hypnosis that I wish to relate here, and the further ones that I will report in the next paragraph exclusively deal with medical hypnosis, and not with stage hypnosis. And it goes without saying that I do not suspect Esteban to be a charlatan, but an integer shaman who applies, as exactly as possible, a tradition that he shares with several tribes of Shuar natives, and that he learnt from an old and experienced senior shaman.

The two experiences of hypnosis that I will relate are quite different while both can be qualified as *medical* hypnosis. Their difference is that in the first experience the hypnosis is a person-to-person one, while in the second experience the hypnosis is a person-to-group one and thus a form of collective hypnosis.

The first experience was taking place back in 1997, when I had just returned to Germany from an exhausting two-year business trip to Asia, with my intestinal flora completely down. I had gone through severe diarrhea and intense dehydration over months and was at that time still consulting medical doctors who gave me high amounts of antibiotics to fight the diarrhea.

The result was that the diarrhea continued despite all but my *intestinal flora was completely destroyed* by the long-term antibiotics treatment.

I was suffering from chronic fatigue and felt very lethargic, lacking motivation and appetite. It was for this reason that I consulted a *homeopathic healer* for help. I got several effective treatments and one of them, the one I remember most vividly, was a treatment with the famous *Bach flower essences*.

The female practitioner who told me she had studied hypnosis and Reiki with a powerful Filipino healer, first wanted to choose the right Bach flower essence for me and my problem. She explained me very patiently the various methods for finding the energy essence corresponding to my organism's *energy code* and asked me which one I preferred. I chose the most direct one, the one that is done through hypnosis, and the experience was going to be a particularly revealing one for me.

She was sitting at a forty-five degree angle at my right and asked me to put my left hand in her right hand. Then she told me to look in her eyes while she would take one flacon after the other in her left hand to *sense* the effect the vibration of the plant essence had on my organism. Never before was I hypnotized so easily, so effectively and so joyfully. It was a *very agreeable condition* and I felt very clearly how each of the essences impacted energetically upon me.

She said I was going to feel either joyful, peaceful, positive and happy, which indicated that the essence was right for me, or I was feeling queer, anxious and negative, which was indicating that the essence was *not compatible* with my aura's vibrational structure. Now, what I wish to report about this experience is something really unusual and that I would call *the hypnotic view*.

What I want to say is that from the moment I was hypnotized I realized that *my perception of ordinary reality shifted* and I saw things differently, in a distorted way, or I even saw things that we ordinarily never see. And what I found most amazing was that I saw on the front of my healer a *huge third eye*, as real as it could ever be, a very intelligent-looking large human eye that did not for the least frighten me. In the contrary, in that special hypnotic condition I knew and acknowledged that I saw her *third eye*, her sixth chakra, only that in this special view I could visualize this eye that all the old mythologies abound of telling us.

And I told her at once about my discovery and she was not the least astonished. She said that other patients had seen it as well and that it was quite a normal experience for her, and that according to her Filipino teacher it showed that she had a great innate potential for healing—and this was really true as her treatment was the most effective one can imagine.

It was almost miraculous; in fact, I was cured within three months, and with only six sessions.

Two years later I started off to another fascinating healing experience, this time directly with a Filipino healer. At that time the magazines in Germany were full of reports about Filipino healers and the photos were absolutely dumbfounding. I saw that the healer had both his hands deep within the belly of a female patient and that there was blood all around, so much blood, and that suddenly he took out something from her intestines, something like a black stone, and threw it on the floor and declared to have found the *evil* in her body. I really thought it was all a dirty trick and wanted to know the truth about it.

Thus I signed up when a befriended natural healer from Hamburg called me and invited me for an audience in a naturopathy practice in Frankfurt where I was going to meet one of the most powerful Filipino healers.

While I studied parapsychology over the years, already during my law studies, I was very skeptical regarding this kind of healing. I told to myself I'd be very watchful to find out what was their trick, while I thought to myself that the soundest hypothesis for all this to happen simply was group hypnosis.

However I was struck by the fact that this hypnosis can affect photographic plates as well, and be taken on video. So, after all, can it be explained with group hypnosis? I had seen this in those magazines even before I went to Frankfurt, and thus it was possible to photograph something that is not to explain within our present reality paradigm. It is and remains a miracle until this day.

I plead for the hypnosis theory here simply because I was experienced with medical hypnosis already and knew how it *felt* and how ordinary perception reacts to it. Because it's really that once you have experienced hypnosis, you know for all times *how it feels* when somebody tries to hypnotize you. You are *aware* that you are being hypnotized in a certain moment, and you can fight it if you don't wish to succumb to it, however pleasurable it may feel. Let me add that indeed, generally, it feels very pleasurable if your general anxiety level is not, like mine at that time, higher than average and you build a resistance against it.

Now, they seemed to try everything to avoid resistance when we were comfortably installed in the natural healer's practice in Frankfurt.

We were being thoroughly prepared for the experience, for more than two hours, during which the healer was still busy with another group. We did not see him and had to remain in a special meeting room where we were being instructed about the strictly spiritual principles that traditional Filipino healers are bound to. We were really well informed and I got to know the first names of most of the participants that were women in their great majority. The atmosphere in the group was friendly and amicable and I felt really relaxed when we entered the room where I saw the healer on the floor, near to a bed and next to a vessel with burning incense. He seemed to be in a deep state of prayer and meditation. In the room several pictures showing the *Holy Virgin* and *Jesus the Christ* were hanging on the walls, and the audience was visibly collected and in a state of respect and awe upon entering the room.

During the whole experience I did not feel the slightest discomfort or fear and I wish to state this right at the start of this report because it so sharply contrasts with my Ayahuasca experience.

Then, all went exactly as I had seen it reported in the magazines. The healer called one of the women to the bed and let her stretch out comfortably, asking her to slightly open the belt of her trousers or skirt so that he could plainly touch her abdomen.

By the way, none of the women felt the slightest discomfort at this demand of the healer. His requesting her to take off her shirt equally did not result in any resistance. Then he *opened* her belly by the navel entry, and virtually penetrated into the navel with the fingers of his right hand, until the navel was an open hole of about the size of the healer's fist.

This opening bled abundantly, and the healer then introduced both of his hands through the navel hole until deep in the woman's intestines. He seemed to search for something in there. Several times, he extruded a part of the large or small intestines, looked at them or rubbed them. He appeared to search for something particular and almost in every case he found it: it was objects like small stones, most of the time of black color, and when he got one he threw it visibly and audibly on the floor.

One of the most interesting details is namely that upon awakening from our collective hypnosis, not only was there no blood anywhere, but there were absolutely no stones to be found on the floor!

Then the woman who was sitting to my left was called. She was a young lady who had complained in our previous talks about a problem with digestion that lasted over many years and that she thought could not be cured with Western medicine, as she had *tried everything already*. With her, the treatment took longer than with any other participant and she seemed to suffer from it, was howling two times very deeply from the depth of her body, like a hurt animal, and gave me a deep regard when she returned, saying:

—I feel *very* hurt, I am suffering great pain!

I was kind of shocked, so much the more as I was called as the next patient. But in my case all went fine and I did not feel anything yet had avoided to open my eyes, somewhat afraid I could be shocked to see blood, yet did not feel any pain. And upon returning to my seat, I immediately asked her if she had seen me bleeding and she replied that, yes, I had been bleeding abundantly and that the healer had put his two hands in my intestines but that in my case the treatment had been a lot shorter than with most of the other patients, and especially herself. I was asking her then if her pain was less and she said that indeed, the pain was gradually decreasing, giving rise to a feeling of comfort that she had not experienced in many years.

Later we were discussing and exchanging about this daring experience but never got a chance to talk directly to the healer. However, the naturopath and owner of the practice offered a free consultation and revealed to be a very good initiate into this practice that he had learned from several Filipino healers. Thus, we all left that experience with a great feeling of delight and amazement, and I can only say with Goethe that school knowledge will not suffice to explain this extraordinary form of healing.

To avoid a misunderstanding, let me be very clear and to the point: I do *not* say that healing induced by hypnosis, related to hypnosis or which may be a veiled form of hypnosis was charlatanism or was not effective. In the contrary!

What I say is that healing which seems *miraculous* to us is in fact a treatment that is so effective that we can't believe it when we compare it to our ordinary, and rather palliative, healing methods. I further say that this *effectiveness* is due to *suggestion* and that suggestion is a command that uses the *power of the word* to impact upon the condition of the body.

The only difference between the normal waking state and the hypnotic state is that in the latter, the body is more suggestible.

Now, what most people don't want to see is that the healing brought about by suggestion is by no means fake healing, but healing that is as good or even better than ordinary healing.

Sometimes we understand certain things when we look at their contrary, or their negative side. So let me give an example that demonstrates what I am saying. It is an old experiment and has been repeated often by *Milton Erickson* to demonstrate the power of hypnosis as a verbal suggestion that directly *impacts* upon the soma. The patient is in deep hypnosis and is told by the hypnotherapist that a sizzling hot iron will be applied to her arm for a few seconds.

Then, the therapist takes the iron which is of course cold, and applies it to the patient's arm. Immediately the body reacts *is if the iron was really burning hot,* and builds a huge watering blister. This blister is still present when the patient wakes up and it takes the same time to heal out as if she was really burnt. It goes without saying that she also experienced some local pain and had to give her full consent before engaging in that really dumbfounding experiment.

Now imagine that what can be done negatively to the body through verbal suggestion can as well done to it *positively*. This explains that under hypnosis healing can be instantaneous and totally effective!

The most important to report in our context is the similarity in the way the hypnotic trance manifests. You will read about it again in the next paragraph regarding medical hypnosis used in psychiatry. Let me summarize so far that this trance usually begins in the arms with a relaxation of the hand and lower arm muscles and then gradually *mounts upwards* into the body, passing region by region like a gentle embrace, thus the upper arms, the shoulders, the face and head, then the chest and the muscles around the heart.

The fear block I experienced was located in my heart region and this already had been confirmed by the homeopathic healer in Germany who, after an extended treatment, told me that from my earliest childhood I had suffered a problem with being abandoned and that my heart chakra was *closed*, whereupon she opened it by slightly touching my heart region with her finger. This slight touch triggered an amazing amount of tears and I suddenly remembered *early childhood feelings* and went through a really difficult moment during about one hour, upon which I was left in total peace and serenity, feeling like *newborn*.

To summarize, I reacted very differently during the inducement of the hypnotic trance. In two instances, with the Filipino healer and the German homeopath, it was a very agreeable and smooth experience, while when I did it with psychiatrists, it was rather anxiety-creating. And with the Ayahuasca it was frightening as well.

I conclude that the fact to experience fear or not depends on the hypnotizer and not the particular kind of hypnosis he or she uses. I tend to believe, and I am open to change my opinion if it should reveal as scientifically unsound, that hypnosis requires a high amount of immediate trust between the patient and the hypnotherapist or shaman, or natural healer.

When this trust is lacking, anxiety will interfere with the depth of the hypnosis or make it a rather disagreeable negative experience.

8) MEDICAL HYPNOSIS

The first time I experienced medical hypnosis was in 1989, in Geneva, with a quite famous transactional and Gestalt therapist, *Dr. Margareta Robinson.*

It was the first time that I ever got in touch with hypnosis, and unfortunately I was *not informed that it was hypnosis* that I was going to experience! When she presented her approach to me, Mrs. Robinson was talking about a combination of transactional and Gestalt therapy that she seemed to have melted into a powerful approach for healing various problems from neuroses to narcissism. I was surprised at the ease of how that hypnosis was brought about. It was by means of using a pet, a *teddy bear*. Indeed, upon holding that magic pet I felt a deep and very *sad* kind of relaxation affecting my body and mind. I suddenly felt extremely tired, and powerless; that sensation was not at all joyful and agreeable, but an experience that left me very depressive. I began to feel apathetic and helpless, *very powerless*, like a baby abandoned at the mercy of some or the other untrustworthy caretaker.

My muscles became weaker and weaker, as if I was given a sleep potion, until I could not lift my arms up any more. Then she asked me to get up, handed me a tennis racket and said:

—Here on this bed your mother is stretched out. She is sleeping. Hit her with this racket as much as you like!

And I could not do it and told her about it. She said:

> —Well, this proves only your problem to me. You have internalized all the violence and resistance against your mother and are for the moment unable to exteriorize it. That's why you suffer from depressions. They indicate the deep hatred against your mother and we would have to work on releasing this energy.

I did *not* agree with her and her approach. I felt she was pushing the therapy in a very hurried and jumpy way that was not bringing me relief while I must say that when coming home from each session, I was seeing the world with other eyes, so much all seemed to have changed for the better.

I then began a hypnotherapy with an American therapist and this therapy progressed *much more carefully,* while I must admit that we never entered a really deep level of hypnosis because of the fear problem I already described earlier in this report.

SUMMARY

The experience with *Ayahuasca* as I made it with the Shuar shaman back in 2004 is in my view supportive for a nonlinear and multi-causative, rather than a linear and single-causative theory of cognition regarding the psychedelic visions and insights subsequent to ingesting the traditional brew.

In addition, in my discussions with the shaman and his assistant, equally a Shuar native, it appeared clear that they themselves rejected the linear and single-causative theory of the kind stating 'it's the DMT that makes for all that Ayahuasca does,' explaining that all the art was in the traditional procedure of preparing the cure and the consciousness focus that forms part of it. In fact, the negative experience of the Polish business man with the brew, and the resulting ineffectiveness of it, shows evidently that the single-causative linear theory of cognition regarding the Ayahuasca is flawed.

The *cognitive experience* with Ayahuasca is probably not a simple direct consequence of the plant-containing DMT, as this has been suggested by Terence McKenna and his brother, the ethnobotanist Dennis McKenna in their book *The Invisible Landscape (1994)*.

In the eight specific particularities that I have brought forward and commented on, there appears to be a certain weight of the evidence for a causation of the cognitive experience by shamanic consciousness acting as a hypnotic agent on the plant matrix that serves as a resilient *transmitter and amplifier of thought energy.*

The specific cognitive elucidation and the insights experienced after ingestion of the brew are brought about by a multi-causative impact of the *consciousness imprint* on my own consciousness interface.

This impact was brought about through the strong focus of the shaman's thought energies on my perception matrix and reception frequency both during the preparation of the brew and at the onset of the intake ritual. This concentration of *thought and attention* is known both from psychic research and clairvoyant experience, and from medical hypnosis to bring about an energy imprint in form of a *consciousness overlay* on the perception interface of the receiver.

I am talking about a multi-causative effect here because the evidence at stake does not allow to exclude any *proprietary additional impact* of the plant consciousness in the process of triggering the consciousness overlay. In fact, there are details in my report that indicate such an additional impact directly from the side of the plant realm, as a *genuine plant-proprietary consciousness* reaching out into my human consciousness.

The most striking detail in this context was that I had myself the clear intuition of being in touch with a proprietary *plant consciousness* or even an unspecific *universal consciousness* that I was in an ongoing telepathic exchange with as long as the trance lasted, and that I was, strangely enough, in state of turning that telepathic communication on and off by simply closing or opening my eyes.

In addition, the obvious parallels with my previous hypnosis-induced alterations of consciousness demonstrate that the focusing of thought energy that the shaman did as a preparation for the ritual in accordance with traditional native tradition has in some way to do with hypnosis, or brings about an effect or imprint on another's consciousness that is similar to a hypnotic injunction.

The most important detail in this context is the fact that there is a *plant-specific matrix* involved in this process, and not just a shaman focusing thought energy on myself as his client. This is the specific contextual link with plant consciousness acting as a *matrix receiver* for *intent*, similar as this has been reported for water, by the elucidating research of the Japanese researcher Masaru Emoto.

As Emoto's water research suggests, it is possible to leave imprints in the memory interface of water by positive or negative affirmations, for example in the form of textual labels glued on the water bottles for some time, that produce or not in the water specific crystals. Typically so, the aesthetically appealing crystals are formed by positive and uplifting intent and correlated affirmations rather than by negative and defeating intent and affirmations.

My argument here with regard to the cognitive imprints received in the form of insights during an Ayahuasca trip is on the same lines of reasoning. My idea is that the consciousness interface of plants, at least of plants that are qualified as *entheogens* or as plants containing mind-altering compounds, serves as a transmitting and amplifying interface for the thought imprint given to it by the shaman's consciousness and thought energy. In how much the plant here participates with its own consciousness-altering compounds, such as DMT, cannot be evaluated from this experience with Ayahuasca, but needs additional, tightly curtailed research. It is namely possible that the plant chemistry, instead of being a unilateral agent of altering human consciousness, serves as a receiver, transmitter and amplifier interface for human intent and thought energy, as this has been reported by Masaru Emoto and others for the *hado*, the specific energy-interface of water.

But even Masaru Emoto has not found, and not even tried to explain the ultimate reason why human intent can have an energetic impact on water, and other substances. The explanation, or one possible explanation is given by Charles Webster Leadbeater in his 1894 booklet *Astral Plane* where he describes the function of elementals in the communication between humans and all realms of nature.

Leadbeater explains that thought is an energetic phenomenon that creates certain vibrations, called thought-forms or *elementals*. These elementals, he says further, gain permanence over time and depending on how much *emotional energy* we invest in those thoughts. And interestingly so, here we encounter the philosophy of the natives who speak about *spirits* when asked what the communicating agents were between humans and plants. And the solution of the riddle is to view the natives' explanation and the theosophical or clairvoyant view together.

The technique consists thus in imprinting intent in the plant matrix by gestating, through the power of thought-energy, certain elementals that function as communicating agents between the human and the plant realm.

These elementals, I suppose, are created during the process of collecting the Ayahuasca liana and carefully preparing the brew, and it is these elementals impacting on the plants' psychoactive substances that are becoming active and *communicative* as it were in the initiate's consciousness.

The Cognitive Experience

When asked to summarize the insights I got through the ingestion of *Ayahuasca*, I can establish the following catalog:

- The intelligence's *alien* noise interface;
- The intelligence's *pulsation* as a cosmic energy;
- The intelligence's attempts for *calling me* in touch;
- Insights about my conditioning through language;
- Insights about relationships and the world;
- Insights about love and life.

These insights did not come up in my consciousness all at once, but rather through little chunks that were repeated several times and with variations, extending virtually until the moment, early in the morning, when I feel asleep.

Interestingly so, the very last insights I got immediately before falling asleep, at around four in the morning, when stretched out on my bed, after the purge eventually had stopped.

It was then that I was suddenly intensely aware of my solitude, my utter lack of relationships, and my general feeling of being disconnected from other people. And it was then that the insights about relationships and about love and life came through.

Another interesting detail is that most insights only came up after I had asked questions to myself or this specific intelligence I was in touch with, while I had not always formulated my questions as questions, but often as affirmations that were then propelled back to me like in a boomerang effect. And what happened was that most of the time the affirmations had been slightly altered in the process.

ALIEN NOISE AND PULSATION

The first phenomenon I noticed about the specific intelligence I felt approaching right at the onset of the trance was its *alien noise*. This noise was clearly distinct from the frog concert and other natural sounds that surrounded me.

My senses were not dulled by the trance but in the contrary sharpened and I could clearly distinguish between the multitude of natural sounds around me in the clear evening air, and the specific alien noise of this intelligence.

When I should put it in words, which is somehow an impossible quest because of the paranormal reality as the contextual background, I would say it's like many, thousands or millions of human voices simultaneously whispering a mantra.

I think it is an important detail that it's not just like a machine-noise, or a tone, but that it bears a resemblance to a whispering human voice multiplied by the millions.

I know that Terence McKenna has spoken of the *machine elves* and their *alien sound* as a typical manifestation during the DMT-induced trance. But what I am saying is that in contradistinction with McKenna's perception, the sound was *not* machine-like but came over to me as *organic*, and somehow related to nature.

I call it *alien* only because there is no sound or anything you could have ever heard in your wake life that bears any similitude to this sound. Actually I prefer the term *noise* over sound because noise is a term used in telecommunications, as something that can either be a background hiss, such as the hiss on vinyl records, or a certain unspecific hum contained in ultra-short wave receivers, or else a term used by graphics designers for the lacking smoothness of an image. All these connotations fit here, in my opinion.

The presence of the *natural intelligence* of the Ayahuasca spirit is related to sound as it manifests not visually in the first place, but audibly, and thus it bears an impact of *resonance*. It has to do with vibration, and with frequency. It has to do with cell resonance and with Sheldrake's notion of *morphic resonance,* as it resonates the mix of nature's frequencies, and comes over as the *Universal Communicator,* and at the same time, the Universal Bearer of all these energies.

—See Rupert Sheldrake, A New Science of Life (1995)

This is exactly what I wanted to convey actually about the *organic quality* of the sound: to me it bears a morphological resemblance with organic life, and organic sounds, only that it overlays many or a multitude of such sounds in its audible presence. So, as with ultra-wave communication, the Ayahuasca intelligence comes through on *a certain frequency,* and not on another, and the frequency is tuned by ingesting the brew, and here the DMT may well be active as the attunement agent.

From the onset of the trance, this *alien noise* was gradually rising in volume, and after some time, I clearly understood that this sound was something like the *pulsation* of the universe, of life, and in that moment I got an intense awareness of the fact that all creation is in fact a result of *sound,* and that life intrinsically is vibration, is sound. This is an insight that I have well today acquired through having studied hermetic and modern literature on sound used for healing, but ten years ago, when I went through this experience, I was not yet consciously aware of this fact.

Hence, I can say that this insight was novel to me. And yet, it sounded completely sound and solid, so to speak, and did not come as a surprise. It is as if the intelligence had not just communicated me something using telepathic touch, but as if it had subtly awakened my intelligence to a novel insight that from that moment could not be unthought any more from my consciousness.

THE FIVE DEPTH LEVELS

From the onset of the Ayahuasca trance, I got clear *telepathic messages* that I should go beyond that first phase during which I saw subtle geometric forms that were of a lesser brilliance and luminosity than those I had seen in some research volumes, such as Pablo Amaringo's *Ayahuasca Visions (1999)*. And I knew in that moment that, contrary to what I had learnt and heard from others about the Ayahuasca trip, the visions were of no importance at all.

I simply *knew* this or it was communicated to me telepathically in that moment. At the same time I was called upon by the intelligence to go beyond that first rather insignificant level and explore into the next depth level, but that for getting there I needed to *relax more* and let go some of the fear that I felt was like a congested knot in my heart chakra. The intelligence also communicated to me that there were in total *five depth levels* in the Ayahuasca experience.

I think it is significant to note that I found this in none of the books I had read when doing my research on shamanism and entheogens, and I haven't found it either subsequent to my experience in any additional books I read about the Ayahuasca quest. What I have well learnt from Michael Harner's seizing account of his own primary Ayahuasca trip, during which he almost died, in his book *Ways of the Shaman (1990)*, was that he had himself experienced, right from the start, the toughest depth level—encountering the primal dragons. But neither Harner nor other researchers and experiencers have given an account of how many depth levels there are, while all seem to agree that there are in fact several levels of intensity to be possibly experienced during the psychedelic trip.

There is something like a *consensus doctorum* in the literature about the ritual use of entheogens that sets a relationship between dose of the substance intake to the intensity of the trip—and here I made a meaningful typo, writing *insensity* instead of intensity. This is true in so far as the experience gets weirder and apparently more insane as a result of our cherished assumptions about reality, and the *sense* that we give to certain experiences being shifted in the course of the strong psychedelic experience.

However, I want to warn here again falling in the trap of single causality and of linear thinking when it goes to evaluate a type of experiences that is intrinsically multi-causal and nonlinear in character. In my view, the *depth levels* that Ayahuasca contains are probably not triggered by the dose alone, but also by the *intensity of the focus and intent* bestowed upon the brew from the side of the shaman.

Now, what is also rather uncanny and that I have not found in any description of Ayahuasca trips anywhere in a book is that the intelligence gave me *signals*. It was like a gentle knocking at my doors of perception. I typically saw a flickering of five red squares at the top upper left corner of my vision, when my eyes were closed.

I intuitively knew in these moments that this was the signal to go deeper in the trance, or jump to the next depth level, only that to my sadness I could not follow the invitation because of my fear block. Every time it happened, the fear came up and prevented me from going beyond. And this blockage was not just mental. If it had been mental only I could have overcome it.

In fact, I wanted to overcome it, but then the blockage somatized and manifested as vomiting, and later also as strong diarrhea. It was not only my mind that resisted the experience, but also, and perhaps primarily so, my body.

CALLING ME IN TOUCH

I was constantly communicating with the intelligence, from the first to the last moment of my Ayahuasca experience. I had prayed already before the onset of the experience, while still on my bed in my hotel room, that through this wisdom quest I might receive guidance for finding my life's mission and for being freed from my constant anxiety, and I kept addressing the Ayahuasca spirit in respectful terms during the experience to assist me in my quest for truth.

And as if it was a final test that this intelligence really understood me, I said this, when I felt I wanted to go back to my room and sleep:

> Dear Ayahuasca Spirit, thank you so much for all the insights, please stop calling me now. I know that I was not able to get over my fear block now, and I hope I can find the courage to continue because I know you will reveal me so much more when I get deeper in the trance. But for now I have decided to stop. It is enough.

And immediately the *calling* stopped, the flickering lights did not appear any more and the *alien* noise was calming down and stopped as well. This alien noise, I understood then, was the *language* of that intelligence. It was something like many people, in some distance, speaking simultaneously, and as if many conversations converged to a chaotic no-sense that was but the secret code or pattern of a deeper, much more unified language of the universe, and of which our human language is only a tiny and almost insignificant part.

FREEING FROM CONDITIONING

The plant intelligence I was in touch with seemed to convey to me telepathically that I was *locked* in language, that all my experiencing of life was conditioned upon language, and that I hardly ever perceived life *directly*, spontaneously, as an immediate connection. At the same time, I received the instant confirmation that this intelligence was *universal* in the sense that it was connected to all, and that it was constantly trying to connect all, such as a total communication matrix of the universe, and third that it was and represented all-that-is.

I became keenly aware that this intelligence was the *Logos*, and that it simply *was*, and it gently invited me to enter this connection, this wonderful all-encompassing love that it irradiated and communicated.

LOVE, LIFE AND RELATIONSHIPS

Before I come to talk about the important insights I received about love, life and relationships at the end of my Ayahuasca trip, I would like to expand a little on that peculiar question-and-answer game that was developing between the intelligence and myself. In fact, I was naturally the one who, puzzled, asked the questions, and the intelligence always *instantly* replied. When I say instantly I really mean that the reply did not even take one second to appear, but it was instantly in my mind upon formulating the question. I think this is quite uncanny as a fact while it is probably known to other researchers.

And the reply could have various forms. It was always economical in the sense that it never wasted even one syllable, and when this was possible, it was just turning around my question, or simply *shortened* it, in order to give the answer. This is something I really have never heard of before, and it reminded me of a higher evolution of certain circus jokes or mind games, and it definitely had a note of humor to it.

The most important experience in this context was that my questions were somehow returned as questions-that-question-again-my-questions so as to give the answer to any question as a result of the question itself—and not as some kind of outside input. So in a way, the phenomenon suggested that the intelligence I was communicating with was altogether *not* an outside or outward or distinct intelligence, but simply a part of my own higher consciousness.

Now, succinctly speaking, this manifested in a way that every thought I had was immediately returned to its contrary and every phrase that I pronounced in my mind was immediately reduced to some more general insight. For example I heard myself thinking:

—I love life …

And it was immediately reduced to:

—I *love* …

Or I heard myself thinking:

—I feel to be alive …

And it was reduced to:

—I *feel* …

And now, when you evaluate the returned, condensed or shortened statements *as answers*, you will notice that they are indeed *highly intelligent answers* to underlying questions. The first statement could be read as an underlying question of the kind: 'What does it mean to love life?'

Now from the returned shortened version, it becomes evident that when I love, I simply love—which means I am in a state of love, and thus as a result I love all-that-is, and thus *also* life. So it's somehow unintelligent to say a sentence like 'I love life' because love cannot be reduced to just a concept like 'love of life' or it is that: a mere concept.

By the same token, to divide love off in concepts such as 'filial love,' 'passionate love,' 'love for children' or 'love for the elder' does not make sense, as what it produces is splitting the holistic notion of love off in tidy compartments that are *concepts of love,* but not *love* any more. So somehow the intelligence politely corrected what I was saying without correcting me! And I immediately understood the hint, like when you solve a *koan* in Zen.

—A koan is a paradoxical riddle that parallels the paradoxes that are the outcome of our intellectual, conceptual look at life. However, please be aware that life or nature is not per se paradoxical, but bound together in infinite harmony. The paradoxical nature of life is an appearance of reality made up through our limited, concept-based and thought-created image of reality—and not reality itself.

Eventually I became quiet and full of gratitude and I said this in my thought, in my German mother tongue:

—*Ich möchte Liebe!* (I want love)

And immediately the response was, in German:

—*Ich möchte lieben* ... (I want to love)

And with all my heart and soul I understood this subtle difference and it was clear to me that in this tiny difference of syntax there was *all the difference*. It was the secret to happiness. I had taken love as a commodity that can be received, stating that I wanted to be loved, instead of understanding that love was not something to receive, but a state of being to develop into, something like an attitude, and this attitude, it seemed to me, simply was *total openness*.

And at that moment I became intensely and acutely aware that I was not in that state of love, that I was not giving love to others, and I also knew *why! It was fear that blocked me off to love.*

And Krishnamurti's saying came to mind that for the first time I really understood: *where fear is, love cannot be.*

And I think this insight transformed something in me. And really, afterwards my relationships changed much for the better.

Literature Review

The first book I read on the subject of shamanism in the 1980s was *Les appeleurs d'âmes* by Sabine Hargous, a French ethnologist. This study published in 1975 with the well-known French publisher *Albin Michel* and that translates in English as *The Soul Callers* is a well-documented thesis on the shamanic universe of the native populations in the Andes. This book clearly centers on one aspect of shamanism only: the healing. The study divides into three main parts *Indigenous Pathogenics*, *Diagnostics* and *Magic Rituals*. However, implicitly, the author expands on virtually all aspects of shamanic spirituality.

After all, it was perhaps a good thing to have begun with this study and not with something that conveys a *felt sense* of indigenous living, as for example the excellent books of Michael Harner, because Sabine Hargous' approach represents decidedly a Western view, with all that this implies. She calls natives *primitives*, as it was the custom in traditional ethnology and that says in one word more than a whole thesis about what quantum physics has taught us about *the observer standpoint*. But for this reason the study is not to be discarded. I would even say this consciousness split is important for some people who else would never read a similar study because their anxiety to *remain fixated in their own cultural belief system* is greater than their curiosity to explore other, and certainly more direct methods to approaching reality. And as, at this time,

I was still working on my international law doctorate and not yet on the daring path to question the Western science approach—while I became more and more critical to it—this was certainly a good book to begin with. As the author was keeping her distance to an alternative worldview, she was nonetheless getting deeply immersed in the world of the natives, and her book is all but a dry thesis paper.

The next book that virtually fell in my hands, as I found it on a garage sale, was Michael Harner's bestseller *Ways of the Shaman (1980/1982)*. This book had a different impact upon me than the first one. It was a revealing new learning!

While I found that Sabine Hargous' study had a rather philosophical touch, Michael Harner's study really moved me into planning myself a voyage, and it was there and then that I took the decision to try out Ayahuasca.

Before I got to read more books by empirically minded researchers, and as I had to wait quite a long time to get the books from Amazon USA shipped to France, I ordered two books by Spanish authors in Barcelona, Spain, that I got within two days only and I did not regret to have read them, as they dealt with the philosophical and conceptional issues.

The first was a book from one of the foremost Spanish authorities on the subject of shamanism, Josep M. Fericla, entitled *Al Trasluz de la Ayahuasca (2002)*. Reading this book, I realized that in Spain there is absolutely no *moralistic bias* against psychedelics such as, for example in France, Great Britain or the USA.

However, compared to France, the legislation even in the United States is still quite liberal. France is really the worst one can imagine in any of the Western nations; this is after all comprehensible when you look at the Cartesian mindset of French people, their extreme left-brainism and their almost total lack of true spirituality.

In Spain, the exact contrary is true which obviously has nothing to do with left or right-wing governments. In Spain, nobody would get the idea to put Cannabis on an index. It is *as legal as Cuban cigars* and perhaps, definitely, more healthy than those. The second impression was that for this Spanish author, the psychedelic quest was a real parallel way of perception, serious not only for freaks and pioneers in consciousness exploration, but also for philosophers.

Fericla is one of the finest philosophers in Spain, and not just for his preoccupation with psychedelics, but in general. Thus, a book from a real authority, and written with a serious mind and true commitment for consciousness exploration. This book confirmed my decision to really take on the voyage I had planned and not just do a theoretical research on the topic of shamanism within the greater project of my research on the *Eight Dynamic Patterns of Living*.

The literary magazine *El Idiota* that I equally had ordered in Spain contained many interesting contributions one of which I wish to mention here as I find it very important. This special issue of the magazine entitled *Visionarios*, contains an article about Carlos Castaneda. *Carlos Castaneda: El Enigma del Último Nagual*, an intriguing study by Cristóbal Cobo Quintas that deals with the somewhat mysterious content of Castaneda's well-known spiritual apprenticeship with the Yaqui sorcerer Don Juan. This Spanish author sees the importance of Castaneda's books—be they invented as a part of the media debate about Castaneda pretends, be they real accounts of the practices of one of the last living witnesses of Toltec culture.

It is noteworthy that Castaneda, *inter alia* on his web site, claims to be the only legitimate last descendant of the Toltecs and spokesman for their culture within a largely ignorant world. In fact, what we learn through visions is more than just the visions; this was already clear to me when I read Castaneda myself, more than ten years ago.

And what all serious studies and reports about visionary experiences, at least those done with Ayahuasca, other DMT derivates or Peyote converge to is to affirm that these visions *enhance our understanding of nature.*

In addition, these studies contribute to helping us understand what is *direct perception* or, as we would call it today, *systems intelligence.*

In my view it's not even the visions themselves that have this impact upon our intelligence but some kind of telepathic code written into the visions, but that we are not aware of, and which is transmitted directly into our DNA or, if already contained in it, thus activated or stimulated.

Eventually the books arrived from the USA and the first one I read was Ralph Metzner's excellent reader *Ayahuasca: Human Consciousness and the Spirits of Nature (1999)* —a sampler that he edited and in which many people related personal experiences with Ayahuasca.

This book, including Metzner's highly interesting introduction, is through and through a masterpiece because it gives so many insights *simultaneously*.

It is all but a dry scientific report, but an exciting adventure to read. In a way, one cannot but feel all those individual experiences on almost a gut level, in order to definitely, and once for all, put aside a Cartesian worldview that tries to split the world off in nice little tartlets called 'science,' 'emotions,' 'perception,' 'experience', etc.

One then begins to understand that awareness is beyond all of this while it encompasses all of this, awareness being the very fact of being aware of being aware. To begin with, it is interesting to see what the primary motivation was for most if not all of the people who contributed to the reader, most of them being involved in natural healing, or otherwise working in social professions.

These people all have in common that they expected some tangible results from the experience, for becoming better healers or advisors, or for solving personal problems, and there was none of them that did not at the end of their statements confirm that the experience had been worth it and helped them to reach this goal.

The next book, that I found even more mind-boggling, was Jeremy Narby's *The Cosmic Serpent (1999)*.

This book, written by a Swiss anthropologist, originally written in French, takes a completely different perspective. Narby, questioning the native shaman's conviction that plants really transfer knowledge during the visions, states:

> First, hallucinations cannot be the source of real information, because to consider them as such is the definition of psychosis. Western knowledge considers hallucinations to be at best illusions, at worst morbid phenomena. Second, plants do not communicate like human beings. Scientific theories of communication consider that only human beings use abstract symbols like words and pictures and that plants do not relay information in the form of mental images. For science, the human brain is the source of hallucinations, which psychoactive plants trigger by way of the hallucinogenic molecules they contain. (Id., 42)

He then puts up the hypothesis that what the plants do is to open a *perception channel* to our own DNA's photon vibrations. Photon radiation of the DNA has been confirmed in recent quantum science but physicists did not go as far as saying that this photon radiation's information flow was in any way consciously *readable* for the human mind. This hypothesis has something daring about it and

Narby makes his point with quite an amount of writing skill. However, I was again and again considering the premises he based his research upon, and in my opinion, Narby made a paramount mistake in failing to question these premises before he set out to write his book. Here is what I would advance against Narby's argumentation:

—Why should mind visions *not* be the source of real information? The fact that this contradicts modern psychiatry means nothing in terms of perception theory, a field that psychiatry has nothing to deal with and does not understand anything about.

—Why should it be important how *Western knowledge* considers hallucinations? To call them *morbid phenomena* is definitely not a scientific judgment, but a moralistic opinion and as such irrelevant for the scientific researcher.

—Who says that plants do *not* communicate like human beings? Who has the knowledge to deny this possibility? The natives do not say that plants communicate like human beings; they say that plants communicate with us using a form of telepathy *that is part of consciousness itself* and that makes that communication can be cross-species.

—Scientific theories of communication consider that plants do not relay information in the form of mental images, states Narby. I want to see the treatise of communication where this is written! This sentence is highly unscientific in itself in that theories of communication deal with human communication only and are generally silent about plant communication. The mere silence of this research regarding plant communication cannot logically be interpreted as a denial of the existence of such communication, in general. Here, Narby clearly committed a logical *faux-pas*.

—Finally, the last sentence in Narby's hypothesis is equally *suggestive*, and not scientific in that it suggests namely that the human mind was seated in the brain and only in the brain, an assumption that is scientifically overthrown. Neuroscience and consciousness research now coincide in acknowledging that the mind or consciousness, while functioning through the physical brain, is not forcibly physically located in the brain, but certainly also in the pineal gland, the pituitary gland, and especially the luminous body or aura. Some go beyond and suggest the mind was located probably everywhere, even in the cells of the skin of the feet, for example, but also *outside of the body,* as psychic research has confirmed since long.

But Narby's study certainly has value in the present discussion be it as a contradicting resource. One thing was namely clear to me from most of the German and American shamanism researchers and their publications: they do not question the possibility of plants being able to communicate information to the human mind in what form however this takes place! They also do not, like Narby, start from a concept of *Western knowledge* but rather take a pioneering, open and experimental approach while sticking to the facts and avoiding speculation. And they all seem to take for granted that the mind and the brain have in common only that the brain functions like an interface for the mind to operate within us, and within all. Thus, I found that Narby was, from the start of his book, much more restrictive and skeptical than, for example Michael Harner, Adam Gottlieb, Ralph Metzner or the McKenna brothers in their respective studies.

On a similar line of reasoning while from a totally different perspective is the DMT research of an American doctor, Rick Strassman, *DMT, The Spirit Molecule (2001)*. Strassman was all but mystic-minded when he began his study with hundreds of patients to experience precisely dosed DMT injections in their veins. The book was quite boring to read, which is certainly not a mishap of the book itself but more of the reader. I just do not find much interest in this kind of soulless research that goes out to understand life from monkey experiments. Okay, a similar marathon study once conducted in France by two sociologists to disproof astrology, was finally exactly confirming its functionality. But for a serious astrologer, such a study is a circus joke for the ignoramus because since thousands of years initiated individuals knew about the cognitive value of astrology and they do not need monkey experiments to confirm this perennial knowledge.

I trust more a critical intelligent and initiated human such as, just to give an example, Michael Harner or Terence McKenna, who have taken DMT and who say with unshaken conviction that they received *real knowledge* through the experience, and not just a kaleidoscope of silly flash lights.

I was glad, then, to read something from a different mind, and frame of mind. Aldous Huxley, the author of the novel *Brave New World* and other great fiction and non-fiction writings, was one of the foremost witnesses in experiments with perception, altered perception and immediate perception. His book *The Doors of Perception (1954)* is an enlightening account of someone who approached the psychedelic experience at first rather as a philosophical curiosity.

Huxley had no or very few preconceptions and his mindset was the one that Zen calls *the beginner's mind*; thus the ideal explorer of an unknown world, at least to our Western mindset.

And Huxley's experience was entirely positive. Reading his account, you are thrilled and charmed and at one point or the other seduced to try it yourself. Huxley is very outspoken about the philosophical implications of his experience and he values it positively, so positively that he is cited in every book published on entheogens; he figures almost like an authority while, reading him, one does not have this impression at all. His style is artful, witty and charming, more than in some of his other books, in my opinion. The book is written from the heart, and there remains no doubt that Huxley loved this mushroom and its hallucinatory compound: *mescaline*. I think it is not a bad idea, for anybody interested in altered consciousness, to read this book as a kind of introduction.

Chapter Three
A Science of Pattern

Introduction

Shamanism is essentially a science of pattern, and interestingly enough, was so already thousands of years ago while modern science only now, through systems theory, has begun to see the paramount importance of pattern in the composure of living, and in the functionality of living systems.

I found *eight dynamic patterns of living* to be present in the lifestyle of most tribal shamanic peoples around the world. These eight patterns, *autonomy, ecstasy, energy, language, love, pleasure, self-regulation* and *touch*, are for the most part shunned and belittled as life-fostering values in most dominator cultures, including our postmodern civilization.

I am saying that it is precisely because we, as the most economically powerful society of the world do not comply with the eight patterns as basic regulators of life that we are at the border of mass destruction, insanity and ecological disaster.

I began identifying the perennial pro-life patterns in living by firstly invalidating the age-old principles that mainstream science declares to be the founding concepts of our universe. To put it more precisely, there was actually nothing to invalidate; I found that these alleged principles were but *intellectual assumptions*, and thus simply invalid as founding principles of life. At the same time, diligent study of the I Ching and the almost daily use of it for divination distilled in me an intuitive understanding of the real and valid patterns that are inherent in all living. I therefore simply call them *patterns of living*.

Let me first of all explain why I use the term *patterns*, deciding to discontinue the use of the term *life principles*. I indeed think that here we are facing a key point that marks the essential difference between *death science* and *life science*.

A pattern is a set of things, a certain arrangement I can make out in the complex scheme of reality, and the main characteristic of this arrangement is that it forms a *relationship* of elements with each other. It is something I can observe. A pattern can be fix or it can be changeable. It can be static or dynamic. By contrast, a principle typically is the start of a down-hierarchy. It's a top-something in a kind of up-to-down order. It is *not* something I can *observe*. Its reality is *merely intellectual:* the outcome of a conclusion I draw in my rational mind *after* observing nature. A principle thus contains my observer point or my judgment about reality.

Death science looks at life through the glasses of principles it has set before it was going to observe. It is essentially blind and proceeds by imposing characteristics upon nature. Western science traditionally has been death science; it gained its conclusions about life by vivisecting cadavers, not by observing the moving changes of living. It is, and remained, a *cadaver science* that is far removed from the changing patterns of reality.

Life science looks at life without any a priori principles or assumptions and observes the dynamic patterns and changes in the texture of life. It is a science that since its start in China, around five thousand years ago, was interested in life, and thus drew conclusions from life, and not from death. Traditional Chinese science together with most other ancient science traditions of the East is a *life science*, one branch.

The I Ching is based upon life science, and is perhaps the highest condensation of it. Needless to add that, as such, it bears no moralistic judgments about human behavior. It looks at human behavior in exactly the same way it looks at all life patterns, and sees the changing nature of it before all. Fritjof Capra in his book *The Web of Life (1996)* explains the importance of pattern when he explores the meaning of *self-organization,* which is a major characteristic pattern of living systems:

> To understand the phenomenon of self-organization, we
> first need to understand the importance of pattern. The
> idea of a pattern of organization—a configuration of

relationships characteristic of a particular system—
became the explicit focus of systems thinking in
cybernetics and has been a crucial concept ever since.
From the systems point of view, the understanding of
life begins with the understanding of pattern. (Id., 80)

In order to scientifically explore the nature of pattern
we need to *change our basic setup of scientific investigation.*
Capra explains:

In the study of structure we measure and weigh things.
Patterns, however, cannot be measured or weighed; they
must be mapped. To understand a pattern we must map
a configuration of relationships. In other words,
structure involves quantities, while pattern involves
qualities. (Id., 81)

This really involves a *radical change* in scientific
thinking because traditionally our science was
quantity-based and measure-oriented, while *systemic
science* is quality-based and relationship-oriented, a truth
that Capra exemplifies when looking at the properties of
pattern:

Systemic properties are properties of pattern. What is
destroyed when a living organism is dissected is its
pattern. The components are still there, but the
configuration of relationships among them—the
pattern—is destroyed, and thus the organism dies. (Id.)

The next important point to understand how nature
thinks is the cell's metabolism, the network that serves

recycling. Capra succinctly elaborates in his book *The Hidden Connections (2002):*

> When we take a closer look at the processes of metabolism, we notice that they form a chemical network. This is another fundamental feature of life. As ecosystems are understood in terms of food webs (networks of organisms), so organisms are viewed as networks of cells, organs and organ systems, and cells as networks of molecules. One of the key insights of the systems approach has been the realization that the network is a pattern that is common to all life. Wherever we see life, we see networks. (...) The metabolic network of a cell involves very special dynamics that differ strikingly from the cell's nonliving environment. Taking in nutrients from the outside world, the cell sustains itself by means of a network of chemical reactions that take place inside the boundary and produce all of the cell's components, including those of the boundary itself. (Id., 9)

But the most revolutionary outcome of the systems view is that our usual habit of dissecting parts of a whole for further scrutiny and scientific investigation *does not work* with living systems. Why is this so? Capra pursues in *The Web of Life (1996)*:

> Ultimately—as quantum physics showed so dramatically—there are no parts at all. What we call a part if merely a pattern in an inseparable web of relationships. Therefore the shift from the parts to the whole can also be seen as a shift from objects to relationships. (Id., 37)

My hypothesis is that our culture has *never* until now applied the *eight dynamic patterns of living* and that it therefore is at the border of chaos, destruction or another kind of worldwide catastrophe. I allege that in contradistinction to shamanic cultures, our culture is suffering from a schizoid mindset, the perversion of love into sadistic hate, rampant violence, the impudent slaughtering of ethnic and cultural minorities, famines that could easily be avoided, and generally a total lack of genuine spirituality which, by itself, already makes for depression and psychosomatic disorders.

What I say is that the *eight dynamic patterns of living* have been respected and applied by all major tribal shamanic cultures including the North American Indians, and that *therefore* they have lived peacefully. With 'peacefully' I do not mean an artificial peace concept which is complete nonsense as it is stuck and rigid, but a *dynamic peace continuum* that includes little fights and small wars as required by the dynamics of *yin* and *yang*, but that is so balanced that it will never trigger a major and global destruction.

The fact that our culture has triggered this destruction in all possible ways, economically, socially, health-wise, militarily and ecologically shows that the *continuum balance* that the eight patterns provide is lacking in modern philosophy, science, military policy, diplomacy, politics and strategy.

The *eight patterns of living* could be taken as a guide concept for being implemented in a new kind of lifestyle to be worked out as part of our presently evolving postindustrial global culture. That is the basic idea. Besides, I think that these patterns are tremendously useful as a base layer for establishing the ground principles of a new peaceful society, as they cover all spheres of life and living.

1) THE AUTONOMY PATTERN

All peaceful shamanic societies have in common that they grant their children an utmost level of autonomy. In *dominator cultures*, that today represent the bulk of large and typically industrialized societies worldwide, the lacking autonomy of the consumer child is a truly pathological phenomenon that often takes the form of parent-child codependence, which I call *symbiotoholism* or emotional abuse and in general the unhealthy fusional clinging of members of the family, or as *collective fusion* through the identification with groups, organizations and ideologies.

In fact, observing the growth processes in nature, we can see that autonomy is something built in all living, and as such takes part in all growth. In order to realize our personal identity and become whole human beings, we have to be able, still in childhood, to form an original personal identity.

This is however impossible if we are reared by narcissistic parents, those namely who are indifferent to helping the blooming of the unique person of the child they have brought to life.

2) THE ECSTASY PATTERN

All peaceful shamanic societies have in common that they have a strong *ecstasy pattern* built in their lifestyle which makes them once in a while enjoy group events where the usual rules of conduct are more or less set aside.

Usually, these events are characterized by magic rituals, the consumption of mind-altering *entheogens*, that is, psychedelics.

3) THE ENERGY PATTERN

Life is energy! This is recognized as a vital life pattern in all shamanic societies, and thus the overwhelming part of the world. Oriental cultures were historically the most wistful in *recognizing and applying energy patterns* for healing, good fortune and positive relationships.

The Chinese science of acupuncture is perhaps the oldest distillation of this holistic knowledge into something we today call a *science* while traditionally people tend to speak rather of *philosophy* when they talk about the perennial science of the bioenergy. However, even in the West, alternative scientists from Paracelsus to Reich have acknowledged the existence of the *bioenergetic functionality* not only of the human organism, but also of the weather, the atmosphere and the cosmos as a whole.

While in substance these researchers observed basically the same phenomena, the way they termed the human energy field varied. Paracelsus spoke of *vis vitalis*, Swedenborg of *spirit energy*, Mesmer of *animal magnetism* and Reich of *orgone*. And since millennia this same energy was called *ch'i* by the Chinese, *ki* by the Japanese, *prana* in India and *mana* with the Kahunas from Hawaii and the Cherokee natives of North America.

Furthermore, parapsychologists universally agree that the motor of all psychic phenomena is to be found in our bioplasmatic and egg-shaped aura, the luminous energy field we carry around our physical body and which can be seen as an extension of our bioplasmatic energy, as it is composed of the same bioenergetic charge that we find in the bioplasma.

Emotions are energetic, streaming currents that are a direct outflow of the cell's bioplasma. I speak about emotional flow.

—See Peter Fritz Walter, Integrate Your Emotions (2014)

These streamings have their seat not in the brain, but in the bioplasma and in the aura.

4) THE LANGUAGE PATTERN

Psychoanalysis has revealed the importance of language as a condition for the sublimation of instincts.

Furthermore, peace researchers found that a lack of language and thus of communication is at the basis of all forms of violence, inner and outer. This insight has not only psychological but also political consequences. For it clearly indicates that only free speech and democracy, both within the family and the nation, can ensure maintaining peace and regulate our natural instincts and desires, so that they do not become asocial and violent through denial.

To everyone who says that we have democracy and yet are a violent society, I reply that we do not have true democracy and never had. For violence only comes up when verbal communication is impaired, and the one major reason why communication is impaired about vital issues is *shame*. When we feel ashamed about certain vital events in life, such as sexuality, we do *not freely communicate*, because we are blocked or inhibited by the nagging feeling of shame that comes up every time we tackle the subject.

Lack of communication leads to violence; where the mouth is defended to talk, the body takes over the role of the mouth—and the fist talks! We all know this from history and from private experience, and yet there is little general conscience in our society about the almost holy importance of dialogue, of communication, not only outside, in relationships with others, but first of all inside, in the relationship with ourselves.

Our large civilizations do very little to integrate the *wistful use of language* because they are hardly conscious of the power of the word. Shamanic cultures, however, are wiser in this respect and generally dispose of an array of rituals that serve exactly the purpose of what in our civilizations we do within a psychotherapy: putting words on things, events and feelings.

5) THE LOVE PATTERN

All peaceful tribal societies have in common that they follow the *love pattern* and not, as most of the larger nations, the morality principle. The present state of violence within and between our larger civilizations, especially those with *high morality* is in my view the result of despising the love principle and the widespread use, also and especially in politics, of moralism. With other words, it is the disregard of one of nature's highest principles, the principle of *biogenic self-regulation*, that brought about the present state of violence and the lack of love and true care among most of the peoples of the earth.

It is the hypocrite manner of preaching peace and democracy by our false and opportunistic leaders while they tread in the dust natural love proverbially like the Biblical serpent.

Wilhelm Reich, in his extensive work on the psychological roots of fascism found that it is the repression of our natural emotions, first of all by prohibiting *our young generations the natural acting-out of their love desires* that brought us at the border of the present abyss of *fundamentalism, persecution, slaughter, genocide, war, civil war and worldwide terrorism.*

—Wilhelm Reich, The Mass Psychology of Fascism (1933)

6) THE PLEASURE PATTERN

All peaceful shamanic societies have in common that they acknowledge the *pleasure pattern,* for example in the way they educate their children. In planning the child's future, what counts is not the *father's job,* that is the typical dominator position, but the natural inclination and interest of the *child* for their later profession. By doing this, instead of projecting upon children their parents' wishes and desires, education ensures that every generation provides for children support for what they really are gifted for. The result is both a high level of skill and motivation for profession and career.

It is not surprising that now also in modern nations the *pleasure function* begins to be seen as the main motivating factor for a person's advancement in life. Suffices to read biographies of great and successful men and women to see that all achievement *is a result of desire and persistent acting upon desire* and that there is no better catalyzing agent than biological self-regulation that is based upon pleasure.

7) THE SELF-REGULATION PATTERN

All peaceful shamanic societies have in common that they follow patterns of self-regulation or *permissiveness* in the education of their small children, and as a result they restrain from inflicting violence in form of physical punishment upon them.

The most peaceful of those tribal nations, the *Trobriands* of Papua New Guinea are completely permissive as to children's sex play and free mating games.

8) THE TOUCH PATTERN

All peaceful shamanic societies have in common that they are conscious about the *touch pattern* and care for maintaining free body touch among family members, nudity, and abundant tactile nutrition for infants and small children in the form of baby massage, baby-carrying, skin-skin contact, and sleeping naked with children. In dominator cultures, life-denying pediatricians were turning down parents' desire for fondling their children and co-sleeping naked with them.

Now we slowly begin to see the macabre results of the *deprivation of tactile stimulation* in infants. Psychosomatic medicine reveals that our immunity against viruses depends on touch and that lacking touch, especially in childhood, leads to more or less acute *immune deficiency* and as a result to higher vulnerability for certain *lifestyle diseases* such as cancer, heart disease, pneumonia, or immune deficiency syndrome.

Furthermore, cross-cultural research has clearly shown that *early tactile deprivation* is one of the major inducing factors for the plague of personal, domestic and structural violence in any given society.

Chapter Four

The Matriarchal Science

Introduction

Shamanism could be called a *matriarchal* science. While the expression seems awkward on first sight, let us look at it from the other side of the moon. If one thinks that the *science of shamanism* could not be qualified as matriarchal, then one must first refute the argument that our modern science tradition was and is, entirely, patriarchal!

That a science may be qualified as 'matriarchal' or 'patriarchal' seems to mess up the scientific methodology and bring in an ideological criterium for measuring what science is. I agree with this criticism.

However, this is not what I am saying when I speak of shamanism as the 'matriarchal science.'

What I am saying is not that science is per se ideological, but that the humans who do science, are well *more* than the science they engage in. In other words, scientists cannot as humans be defined by the science they are doing, but rather, they define, as observers, what kind of science they are going to create.

Quantum physics has left no doubt about the fact that the observer is always entangled with the object of observation and that there is no such thing as 'detached' observation.

As a result, because of this entanglement, the science we humans create cannot be neutral in the sense to be detached from us, from our humanity. On the contrary, it is *impregnated* by our humanity, and if we follow certain ideologies, our science will reflect it in one way or the other. *This is not a matter of ideology, but a matter of consciousness.*

The transition from matriarchy to patriarchy, and the correlating change in symbolism, was not just a historical or psychohistorical event, but something that has affected human consciousness as a whole. This change or transition deeply impacted upon wake consciousness, while visionary and psychedelic experiences, as well as experiences with hypnosis have given repeated evidence to the fact that the matriarchal symbolism is still deeply rooted in our subconscious mind and its pictorial vocabulary.

These visions are not just visual effects that show the energetic impact that encountering cosmic spiritual entities has on those who go through such transformative experiences. In fact, the amazing and almost miraculous healing that most have experienced who encountered *mythic creatures in the trance state* that is induced by entheogens can only be explained when we assume a *direct infusion of bioenergy* from these sources—whatever the explanation one may give as to their origin.

What I wish to demonstrate in the present chapter is that the large rhetoric about the matriarchy-patriarchy dichotomy is but an *intellectual problem,* as on the soul level or the level of super-consciousness, such a dichotomy simply does not exist.

The patriarchal gods may have taken their place in our churches, but they were fortunately not able to penetrate in our hearts and the larger parts of our consciousness that are accessible for the spiritually awakened individual.

Here, we have the whole of the Olympus, so to say, and not only the official part of it. And for everybody who has once entered that dimension, I do not need to mention the fact that the matriarchal symbolism is the only one that really stands out on that level of consciousness, while the patriarchal gods may well exist also on that level, but have a minor importance. The psychological reason for this fact was clearly acknowledged by Joseph Campbell. He writes:

> [A]s all schools of psychology agree, the image of the
> mother and the female affects the psyche differently
> from that of the father and the male. Sentiments of
> identity are associated most immediately with the
> mother; those of dissociation, with the father. Hence,
> where the mother image preponderates, even the
> dualism of life and death dissolve in the rapture of her
> solace; the worlds of nature and the spirit are not
> separated; the plastic arts flourish eloquently of
> themselves, without need of discursive elucidation,

allegory, or moral tag; and there prevails an implicit confidence in the spontaneity of nature, both in its negative, killing, sacrificial aspect (lion and double ax), and in its productive and reproductive (bull and tree).

—Joseph Campbell, Occidental Mythology (1991), 70.

In a society with predominantly patriarchal values, the soul will keep the counterplayer inside, hidden, and in the dark. Thus in a solar culture such as ours, the *counterplayer* is the lunar principle, or, as it was called in antiquity, the *Lunar Bull*. If we want to become whole so as to embrace *our genuine soul values,* we have to heal the phylogenetic split between patriarchal and matriarchal culture.

This split was a historical fact and it has left imprints in our soul and our psyche.

But while this may have been so as a matter of history, while there have been matriarchal cultures first and patriarchal societies thereafter, this is not how the soul has experienced these matters. Recent research has corroborated that things are really not as clear-cut as historians for centuries thought they were. When questioned about *patriarchy* and *matriarchy*, many people, and among them even researchers of repute, tend to jump to quick conclusions.

They take either-or positions or they question the whole dichotomy calling it a historic bluff.

And there are those who try to find a way out of that hide-and-seek game that leaves important questions open by declaring them as obsolete. There is one author who stands out, Riane Eisler.

—See, for example, Riane Eisler, The Chalice and the Blade (1995) and Sacred Pleasure (1996).

She has not declared the dichotomy as a historic bluff, but showed with a lot of evidence that both of these concepts never have existed in a pure form, but that in a way they are complementary. However, in a second step, that was perhaps more important than the first, she has looked at the basic ingredients of each of these cultural opposites and found remarkable, if not striking, differences. There is one main difference that she peels out and that, once you know about it, cannot be unthought.

It is the discovery that, deep down, the two concepts differ by the way they look not at one gender, but by the way they look *at both*.

More precisely, Riane Eisler found that matriarchy is predominantly a paradigm that favors *partnership relations* between the two sexes and generally between all members in a given society, while patriarchy favors dominance and oppression, male over female, and above over below, in the sense of strict obedience-based hierarchies, which means in clear text powerful over powerless.

Without knowing more, here already, with this kind of rudimentary knowledge as the essence of Eisler's in-depth research, we see that there is something of an automatism built in patriarchy. *It's the automatism of abuse.* It's as if all was setup for it to occur. It's as if the cultural and social framework was exactly drafted for abuse to happen, while abuse is of course eloquently fought, in patriarchal terms, as a sin and an abject behavior. While matriarchy tolerates it and has built rape right in most of its cultural myths. But patriarchy has *institutionalized rape,* in all its forms, sexual, social, racial, ethnic, military and commercial. That is the difference.

Riane Eisler's amazing research has brought to daylight that maintaining the age-old dichotomy of matriarchal versus patriarchal is only accurate when we describe their psychological content, but not when we describe evolutionary changes in the human setup. In reality, Eisler explains, we are dealing with a *partnership-oriented paradigm versus a dominator paradigm,* the first coming close to the idea of matriarchy, the latter more or less synonymous with patriarchy. The merit of Eisler's approach is that we can get away from extreme positions: because there never was a really pure matriarchy or a really pure patriarchy in human history.

When we look, for example, at the mythology of highly patriarchal tribes, such as the ancient Hebrews, we find matriarchal elements, and therefore must conclude that we got a mix rather than a pure soup. In that mix, to rest with the example of the Hebrews, are predominantly patriarchal elements and a few matriarchal elements, as in *yang* is a small portion of *yin,* and *vice versa.* And as Johann Jakob Bachofen found in his classical treatise on matriarchy, even in highly matriarchal cultures there are to be found a few elements of patriarchy.

—Originally in German language, Johann Jakob Bachofen, Das Mutterrecht (1948).

Therefore, when we use the dichotomy matriarchal-patriarchal, we are arguing not from a real-life perspective, but rather from our ideological understanding of *patriarchy* or *matriarchy*. What counts for us within the purpose of this book is the *spiritual significance* of matriarchy as a psychological and archetypal complex in the collective unconscious of humanity not the historical or psychohistorical evolution of humanity.

—See Lloyd deMause, Foundations of Psychohistory (1982).

Regarding the evolutionary aspect, Joseph Campbell writes in *Occidental Mythology (1973):*

> For it is now perfectly clear that before the violent entry of the late Bronze and early Iron Age nomadic Aryan cattle-herders from the north and Semitic sheep and goat herders from the south into the old cult sites of the ancient world, there had prevailed in that world an essentially organic, vegetal, non-heroic view of the nature and necessities of life that was completely repugnant to those lion hearts for whom not the patient toil of earth but the battle spear and its plunder were the source of both wealth and joy. In the older mother myths and rites the light and darker aspects of the mixed thing that is life had been honored equally and together, whereas in the later, male-oriented, patriarchal myths, all that is good and noble was attributed to the new,

heroic master gods, leaving to the native nature powers
the character only of darkness - to which, also, a
negative moral judgment now was added. For, as a great
body of evidence shows, the social as well as mythic
orders of the two contrasting ways of life were opposed.
(Id., 21)

It is not difficult for us today to see that the symbolism
of mythology bears a specific psychological scripting.
Particularly under the perspective of *psychoanalysis*, and
psychosynthesis, there is little doubt that the old sagas are of
the nature of dream, or that dreams are symptomatic of the
dynamics of the psyche. Sigmund Freud, Carl Jung, Joseph
Campbell, Otto Rank, Karl Abraham, Géza Róheim, and
many others have in the last century developed a vastly
documented modern lore of dream and myth
interpretation. With our modern-day discovery that the
holistic patterns of fairy tale and myth correspond to those
of dream, the long discredited ideas of 'archaic man' have
returned dramatically to the foreground of consciousness.
One of those archaic symbols or archetypes is that of the
Lunar Bull, for there is a direct relationship between
mythology and astrology. It can be said that astrology uses
mythology to a large extent in order to make spiritual
energies more visually comprehensible.

When explaining the nature of the planetary energy of
Moon, for example, astrology will use certain metaphors.

These metaphors are embodied in symbols, and the
symbols, as such, build a necessary vocabulary for

anybody to study who wants to practice and explain astrology.

For example, the main symbols traditionally associated with the Moon energy are: *Cancer, Bull, Female, Shell, House, Black, Water, Shadow.*

As the mythic bull's characteristics are associated with the *lunar* energies, it was called, in Antiquity, the *Lunar Bull*. This expression is not a fancy, even today, because the *bull fighting tradition* that dates from patriarchy, has put the whole bull mythology completely upside down. The killing of the bull that was once a ritual sacrifice for the Goddess as the tutelary divinity of the bull was transformed into a sport in which the stabbing of the bull is a *symbolic rape* expressing the subordination of the female under the male's sexual dominion.

Thus, by analogy, the bull that is stabbed and killed by the Matador within the traditional bull fighting has quite little or nothing to do with the matriarchal mythic or lunar bull. The lunar bull was the object of worship prevalent in the age when our sun was passing through the sign of Taurus.

What was preserved from that time were the mysteries of *Mithras*. The horns of the bull were generally a symbol of fertility and bountiful riches in many cultures for thousands of years. The constellation Taurus may also allude to the Greek story of *Europa and the Bull*.

Europa was daughter of King Agenor. One fine spring day, accompanied by her hand maidens, *Princess Europa* went to the seashore to gather flowers.

Zeus, who had fallen in love with Europa, seized the opportunity. Zeus transformed himself into a magnificent white bull, and as such he joined King Agenor's grazing herd.

Europa noticed the wonderful white beast, who gazed at them all with such a mild manner that they were not frightened. Europa wove wreathes of flowers for the beast, and wrapped them around his horns. She led him around the meadow, and he was as docile as a lamb.

Then, as he trotted down to the seashore, she jumped onto his shoulders. Suddenly, to her surprise and fright, he plunged into the sea and carried the princess to Crete. As they reached the Cretan shore, Zeus then turned into an eagle and ravaged Europa.

She bore three sons, the first of which was Minos, who is said to have introduced the bull cult to the Cretans. He had Daedalus build a labyrinth in the depths of his palace at Knossos, which became the home of the Minotaur, the offspring of Minos' wife Pasiphae, and a bull. Seven young boys and seven maidens were ritually sacrificed to the Minotaur every year, until Theseus killed the monster.

The Lunar Bull

What does this myth tell us? Which psychological truth does it reveal? Let us have a deeper look at this intriguing story. We got a seducer here, we have an abduction, a rape, and then, as a result, a child-eating monster that eventually is killed. And we have a bull. What does this bull stand for, psychologically?

Experts of mythology and psychiatrists agree that the bull, despite of his phallic horns is a *symbol for matriarchy*, and this because the bull cannot be seen isolated from the Goddess that, metaphorically and from the visual depictions, stands on the shoulders of the bull.

This is a metaphor because we would not be interested in that bull if it had only a historical meaning for us. We are interested in that bull because we have its energy within us. Joseph Campbell affirms that all the gods are *within us*.

Hence, the bull, as a sort of matriarchal god, also is within our own unconscious, a part of our male love instinct that can enjoy to conquer and rape, abduct and possess, enclose and abuse.

We are used today to a psychological language that suggests all these longings were abysmal and abject and we tend to project them, as a result of our blinding them out, onto others that we call *the monsters, perpetrators, rapists or sex offenders* and that our morning papers abound of. And yet, all this psychological hide-and-seek is useless:

we are facing but parts of ourselves when dealing with these well-hidden issues that often are wrapped into the folder of our best-kept family secrets.

When in *The Power of Myth (1988)*, which is actually a wonderful example of human dialogue, Bill Moyers asked Joseph Campbell about the serpent as the seducer in the biblical story of the genesis, Campbell replied:

> That amounts to a refusal to affirm life. In the biblical tradition we have inherited, life is corrupt, and every natural impulse is sinful unless it has been circumcised or baptized. The serpent was the one who brought sin into the world. And the woman was the one who handed the apple to man. This identification of the woman with sin, of the serpent with sin, and thus of life with sin, is the twist hat has been given to the whole story in the biblical myth and doctrine of the Fall. (Id., 54)

Joseph Campbell basically affirms that patriarchy is but a form of life-denial, a collective neurosis, not a lifestyle, philosophy, or *Weltanschauung*. It's a disease, a *twist* given to life that perverts its very nature and that had a more or less destructive influence upon the survival of shamanic cultures, because the latter tend to be more matriarchal in nature. And ultimately, therefore, it's a refusal of humanity. Campbell develops the theme further by alluding to the *Star Wars* plot:

> Darth Vader has not developed his own humanity. He's a robot. He's a bureaucrat, living not in terms of himself

but in terms of an imposed system. This is the threat to our lives that we all face today. Is the system going to flatten you out and deny you your humanity, or are you going to be able to make use of the system to the attainment of human purposes? How do you relate to the system so that you are not compulsively serving it? (Id., 178)

Patriarchy, with its craving for obedience to the father, is a sort of compulsion neurosis. Not only are individuals *flattened out* by systems that are eternal replacements of *real fathers*, those that have typically abandoned their roles as true caretakers, having become troublemakers.

These authority-craving individuals have *flattened out* their better halves, their right brains, so as to serve the system even more.

The bull story tells us that rape desires as part of sexual longings are not destructive *per se*, but become destructive when they are enclosed, repressed, tightly controlled and discarded out of life by strict moralistic rules rules. The Minotaur became a *child-eating monster* because it was enclosed in a tower, because King Minos was afraid for his reputation and wanted to hide the monster from the populace.

We have the symbolism written into the Tarot where *The Tower*, the 16th Arcane, is a symbol of something that is too tightly controlled, to a point to explode, with all that usually accompanies those explosions—be it a scandal, a public outrage, the revelation of a family secret, an abuse story, or criminal conviction as a *sex offender*.

—See, for example, Sallie Nichols, Jung And Tarot (1986)

And then, we ask '*Why has this happened?,*' and we are again regressing in childhood longings for autonomy that were thwarted by over-controlling parents or educators, and we face our *rage*—eventually. The public outrage we encountered was but a projection of our *own inner rage* that we had repressed. We had forgotten about the library with the books that can talk, and the wizard, and magic houses that endure.

The Autonomy Pattern

There is namely one sociologically relevant difference between shamanic cultures and dominator cultures. It is the fact that in the former, the child—especially the male child—is granted an abundant amount of autonomy, while the contrary is true within modern industrialized societies. What is the importance of autonomy? We have seen that the *Autonomy Pattern* is one of the eight dynamic patterns of living that I have discovered to be prevalent in shamanic cultures. And I believe it's the most important of them for the following reasons.

Autonomy is fundamental for every being-in-growth. Without autonomy, there is fusion, symbiosis, and dependence. While for certain organisms, such as the human newborn, symbiosis for a certain time is a biological necessity, this symbiosis is time-bound and should gradually give rise to autonomy. While the natural symbiosis is needed for the first eighteen months of the newborn, it should gradually come to an end after that period. Unfortunately, postmodern international culture is more or less completely dysfunctional regarding this primal movement from fusion to autonomy that should take place, dynamically, in the growth process of the human baby.

What happens is that the necessary biological symbiosis with the mother, *eighteen months from birth*, is neglected for various reasons; babies suffer from a more or less stringent tactile deprivation that will leave scars for their whole lives.

In order to compensate for the lack of care bestowed upon the infant, as a guilt-reaction and for various other reasons, the post-symbiosis condition is not better for the child: instead of growing into autonomy most children in our culture grow into codependence with their parents and caretakers; instead of building a gradually larger extent of autonomy, parents tend to gradually entangle their children in a tight net of stiffening dependencies. This form of *emotional vampirism* is so rampant especially in modern Western societies that I have called it *emotional incest*.

I further argue that the present defamation and persecution of affectionate and nurturing erotic love between children and adults and its manipulatory confusion with child-endangering sexual sadism have their origin in shame and guilt our society is suffering from because of its deprivatory and dysfunctional childrearing paradigm that endorses and purports emotional and, in a hidden way, sexual incest by holding children dependent, helpless and infantile as long as possible so as to *compensate for the crippled emotional structure of their parents and caretakers.*

This is how an ever new generation of emotional and sexual cripples will raise an ever next generation of dysfunctional water-headed babies that are going to live with a perverted bioenergetic base structure. Such a situation is *shameful* for a society based upon *egalitarian principles* and that pretends to respect the *person of the child;* however, this reality is veiled, because shame tends to bring about defensive and projective reactions.

T demonstrate what is right and what is wrong here, I have to dig a little deeper and get back to the foundations, not of psychohistory, but of *psychoanalysis.* In fact, Freudian psychoanalysis affirms the latent sexuality of the child, and newer research has shown that even the fetus is sexual in an auto-erotic manner. In fact, when you read psychoanalytic writings, you are quickly overwhelmed by the extreme focus of these people upon *incestuous wishes* of the child or both the child and the parents. The Socratic error here is to assume that this view was *scientific* in any way, while it is truly the consequence of a cultural, and in addition a professional *bias.* The cultural bias is the fact that in patriarchal societies, *natural* sexuality is forbidden for children with the result that *unnatural* sexuality is brought about, mainly in the form of rape-centered pornography, sadomasochism and violent child rape, abduction and murder. The professional bias is the fact that psychoanalysts typically deal with neurotic, and not with sane people.

The final and quite far-reaching results of this fundamental position of mainstream psychoanalysis are the following. The regard upon sexuality is distorted in that incest and incestuous wishes are viewed upon with an exaggerated and unnatural focus that veils the fact that the human being, if raised freely, naturally projects sexual wishes outside of the family. The factual *oedipal touch* of the modern nuclear family and the really widespread problem of incestuous wishes, and factual emotional and sexual incest, is the result of patriarchy's denial of *child-child sex* outside of the family; anthropological research in shamanic tribal cultures that give their children full emotional and sexual freedom for copulating with other children corroborates that in these societies incest is *absolutely non-existent;* interestingly enough, what also is practically non-existent in these cultures is violent crime and sexual dysfunctions, as well as homosexuality.

As modern society says violence is good, and sex is bad, it by the same token says incest is the rule for the child, while sex outside of the family is the exception as it is invariably considered as criminal and allegedly damages and traumatizes the child. This is how patriarchy has put nature upside down: it focuses upon the sick and dysfunctional and disregards the plain, healthy and natural.

The late French child psychologist Françoise Dolto did not agree with Freud. She wrote that not sane, but only neurotic children had incestuous wishes toward their parents. In a seminar for young psychoanalysts during one of her workshops on child psychoanalysis, she voiced:

> You as psychoanalysts have to deal, in your daily practice, with neurotic children. Of course, neurotic children are incestuously fixated, because the very etiology of neurosis, as we know since Freud, is sexual. So, with this bias in your mind, you wrongly assume that the same was true for the healthy child.
>
> —Françoise Dolto, Séminaire de Psychanalyse d'Enfants, Tome 2, (1985), 21 (translation mine)

What is true for sexuality is equally true for *autonomy*. A naturally sexual child is *typically more independent* and more autonomous than a neurotic and incestuously fixated child. The frequently observed *clinging behavior* of modern city children, their helpless, infantile and irresponsible behavior, even when approaching puberty, their immaturity in handling sharp or fragile objects such as knives or glasses show well their incestuous fixation, their neurotic blockage and the pathological codependent entanglement with their parents; all this demonstrates the *early psychosexual damage* a life-denying and pleasure-hostile education inflicted upon them.

There is a *natural striving for autonomy* built into every growing life. A child of three years of age needs more autonomy than a child of fifteen months of age. A toddler of eighteen months needs more autonomy than a baby of five months. Many parents ignore that babies, toddlers and pre-schoolers, already before reaching the age of primary school, need to develop autonomy.

Many adults believe that children grew through magic shifts, like the one from babyhood to childhood, from childhood to youth and from youth to adulthood. The first shift is believed to take place around seven years of age, the next one around twelve years of age and the final one around eighteen years of age.

Sorry, but this is really speaking about myths. These shifts don't exist in real life as all growth is gradual and smooth. This is why all education should be gradual and smooth. While it is a good thing to have certain initiation rites or ceremonies that mark important steps in the growth of children, these rites are what they are: mark stones that border an otherwise seamless road. I arrive at a mark stone, I see the mark stone, I touch the mark stone, I pass the mark stone, I remember the mark stone. My passing the mark stone is gradual, and smooth in time, and the mark stone itself is of lesser importance than my passing it. What is important is that I constantly grow, that I remain *moving*. We learn the basic *movement into autonomy* during our *first year of life*, and not later on during adolescence or when we allegedly *turn into* that magic world of adulthood.

I do not belittle the important changes that take place in the life of adolescents, and their sometimes passionate focus upon getting more autonomy, nor do I belittle the marking shift from adolescence into final adulthood. But often we observe that especially those adolescents who have rather repressive and possessive parents get onto the obnoxious track and really push it through for every millimeter of increased autonomy. There is a logic in every behavior and adolescents who put high stress on autonomy *have a reason* to do so. The reason is rooted in much earlier years, in the years of babyhood.

There is no alternative to autonomy. To make down or belittle children's need for autonomy is to open the door to emotional and power abuse *large scale*.

This form of rampant child-abuse is not perpetrated by the proverbial *stranger*, but by *mothers*, first of all mothers, and more and more also by professionals who are working for, affiliated with, or sponsored by the international *child protection* industry.

In tribal shamanic cultures, children grow into autonomy gradually and naturally. They are not held back from experiencing life, from meeting challenges. In many tribal cultures children are taught early how to cope with their dreams, how to attack monsters in their dreams, how to cope with nightmares, and how to go out victorious.

This is especially true for male children, and it is especially important for male children as the deprivation of autonomy has rather undesired consequences in males. Notably, rape desires are one of the most striking of those aftereffects.

When autonomy was denied to a boy and the psychic umbilical bond with the mother was not cut through the aid of initiation rites, or else early access to a sexual mate during adolescence, the coming up of rape desires is inevitable.

The Dominator Quest

And back where we came from, we can eventually ask what we really want when we want to rape, to possess, to abduct, to ravish. And we gradually, very gradually, find out that, then, we want to find unity with our soul, and *make the split undone* that was forced onto us by patriarchal life-denial, by moralism, by a schizoid education that we suffered, individually and collectively. After all, to copulate means to *link!* And then we might finally ask the pertinent question: 'How has patriarchy come about—and what was before?' It all started with a murder. The murder of the Goddess. Which is ultimately a matricide, and implicitly a mother-rape. And it became the foundation of what is called *a culture*. It became the foundation of what is called 'religion.' Joseph Campbell explains in *The Power of Myth (1988):*

> [I]n biblical times, when the Hebrews came in, they really wiped out the Goddess. The term for the Canaanite goddess that's used in the Old Testament is *the Abomination*. Apparently, throughout the period represented in the Book of Kings, for example, there was a back and forth between the two cults. Many of the Hebrew kings were condemned in the Old Testament for having worshiped on the mountaintops. Those mountains were symbols of the Goddess. And there was a very strong accent against the Goddess in the Hebrew, which you do not find the Indo-European mythologies. Here you have Zeus marrying the Goddess, and then the two play together. So it's an extreme case that we have in the Bible, and our own Western subjugation of the female is a function of biblical thinking. (Id., 215-216)

It seems that when man began to preach *high morality* and confessed to strive 'for goodness', he began to really become diabolic. Campbell writes that *the vandalism involved in the destruction of the pagan temples of antiquity is hardly matched in world history*. (Id., 248)

Again we may reflect on the teaching of the Lunar Bull. Zeus married the Goddess by raping her, and that rape ultimately was union and creation. While patriarchy, with its strong emphasis about the *abomination* (sic!) of what it labels *sexual crime* is exactly embodying the perversion that it so strongly projects upon matriarchal cults, and, today, upon *matriarchal peoples*.

The *true abomination* is not matriarchy or Goddess cults, and not rape, but *a cult or religion or cultural paradigm that perverts nature into a total repression of the living impulse* and that puts a single male god as the creator principle, thereby annihilating the eternal *balance of polarities*, manifesting as *yin* and *yang*, female and male, Moon and Sun, red and blue, cool and hot, dry and moist, and that restricts life to a *dead morality*. Campbell explains in *Occidental Mythology* (1973):

> The patriarchal point of view is distinguished from the earlier archaic view by its setting apart of all pairs-of-opposites—male and female, life and death, true and false, good and evil—as though they were absolutes in themselves and not merely aspects of the larger entity of life. This we may liken to a solar, as opposed to lunar, mythic view, since darkness flees from the sun as its opposite, but in the moon dark and light interact in the one sphere. (Id., 27)

Many people, even in our days of feminism, women rights and open criticism of patriarchal tradition and values do not really grasp the implication of patriarchy upon our sexual mores and sexual laws.

Or they are simply afraid to question the reigning system as deeply as that, scratching the surface with their research.

I have been in touch with researchers from Germany and the United States who openly unveil and criticize the trap of patriarchy and who also defend the sexual freedom of children. But their rhetoric has only one leg when it goes to see what *sexual freedom* for children really means!

It means *free partner choice*. It means that a child can also choose *an adult as a partner* for play, including sex play.

When faced with that argument, all those researchers that from their books sound so well-bred, well-educated and well-groomed *backed off*. They cease to argue and suddenly become dogmatic and declare that in such a case we could not speak any further of child sexuality but about *pedophilia*, and that the latter was invariably rape, violence and abuse. They assert this without having anything in hand for the backup of their unscientific rants. *That is how far our science goes, all science goes.*

We cannot access knowledge that we are not ready to get because we are *emotionally not mature for it*. These men, while they may have many letters behind their names and while they may be accredited at famous universities, are anxious children who, when it goes to open the forbidden door, shy away and declare that there are no forbidden doors because we lived in a *democratic* society. A society so democratic obviously that it incarcerates people for love and has genocided in its 250 years of existence more people than all other cultures around the world in the last 5000 years!

> I refer here to the courageous research of Professor Noam Chomsky, from MIT, as I honestly did not know about this fact. See for yourself what you think of America's claim to be the 'most moral culture of the world …

These apparently so liberal scientists would thus forbid their child to have an adult sex partner, while they would allow their child to have sex with a peer. What a high form of respect indeed! A slave is forbidden to make love with a noble while he is graciously given the right, by his master, to love his brothers-in-fate. *What, then, is that modern childhood else than slavery?*

And in what those liberal parents really differ from our patriarchal house tyrants of old?

What Joseph Campbell calls a *solar worldview*, I call a worldview where *stupidity has become the order of the day*. To deny our shadow is suicidal, and it's exactly what a solar worldview is all about. It denies shadow.

A picture without shadows is a one-dimensional drawing of life, a shallow affair. It's sketching a life that is not worth to be lived, because all is on one level, without ups and downs, without excitements, the shallow boredom of a moralist who *goes to Church* at fixed hours or who bows to the ground to lick the feet of his cosmic monstermind.

The phantasmagoric incest that in ancient matriarchal rituals was put on stage in dance and chant as a celebration of creation has quite little to do with actual incest, the prototypical father-daughter incest so ingrained in patriarchy. It is *not a sexual incest,* but symbolizes the need of the young male for a healthy symbiosis with his mother, if he is to develop his full psychosexual potential.

An important detail in those old representations of the Goddess and her Bull is that the bull is actually in a supportive role: the Goddess stands on him. He thus

212

supports the Goddess. *The male supports the female.* That is the quintessential message of matriarchy.

That does not mean he's a servant of the female. In patriarchy these poles have not just be reversed. The female is not just supporting the male, but *serves* the male. That is the substantial difference.

In matriarchy, the son supports his mother, but he is not her servant and slave-partner. In patriarchy, the daughter is not just supporting her father, but she's supposed to be his sex servant.

We have that incarnated both in the household-female and the love-female. The wife is supposed to serve her husband. The prostitute is supposed to serve her client.

Both are in not just a supportive role, but hold actually slave roles. That is why we can say that patriarchy has not just reversed matriarchy. It has distorted it to a caricature of life in which roles are no more naturally taken by people, but artificially forced upon people. Joseph Campbell writes in *The Hero with a Thousand Faces (1973):*

> This recognition of the secondary nature of the personality of whatever deity is worshipped is characteristic of most of the traditions of the world. (...) In Christianity, Mohammedanism, and Judaism, however, the personality of the divinity is taught to be final—which makes it comparatively difficult for the members of these communions to understand how one may go beyond the limitations of their own anthropomorphic divinity. The result has been, on the one hand, a general obfuscation of the symbols, and on

the other, a god-ridden bigotry such as is unmatched elsewhere in the history of religion. (Id., 258-259, note 5)

Historical Turn

To come back to our initial question, how was it possible that science in dominator cultures *became aligned with the patriarchal or solar principle,* while the oldest, and most original science, the science of shamanism, was organized along the lines of the lunar principle? This is really an intriguing question for it explains so many things, to mention only one here.

Shamanism's science is much more holistic, more right-brain, because the lunar principle allows feminine values with much more ease than the solar principle. This is why shamanism is Gaia-friendly and cares about *ecology* and harmony between man and nature. The solar principle, by contrast, is responsible for the fact that science in all dominator cultures, the modern industrial nations on top of the list, is left-brain, reductionist and nature-hostile, and has done more for destroying nature than for preserving it.

If we want to understand how the split came about between the original science and the modern sciences, we can make out certain events or a group of events that are typically considered to be the *turning point,* or historical turn. Riane Eisler Eisler usually associates it with the beginnings of patriarchy and the introduction of the school system. If we take Europe as an example, why and how schools came up? In the Middle Ages, when the Church tried to gain as much power over people as possible and indulged in human rights abuses of all kinds, monks and nuns opened the first schools.

These schools were recruitment centers for the monasteries. From the beginning, boys and girls were separated in different schools. From the boys' classes, the monks the recruited, from the girls' schools the nuns.

When you read history books, the Church is cited as the great benefactor of mankind in implementing the school system. But the Church's intention was first of all an effort to sustain the power of its own worldly hierarchy and oppression system, and second, and most importantly, *direct perception of truth* was going to be wiped out from civilization from that point in history.

Before the existence of schools, children were raised by their parents and the other adults of the extended family.

They learned primarily by observation and *direct perception*. They *picked up* what they needed for their later career, from their early environment. It is interesting to remember, in this context, that early language learning takes place in exactly the same way. The young child picks up whole patterns from the language spoken around him or her.

Research in recent years provided evidence for the fact that this form of learning is perfectly adapted to the *passively organizing intelligence* of the human brain. Humans generally learn their mother tongue perfectly, whereas they cripple along learning a second or third language later in school or at college. Only relatively recent learning methods such as *Superlearning®* have taken serious the wisdom of nature present in every learning experience. Think tanks such as Edward de Bono have in addition shown us the relevance of the brain's functioning as a passively self-organizing system.

—See, for example, Lynn Schroeder, Sheila Ostrander & Nancy Ostrander, Superlearning 2000 (1997)

From his experience as a corporate trainer, Edward de Bono found that our usual learning processes, such as curricula in schools, universities or, more specifically, in management training, are *awkwardly maladapted* to the way our brain organizes and stores information. De Bono, much in the same way as Dr. Georgi Lozanov, originator of the *Superlearning®* method, found that only in early childhood learning, and especially in the way young children learn their first language, we see nature's full intelligence at work. It is a well-known fact that geniuses such as Albert Einstein, Pablo Picasso and many others among our creators never finished school, dropped out or flew it. They knew that they knew better and followed their inner instinct rather than an artificial learning system which involves *a considerable waste of time and resources* and which violates human dignity in the most flagrant way. With one word, they followed their *soul* and thereby realized their soul reality without perhaps reflecting about it.

They did not let society condition their inner mind to a point to crush their creative impulses. They were *marginal* in just the same way as we are all marginal on the soul level, or as an autistic child is marginal, and as we as creative souls are all marginal in front of the herd of school-fed morons.

It is not a matter of research or of statistics to draw out the human potential, and still less when we talk about the human soul.

Every soul is marginal in the sense that it can't be measured on the lines of science, the usual whitewash of complexity for the masses, the *perennial fascist cover-up of true human genius.*

Murder of the Goddess

Joseph Campbell's research on the *religious roots of culture* is not new, but for this reason it is not less a theme of the day.

—See, for example, Joseph Campbell, The Hero With A Thousand Faces (1973), Occidental Mythology (1973/1991), and The Power of Myth (1988)

For it is counteracting fascism, as it shows with such strong evidence not only how complex the human soul is, but also that this *has to be that way* if man wants to maintain psychic health, individually and collectively.

This astounding holistic information opens infinite insights into how to live peacefully, resourcefully and respectfully. The *historical shift* toward patriarchy was a profound shift in human consciousness, opening a *deep schizoid split* that some explain esoterically with an alien manipulation of the human DNS. But even if we stay with the historical facts alone and see their symbolic and archetypal content, we will see that something went wrong at that point in human evolution.

Riane Eisler, in her best-selling study *The Chalice and the Blade (1995)* called it the *truncation of civilization*. It was the unwritten historical vow of many to deny their humanity and follow the course of atrocious violence that began with the slaughtering of peaceful and nature-abiding cultures by the new arrogant patriarchal hordes and their violent, jealous and blood-thirsty God Yahweh, and psychologically a turn from permissiveness to moralistic repression.

Wilhelm Reich called it the *irruption of compulsory sex-morality*, title of one of his books, whereas Campbell qualifies it as 'the power impulse [being] the fundamental impulse in European history [that] got into our religious traditions.'

—Joseph Campbell, The Power of Myth (1988), 248

As Reich and other psychoanalysts clearly showed, this power obsession, that lasts until today in our Western culture, was from the start a sort of cultural cancer as the result of the *denial of nature* and man's arrogant claim to *improve* creation and make it better, thereby destroying it.

And that is exactly what I said earlier in this book, it is by repressing *primary power and breeding depression* that the thirst for power was taking immense dimensions in our culture, until this day. It was the denial of primary power that was at the origin of this cultural perversion. Joseph Campbell observed that the gravity of this historical shift was so deep and lasting that even the mythological and archetypical symbolism changed with it:

> The new age of the Sun God has dawned, and there is to follow an extremely interesting, mythologically confusing development known as solarization, whereby the entire symbolic system of the earlier age is to be reversed, with the moon and the lunar bull assigned to the mythic sphere of the female, and the lion, the solar principle, to the male.'
>
> —Joseph Campbell, Occidental Mythology (1973/1991), 75.

It was the real beginning of the apocalypse, for all that came later and that we face today are but results and consequences of the profound shift that took place at this time.

It was the shift from matriarchy to patriarchy or, in new terminology, the shift from a partnership culture to a dominator culture.

—The great majority of authors before the new perspective brought up by Riane Eisler were founding their terminology on Bachofen's study about Das Mutterrecht (The Matrilineal Order) that was first published as early as in the 1920s and similar studies by Bronislaw Malinowski and Wilhelm Reich in the 1930s. All these authors spoke about a shift from matriarchy to patriarchy.

Joseph Campbell acknowledges the dominance of the patriarchal gods since then in our Western cultural paradigm, but he considers the goddess as *the counterplayer* in the collective unconscious and thus assigns her at least a shadow role. In *Occidental Mythology (1973/1991)*, Joseph Campbell remarks:

> I am taking pains in this work to place considerable stress upon the world age and symbolic order of the goddess; for the findings both of anthropology and of archeology now attest not only to a contrast between the mythic and social systems of the goddess and the later gods, but also to the fact that in our own European culture that of the gods overlies and occludes that of the goddess—which is nevertheless effective as a counterplayer, so to say, in the unconscious of the civilization as a whole. (Id., 70)

This shadow role of the *Goddess* in Christianity is symbolized by the *Holy Virgin*, and it is sexually fantasized about as a secret wish to defile, debauch and rape virgins.

See R.E.L. Masters, *Forbidden Sexual Behavior and Morality (1951)*, who observes:

> It is ironic that where the desire to defile, humiliate or otherwise sadistically abuse children is concerned, it is so often the very notion of the child's purity and innocence that leads to the violation. (Id., 387)

In fact, how can a deity that originally stood for fertility become an eternal virgin? When we study Greek mythology, we see that the *original mother goddess* was Demeter, while the Church's virgin cult suggests that her daughter Persephone, a girl abducted by Hades, god of the underworld, became the new, castrated, Virgin Mother.

—In Greek mythology, Persephone, daughter of the earth goddess Demeter became the queen of the underworld after her abduction by Hades.

And Hades represents the psychologically and socially rejected sexual longing for *virgins*, for little girls, that became suppressed in our personal and collective *underworld*, the unconscious. We can thus see that the virgin cult is a *direct consequence of patriarchy* and already well present in the Hellenistic and Roman cultures, and not an invention of the Christians.

—As R.E.L. Masters reports, it was in the Victorian Era that the virgin cult became a real sexual obsession or mania, a cult for well-to-do men to rape and defile young girls, when those were available, for example, in the worker classes of the poor quarters in industrialized London and other major cities of that time of the early Industrial Revolution.

The female, to become acceptable in an entirely man-dominated world, had to be deprived of her own desire, castrated, relegated to the role of the 'obedient little girl.'

Without desire herself, the girl-female became *undesirable* as an unconscious reflex of the superego's copulation prohibition. She was no more desired as a child to be lovingly procreated by her parents, but her birth *was largely considered an accident;* in many cases a man who procreated only girls or too many girls was considered weak in Antiquity and even through the Renaissance.

Hence, the undesirable girl-female became a sexual taboo; for the unconscious, in fact, there is no difference between the desire of a couple to have a child and the sexual desire for copulation with a child. In French, this is more obvious than in English. *Je désire un enfant* in French both means 'I wish to have a child (to be born)' and 'I desire a child (sexually).' This linguistic particularity in French language reflects the fact that for the unconscious there is no difference between the desire to have a child born as a companion for a couple, on one hand, and the desire to have a child as a companion for bed, on the other. Both is *desire pro creation*, both is sexual desire in its larger cultural sense. What I am saying is that with the psychological castration of the female and the moralistic prohibition of her being desirable sexually, human sexuality became forever damaged, and perverted into a voyeuristic cult that hypertrophies the visual and neglects the tactile: the psychological roots of pornography are to be found in the taboo to touch a female child sexually.

The more sexuality with female children became tabooed, the more the sexual female child became a *haunting sex obsession* for males, and led to the criminal definition of rape, originally a property offense.

—See, Florence Rush, The Best Kept Secret (1980), and Riane Eisler, The Chalice and The Blade (1995)

Etymologically, the word 'rape,' derived from the Latin word *rapus* originally meant theft, and this can be well shown in French, where the word for theft is *vol* and for rape *viol*. In Antiquity, to possess a female child sexually meant in most cases to abduct her, a fact that is well established in Greek mythology in the story of Hades abducting *Persephone* for enjoying and possessing her sexually.

In ancient patriarchy, the rape of a little girl was an offense against her father, a kind of *property damage* that could be repaired by paying an *indemnity* to the father, but not a crime against the person of the child.

From the Church's modified goddess doctrine, its virgin cult becomes understandable. While the god-mother is a very old idea and existed long before Christianity, this god-mother, for the Christians, had to be a virgin, and even a Holy Virgin. Joseph Campbell writes in *The Power of Myth (1988):*

> The virgin birth comes into Christianity by way of the Greek tradition. When you read the four gospels, for example, the only one in which the virgin birth appears is the Gospel According to Luke, and Luke was a Greek. (Id., 217)

Behold, the doctrine of *Immaculate Conception* was only valid for the conception of the *Son of God*. All other children were born in sin, from ordinary, non-virgin mothers. I can't think of a greater *perversion and distortion of nature* because this mental construct means in fact *that nature is wrong and faulty* and that the very denial of nature is right and holy.

If the Church had integrated the small female as a desirable love object, we would probably not face such terrible amounts of female children raped, abducted and killed every month in many countries that follow the patriarchal dominator paradigm.

And we would not have had such a raise of homosexuality in our culture because homosexuality is the result of an unconscious blinding out of the desire for small females. Thus, the Church, by the same token, would not have had to invest so much energy for fighting homosexuality during several centuries in its existence.

The large fallback into paganism today is the result of this *denial of responsibility* of the Church to integrate human sexual desire in all its forms. And by doing so the Church missed the sense of the Grail—as according to Campbell, the grail symbolizes the respect not of abstract rules and regulations (sexual or other ones) but respect of nature, of creation. The Babylonian *Epic of Creation* amply demonstrates this fact. As Campbell writes in *Occidental Mythology (1973)*:

> [It is] a forthright patriarchal document, where the female principle is devaluated, together with its point of view, and, as always happens when a power of nature and the psyche is excluded from its place, it has turned into its negative, as a demoness, dangerous and fierce.

And we are going to find, throughout the following history of the orthodox patriarchal systems of the West, that the power of this goddess-mother of the world, whom we have here seen defamed, abused, insulted, and overthrown by her sons, is to remain as an ever-present threat to their castle of reason, which is founded upon a soil that they consider to be dead but is actually alive, breathing, and threatening to shift. (Id., 86)

On the other hand, Campbell reports in *Oriental Mythology* that in most non-Western cultures the very opposite paradigm was being in place, isolating Christian life-denial as something unique and atrociously perverse in human evolution:

The dreamlike spell of this contemplative, metaphysically oriented tradition, where light and darkness dance together in a world-creating cosmic shadow play, carries into modern times an image that is of incalculable age. In its primitive form it is widely known among the jungle villages of the broad equatorial zone that extends from Africa eastward, through India, Southeast Asia, and Oceania, to Brazil, where the basic myth is of a dreamlike age of the beginning, when there was neither death nor birth, which, however, terminated when a murder was committed.

—Joseph Campbell, The Masks of God (1962), 4

The synthesis is to be found in what the Taoists called *The Tao* and that Campbell calls '*the perfume, the flowering and fulfillment of human life, not a supernatural virtue imposed upon it.'*

—Joseph Campbell, The Power of Myth (1988), 245.

And like the Taoists, Campbell says that *'heaven and hell are within us, and all the gods are within us.'* Campbell makes his point succinctly by telling us to overcome the schizoid split so deeply rooted in the patriarchal shift that occurred five thousands years ago and reminds the myth of the Grail as a syncretic doctrine of love allowed to grow beyond all borders:

> The Grail becomes symbolic of an authentic life that is lived in terms of its own volition, in terms of its own impulse system, that carries itself between the pairs of opposites of good and evil, light and dark. (Id.)

And he emphasizes that love *'is not expressing itself in terms of the socially approved manners of life because it has nothing to do with the social order.'* (Id., 254)

Even more clearly, Thomas Moore, in his book *Care of the Soul (1994)* states that *'[m]oralism is one of the most effective shields against the soul, protecting us from its intricacy'*. Thomas Moore pursues:

> The soul's complex means of self-expression is an aspect of its depth and subtlety. When we feel something soulfully, it is sometimes difficult to express that feeling clearly. At a loss of words, we turn to stories and images. Nicholas of Cusa concluded that we often have no alternative but to live with *enigmatic images*. Since soul is

more concerned with relatedness than intellectual understanding, the knowledge that comes from soul's intimacy with experience is more difficult to articulate than the kind of analysis that can be done at a distance. Soul is always in process, having, as Heraclitus says, its own principle of movement; so it is difficult to pin down with definition or a fixed meaning. When spirituality loses contact with soul and these values, it can become rigid, simplistic, moralistic, and authoritarian - qualities that betray a loss of soul. (Id., 17)

Reich stated this fact in similar terms in his book *Children of the Future (1950)*:

Moralism only increases the pressure of crime and guilt, and never gets at or can get at the roots of the problem. (Id., 44)

Finally, I wish to address the senseless control paradigm of life-denying society that has brought about the split between so-called erós-inspired and agapé-inspired love. Reich appears to anticipate Riane Eisler's research for almost a century:

The splitting of sexuality into debased sensuality and transfigured love, which generates entire systems of philosophy on the problem of *sexuality* and *eroticism* is nothing more than an expression of the dominant position of the man and, in addition, a consequence of the efforts of distinguished hypocrites to set themselves apart from the masses by adopting a special morality. (Id., 204)

> The moralists, however, only have eyes for what occasionally, in their opinions, confirms their theory. They do not see and do not even want to see that their doctrines do not apply to the mass of young people, and they duck responsibility for what will happen in the future if people follow their teachings. (Id., 197)

Reich explains something very important for our quest to reunite with nature's wisdom and overcome our socially programmed and culturally sanctified alienation, our split existence; it is the fact that when the emotional nature of humans is not bent and has not been thwarted early and life, we are naturally sane, both emotionally and sexually.

To say it crudely, and with Reich, men and women who are sane and natural won't abduct, rape and murder children because of lust for child sex; hence, moralism's reasoning about the 'impossible human' is essentially a *perception error,* and so are our sex laws and the whole body of behavior rules that more or less *implicitly assume* that when people are unobserved, and let free, they will indulge in perverse acts of all kinds and jeopardize the friendly togetherness of the community. Reich counters:

> Sexual responsibility is automatically present in a healthy, satisfying sexual life. (Id., 208)

> It is this dependence on parental care and authority which the Church immediately enters the fray to defend, equipped with all the machinery of stultification and platitudes about an avenging God, his eternal will, and his wise foresight in its attempt to translocate marriage

and family to divine regions far removed from the real world. (Id., 214-215)

Reich's position is clearly for a *free emotional and sexual life of children as a conditio sine qua non* for overcoming the life-denying patriarchal plague:

> The means which such parental homes use to bring their children to heel consist essentially of sexually intimidating and crippling them and making them afraid of their sexual desires, thoughts, and deeds. (Id., 215)

When the Tao was lost, Lao-tzu wrote in the *Tao Te Ching*, the schizoid spirit of dualism began to build images of *ideal substance.* Instead of recognizing substance as eternal change, expressed in the *yin-yang alternation* of ever-changing evolution, the schizoid thinkers began to split the world into what they called *the miserable state of the world*, on one hand, and the *ideal paradise-like state of heavenly existence,* on the other. Despising the origin of their very existence, that is mother earth or *Gaia*, they began to despise and fear the essence of earth, the sparkling spirit of abundant creation, naming it *serpent* or *devil*.

Having condemned the source of their bliss, the new inhabitants of a split world were making for the ground of their profound unhappiness, paranoia and the ultimate destruction of their basic life continuum.

Instead of striving for harmony and accepting all-that-is, they transformed in their madness peaceful togetherness into innumerable wars that they proudly proclaim as:

- ▸ war-of-the-sexes

- ▸ war-for-survival

- ▸ war-against-evil

- ▸ war-against-islamism

- ▸ war-against-terrorism

- ▸ war-against-perversion

- ▸ war-against-drugs

- ▸ war-against-pedophilia, and so forth.

The result is a world full of strife, war, destruction and a perverse rat-race for material gain and dominance.

This new, and even larger, international dominator culture is currently spreading all over the world and our modern global consumer culture is its latest and most appalling offspring.

Taoism, by contrast, teaches that a seeker of truth does not will to consume or dominate the object of his love. The lover of the original state of existence who studies the Tao, the spontaneous principle of creation, is a *lover of unspoiled nature*, a *lover of small children* as they represent the original inhabitants of the non-split world. This was recognized in olden times all over the world, but has been forgotten and is today carefully veiled behind the lies of violent moralism.

This is however not a new phenomenon, as the same, only regionally limited, was occurring when China became a feudal state. Lao-tzu then retired into the mountains and wrote in the *Tao Te Ching:*

> The more laws and restrictions there are,
> The poorer people become.
> The more rules and regulations,
> The more thieves and robbers.

The wise does not discriminate between the sexes, recognizing that *yin*, the female principle, was first in creation and is more encompassing than *yang*, the male principle.

That is why the wise who is inspired by the Tao will celebrate and worship little girls as protector-goddesses of his universe. He will not nourish an exclusive preference for one of the sexes because he knows that in relating only to *yin*, his *yang* force will overflow and damage his inner *yin*, and that by relating only to *yang*, his *yin* force will overflow and damage his inner *yang*. As a result of this fact, and because of his self-knowledge, the sage does *not reject* anything; he is not influenced by the split-paradigm that says 'There are adults, and there are children,' as if talking about two different races.

Knowing that all things are nourished by the Tao of spontaneous creation and change, the wistful lover recognizes the values of care, love and parenthood in other adults; he does not attack the family order nor the order of the state. The wistful lover does not reject the world, nor does he need to make for an ideal or paradise-like state of happiness. He is happy by accepting all-that-is, and the world as it is, by not trying to do creation better than the Tao.

We have created total confusion in our relationships, and put the *love principle* upside-down, demonized what is naturally beautiful and enriching and put up *false values* that render us shallow and mean, and full of suspicion and fear.

When we justify the mess we see all around is in modern society, we are producing still more confusion and destruction, and in order to veil our millenary stupidity, we blame nature and human nature.

While it is so obvious that it's the perversion of nature and human nature that has created the mess and brings about the destruction, but not nature herself, we go on affirming that nature was wrong and not to be trusted and our so-called *scientific* mind could *correct the errors supposed to be inherent in nature.*

The Murder Culture

No murder can happen without being preceded by a murder inside of us way before we set out to kill in the first place. The desire to kill comes about through the schizoid split created by killing something within ourselves.

Our past millennia of collective murder and genocide were preceded by the killing of one of our internal opposites and thus upsetting the *natural balance of yin and yang* within us: by condemning and tightly regulating *sexual pleasure or certain forms of it*, by achieving to interfere with and repress the natural emotional flow in the lives of our children, we have distorted the natural order, and turned upside-down the subtle energy flow, not only in the human being but, as all is connected, also in the stratosphere of the earth, the planetary energies within our galaxy and the intergalactic energy balance within the whole of the cosmos.

And we had no right doing so because the bodies of our children are not *our* bodies, as we do not own our bodies. The human body as the whole of life cannot be owned. Lao-tzu said the human body is 'the eternal adaptability of heaven.' Other philosophers said that the universe as our mother earth lends us a body that we have to give back when we go back to the subtle realms of existence. In fact, even the dullest of the dull must admit that we cannot take our bodies into the afterlife. Minutes after our spirit has left our body, the body begins to decay and in a few days it is but a peace of rotten flesh that is virtually eaten up by a multitude of birds, insects, worms, beetles and other animals and plants that mother earth sends out to embrace back in her substance what she has so generously granted us as a vehicle for our spiritual advancement.

Life is created by pleasure and natural death equally is pleasure as it opens an illuminated path into a subtle *vibrational* existence. Killing natural attraction was the foremost tool of dominator culture to get hold of humans and to manipulate and control them into the literal essence of their flesh and their bones. By the same token and with the same goal, dominator culture repressed the truth about the cyclic nature of birth-and-death, and invented the myth of a linear one-time life that supposedly ends in death as ultimate shock and destruction. The three dominator religions have coincided in suppressing the teaching of *natural reincarnation* that is an essential element of perennial philosophy.

There is a *new culture* now raising especially in highly civilized societies that refuses to stay with analyzing and blaming the terrible state of affairs we are in, and instead practices a new way of living. While these movements are very diverse, what they have in common is that they attempt to become germs or living cells of what could be realized on a larger scale within a truly humane, society and culture.

While communities were existing already in the 1960s, they were overruled by a new wave of fascism from about the mid 1980s, but the basic idea is familiar with all those who practice one or the other alternative lifestyle.

Young people today who subscribe to what could be called a *love culture* seem to be inspired by a deep quest for innocence. They tend to accept and understand the spiritual significance of matriarchy and respect what they call the *Gaia* principle, a deep veneration of *Mother Earth.* They are often involved in professions that either involve art, drama, dance and music, or the professions that deal with natural healing, body work, healthy diet and integral living, or else they are unconventional psychiatrists or psychoanalysts, astrologers or numerologists as well as those who engage in one or the other spiritual path such as Yoga or Zen. But there are also people from other professions who individually join these circles, temporarily or permanently.

This brings me to explain more in detail what I exactly mean when I am talking about the spiritual significance of matriarchy. In *Occidental Mythology (1973)*, Joseph Campbell observes:

> In the older mother myths and rites the light and darker aspects of the mixed thing that is life had been honored equally and together, whereas in the later, male-oriented, patriarchal myths, all that is good and noble was attributed to the new, heroic master gods, leaving to the native nature powers the character only of darkness—to which, also, a negative moral judgment now was added. For, as a great body of evidence shows, the social as well as mythic orders of the two contrasting ways of life were opposed. Where the goddess had been venerated as the giver and supporter of life as well as consumer of the dead, women as her representatives had been accorded a paramount position in society as well as in cult. Such an order of female-dominated social and cultic custom is termed, in a broad and general way, the order of Mother

Right. And opposed to such, without quarter, is the order of the Patriarchy, with an ardor of righteous eloquence and a fury of fire and sword. (Id., 21-22)

In simple words, whenever we face a life paradigm that does away with the changeability of life and thereby reduces the concept of living to a *monistic, monolithic principle,* we are facing not human saneness, but insanity at its peak, and the result, invariably, is violence.

All the eloquence of Biblical preachers cannot betray the truth seeker's intuition of what is naturally sane, and the more missionaries preach and exhort, the more violent, the more dangerous, the more genocidal they are. Human colonial history has given abundant factual proof for that sad psychological reality.

Ours is undoubtedly a *murder culture* because those who founded it were themselves based upon murder, the rape and extinction of their surrounding out-groups which was, at that time of much more limited population compared to today, *already a mass-murder to be qualified as genocide.* I do not know on which mountaintop today's conservatives gather to acknowledge that their worldview if founded on *goodness* or were inducing goodness in people?

What *goodness,* the hell, comes from a worldview in which only the in-group enjoys respect and where everybody else, including their children, is subjected to torture, rape, murder and genocide? It is here where the spiritual significance of matriarchy comes in as a regulatory principle. Joseph Campbell affirms:

> I am taking pains in this work to place considerable stress upon the world age and symbolic order of the goddess; for the findings both of anthropology and of archeology now attest not only to a contrast between the mythic and social systems of the goddess and the later gods, but also to the fact that in our own European culture that of the gods overlies and occludes that of the goddess—which is nevertheless effective as a counterplayer, so to say, in the unconscious of the civilization as a whole. (Id., 70)

What has the female become under patriarchy? A split concept, how could it be otherwise, a breed of dualistic thinking. A *virgin* to be defiled, raped, abducted and killed, on the subconscious level, and a *daughter of good breed*, the obedient slave-girl, at the apparent or outside level, the princess to be married off for material riches paid to the father. An *investment* at best, when older, a household item. When old, a nuisance. Patriarchy instituted *correction homes* for the young, prisons for the free thinkers and retirement homes for the elder. All those who fall outside the in-group, which is the 20-40 majority, have to be taught that sex is a shame, and has to be repressed. They are deprived of it as a matter of social duty, just as prisoners are. That is the respect patriarchy has in front of the child and old age.

The rest is lip service and sentimentalism. *The reality of life speaks in facts, not in cathedral speeches.*

An old female, once the person of highest regard and social status in matriarchy, under patriarchy has become a double form of plague, the plague to be a female and the plague to be old and *useless* within the greed machinery of patriarchal making.

The Spiritual Laws of Matriarchy

The *spiritual laws of matriarchy* are the counterplayer in the collective subconscious that Campbell intuits, not the imaginative embodiment of patriarchal minds because it will be debased until the, probably catastrophic end of patriarchy! But patriarchy cannot alter cosmic laws and this, and not human wit, is what I am talking about here.

Matriarchy is based upon a whole range of laws regulating the relationship between the human realm and the animal and plant realms. Patriarchy, by contrast, is based on the violation of these spiritual laws. It cannot last because it dethrones nature and, by doing so, debases creation itself. It is blasphemic, in last resort. And patriarchy's monotheism was born on the blood-soaked linen of raped and massacred nations and populations that have been *sacrificed* for Yahweh's *cool walk in the garden.*

Thomas Moore has spent more than a decade in monastic seclusion as a Catholic monk and he finally quit religious life with all its restrictions, only to discover that life within the busy world of modern international society can guard and purport the same soul values and the same sensitive and lucidly intelligent approach to life he once discovered and implemented by spending long years in monasteries. In his bestselling book *Care of the Soul (1994)*, Moore writes:

> Moralism is one of the most effective shields against the soul, protecting us from its intricacy. (…) I would go even further. As we get to know the soul and fearlessly consider its oddities and the many different ways it shows itself among individuals, we may develop a taste for the perverse. We may come to appreciate its quirks and deviances. Indeed, we may eventually come to realize that individuality is born in the eccentricities and unexpected shadow tendencies of the soul, more so than in normality and conformity. (Id., 17)

Caring for our soul, being connected to all-that-is, implies to pay attention to detail—*all detail in life.* Moralism, in last resort, is a form of shallowness, an ingrained laziness to deal with all the stuff that makes our daily life, including our oddities and difficult-to-admit perversities.

Moralism is the banner of patriarchy and for good reason it never had a stand in matriarchal cultures. Whoever is really soulful, and *spiritual*, pays attention to all-that-is and does not make up a phraseology of ought-to's that fills his mind in order to put his soul at rest, so that it does not become too virulent and inquisitive.

The highest spiritual law is *total attention*. The moralist does not deal with detail. He haughtily rushes over all detail in life, declaring that 'little daily matters' did not count for a 'spiritual' man, a man of word, of honor, of principles, a man whose life was based upon *values*. In reality, there are no *little daily matters* as all matters, as all is important for the one who pays attention to detail. Love is detail. For the truly spiritual person, there is no shame connected to talking about his perverse sides, fantasies, longings or deeds. He knows that the energy can flow in one direction and also in the other direction, that energy can retrograde and pent-up and that this brings about perverse reactions, desires and needs. But to recognize this means to be freed of the obsession to follow-up to these delusional needs.

To admit perversity means to deal with it, while moralism entangles one who arrogantly wipes off the idea of admitting perverse desires, making him a slave of his repressed perversions. That is why non-judgmental, permissive cultures, which are those that are more matriarchal in their base setup really can deal with human perversity, and constructively so, while human history shows with all evidence that patriarchal moralism brings about emotional stuckness that puts on stage a *clean* reality, while behind the stage all the devils are playing hide-and-seek. Moore explains:

> Care of the soul is interested in the not-so-normal, the
> way that soul makes itself felt most clearly in the

unusual expressions of a life, even and maybe especially in the problematic ones. (...) Sometimes deviation from the usual is a special revelation of truth. In alchemy this was referred to as the *opus contra naturam*, an effect contrary to nature. We might see the same kind of artful unnatural expression within our own lives. When normality explodes or breaks out into craziness or shadow, we might look closely, before running for cover and before attempting to restore familiar order, at the potential meaningfulness of the event. If we are going to be curious about the soul, we may need to explore its deviations, its perverse tendency to contradict expectations. And as a corollary, we might be suspicious of normality. A facade or normality can hide a wealth of deviance, and besides, it is fairly easy to recognize soullessness in the standardizing of experience. (Id., 18)

The spiritual laws of matriarchy are of course no written laws. They are no worldly statutes or regulations. They are truths valid on a cosmic level, and on a soul level. But they are observable in the lives of those who live in close relation with nature, for example, shamanic tribal peoples who maintain a living spiritual contact with all natural forces through their *shamans*, and their long-standing traditions of dialogue with nature's wistful energies.

When I talk about the *spiritual laws of matriarchy*, I do not mean general spiritual laws such as the law of attraction, the law of prosperity, the law of harmony, and others. I am rather talking about *patterns of living*, directly observable in the lifestyle of wistful peoples and that are no secret knowledge, but to be verified by any serious researcher on shamanism. For there is no occult hermetic tradition to be studied, as these patterns are directly applied, by tribal peoples, in their daily life and relationships.

Bull and Serpent

The spiritual significance of matriarchy is not just a matter of mythology, of energies, of symbols. Its meaning goes beyond the mythic bond of humans with nature and all the forces that have their imprint upon us and the whole of the universe. The matriarchal laws have a direct impact upon our soul. I dare to say that if the soul itself obeys to certain laws, then to these matriarchal laws or patterns that I was talking about in the previous chapter.

Our soul is at odds with the *normalcy* concept that is at the basis of patriarchal laws and their underlying morality code. As Moore expresses it:

> Care of the soul sees another reality altogether. It appreciates the mystery of human suffering and does not offer the illusion of a problem-free life. It sees every fall into ignorance and confusion as an opportunity to discover that the beast residing at the center of the labyrinth is also an angel. The uniqueness of a person is made up of the insane and the twisted as much as it is of the rational and the normal. To approach this paradoxical point of tension where adjustment and abnormality meet is to move closer to the realization of our mystery-filled, star-born nature. (Id., 20)

The soul really follows the *self-regulation* pattern of living; it cannot be forced to adopt other than its own rules, and its intelligence is not rational, but the *emotional intelligence of the heart.* The soul's major longing is balance, harmony, wholeness, and its major effort is the one of healing fragmentation. Carl Jung writes in *Religious and Psychological Problem of Alchemy (1993)*:

> But the right way to wholeness is made up, unfortunately, of fateful detours and wrong turnings. It is a *longissima via*, not straight but snakelike, a path that unites the opposites, in the manner of the guiding caduceus, and whose labyrinthine twists and turns are not lacking in terrors. It is on this longissima via that we meet with those experiences which are said to be *inaccessible. (Id., 541)*

The soul and its superior knowledge about life and happiness is indeed inaccessible if we *think* life, instead of *living* life, applying only our left brain and considering only logical thought as being relevant for understanding life and living processes.

It can be said that this kind of lifestyle, that today is widely adopted, is lacking shadow, rendering life as a one-dimensional drawing, a *solar* worldview in the words of Joseph Campbell, where shadows are *lighted away* by the sun rays of the purely rational mind. Thomas Moore explains:

> A neurotic narcissism won't allow the time needed to
> stop, reflect, and see the many emotions, memories,
> wishes, fantasies, desires, and fears that make up the
> materials of the soul. As a result, the narcissistic person
> becomes fixed on a single idea of who he is, and other
> possibilities are automatically rejected. (Id., 67)

For the narcissist, all in life is about statistics. Love is
expressed in percentages and probabilities. But what is the
daily life taste of it? Never known, never seen. The
narcissist talks about principles, rules and facts: he
suggests love could be measured, quantified and
scientifically *demonstrated*. Nay, such a thing cannot be,
otherwise it would not be love, but the shallow soup that
today is yelled from all megaphones of international
consumer stupidity. *Love me forever!* The soul knows that
love is not a concept and cannot endure according to the
mind and will. It has its own life span, and it knows its
own death.

The narcissist flies in the air and cherishes lofty
Apollonian ideas. But where is their Dionysus? The truth is
encoded in that part of them, and carefully hidden from
their public appearance. Care of the soul, for most of us,
means care for the Dionysian principle in us, the *Sad King*,
as I called it. Narcissism is an inevitable by-product of
patriarchy, and its etiology as *wrong relating*. Wrong
relating to self, and as a result, wrong relating to others. It
is built on the preclusion of the shadows of the soul—
thereby ignoring its own shadow. Narcissists, therefore, are

tragic figures. They are tragic in the sense that they run into the abyss without the slightest idea of what they are doing., because they are not grounded and have their feet in the air, like the *Fool* in the Tarot. They are lunatics, because they have not integrated their own *Luna*, their Moon energy. They are the eternal Peter Pan's of sunshine movies, and present themselves to the public smiling, broadly smiling, most of the time, but in haphazard moments you see their true face —while they themselves ignore it.

Thomas Moore observes that narcissism, in our times, is a problem that by far surpasses the individual and has become a societal concern:

> America has a great longing to be the New World of opportunity and a moral beacon for the world. It longs to fulfill these narcissistic images of itself. At the same time it is painful to realize the distance between the reality and that image. America's narcissism is strong. It is paraded before the world. If we were to put the nation on the couch, we might discover that narcissism is its most obvious symptom. And yet that narcissism holds the promise that this all-important myth can find its way into life. In other words, America's narcissism is its refined puer spirit of genuine new vision. The trick is to find a way to that water of transformation where hard self-absorption turns into loving dialogue with the world. (Id., 62)

Narcissism is destructive because it believes in shortcuts, quick fixes and once-for-all solutions.

The soul however, and evolution in general, proceeds in a spiraled movement, which is something like a circled forward movement. Thomas Moore describes it in the language of alchemy:

> All work on the soul takes the form of a circle, a rotatio. (…) I keep in mind the alchemical circulatio. The life of the soul, as the structure of dreams reveals, is a continual going over and over the material of life. (Id., 13)

The spiraled movement is more holistic than the linear movement because it carries our base all along from here to there. That means we do not leave our origins, but remain firmly rooted in where we came from. These roots are essential for providing us with *living energy.* It's a serpentine movement, the movement of a snake. However, our quick efficiency, our stress on immediacy, our lack of time, our focus on straight solutions prevent us from integrating, rooting, personal evolution in the soul. As a result, our progresses are merely peripheral and remain at the surface of the personality.

All this, while it sounds commonplace, is the inevitable result of patriarchal morality because it circumvents the soul. To explain this on a mythological level, let me introduce another symbol, as important or even more important in world mythology than the bull: it's the *serpent.* Ralph Metzner, in the introduction to his reader *Ayahuasca: Human Consciousness and the Spirits of Nature (1999),* observes:

Not only among Amazonian shamans, but throughout
the world, in Asia, the Mediterranean, Australia, serpent
images are used to represent the basic life force and
regarded as a source of knowledge—the wisdom of the
serpent. The serpent image is seen often as a link
between heaven and earth, and in this regard the snake
is often found in association with other images of ascent.
(Id., 34)

Joseph Campbell reports two crucial turning points for
the cosmic serpent in world mythology. The first occurs in
the context of the Iron Age Hebrews of the first millennium
B.C where the mythology became inverted, so as to
represent the opposite to its origin, the second is to be
found in the creation myth where the serpent who had
been revered in the Levant for at least seven thousand
years before the composition of the *Book of Genesis*, plays
the part of the villain.

Yahweh, who replaces it in the role of the creator, ends
up defeating *the serpent of the cosmic sea, Leviathan*. For
Campbell, the second turning point occurs in Greek
mythology where Zeus was initially represented as a
serpent, but then, when the myths changed, Zeus became a
serpent-killer.

From that time, Zeus was depicted to secure the reign
of the patriarchal gods of Mount Olympus by defeating
Typhon, the enormous serpent-monster who is the child of
the earth goddess Gaia and the incarnation of the forces of
nature.

—See Jeremy Narby, The Cosmic Serpent (1999), 66, with further references.

It is in accordance with this fundamental change in mythology that, as I mentioned earlier, the significance of the bull equally *changed from a matriarchal to a patriarchal meaning,* and the Hispanic tradition of *bull fighting* clearly reflects the perverted patriarchal tradition rather than, as some pretend, representing a matriarchal base structure in Hispanic machismo.

While the female principle in the Babylonian epic of creation has been devalued, we can still find it associated with the serpent, the boa, the *Great Mother,* in the natural philosophy of most tribal peoples, as reflected by shamanism.

In Ralph Metzner's *Ayahuasca* reader, already quoted, we find a range of reports contributed by people from all walks of life who have taken the traditional Ayahuasca brew in order to encounter the plant teachers or *spirits* of the plant. Two of them report visions of the cosmic serpent. Raoul Adamson entitled his experience *Initiation into Ancient Lineage of Visionary Healers* and writes:

> I become aware of a morphic resonance between serpent and intestines: the form of the snake is more or less a long intestinal tract, with a head and a tail end; and conversely, our gut is serpentine, with its twists and turns and its peristaltic movement. So the serpent, winding its way through my intestinal tract was *teaching*

my intestines how to be more powerful and effective—
certainly a gut-level experience! (Id., 48)

Ganesha, in her *Vision of Sekhmet*, reports:

As I read about Sekhmet and assimilated my experience
with her, the understanding that formed in my
consciousness was that Sekhmet is a Great Mother
Goddess, one that spans all time. With the sun disk at
her head and the snake around it, she symbolizes the
serpent power of the root chakra having risen to the
crown. Thus, she encompasses both heaven and Earth,
and demonstrates the way to unite the heaven and Earth
of our own nature, Spirit and Form, through the
awakening of the kundalini power in the muladhara
chakra and its arising to the sahaswrara chakra. (Id., 83)

Raimundo D., in his *The Great Serpentine Dance of Life*,
writes:

The plumed serpent is masculine, involves outer
impression and show of power; the unplumbed serpent
is feminine, involving inner expression and statement of
strength. (…) I experienced my entire body being
reprogrammed and rearranged, even reconstituted at the
deep cellular level. This resulted in an incredible feeling
of openness, solidity, wholeness and openness. (Id., 130)

We can thus summarize that the association of the
serpent as a *matriarchal symbol* for the Mother Goddess is
not only a recurring theme of world mythology, but can be
experienced, with the use of entheogens, as a spiritual

vision that impacts directly on the soul and super-consciousness.

As it can be argued that what is seen in psychedelic visions is but the content of the collective unconscious of humanity, there is truth in Campbell's statement that the Goddess still today acts as a *counterplayer* to patriarchy, on the level of the unconscious, and this independently of personal beliefs or intellectual understanding of shamanism or nature religions.

Chapter Five

A Scientific-Shamanic Approach to Religion

Introduction

In the present chapter, I will present a somewhat uncanny approach to religion. It is scientific because it proceeds empirically and without any preliminary assumptions. What I am going to show is that there is a way to our inner resources that is accessible to each and everybody. To get there, no casebook is needed, no classes need to be attended, and no library needs to be researched. All that is to know is contained, in form of holographic patterns, within the unique Self. *It is a shamanic quest.*

If then the unique Self is the guide, as for example Ramana Maharshi affirmed it, I don't know why anybody should spend their money on expensive workshops for healing and self-transformation? Most of those books only repeat verities that you possess, literally, within yourself.

After all, a guru can only speak about his or her own experience, but yours will be different, for sure. You can never do what the guru did, simply because your action is a different one, because you are a different person. Thus, how can you think a guru can be of help to you, given that the guru can only speak for his own spiritual pathway, not yours? Why should you not ask your inner guide, the unique self? This is what I am going to write about in this chapter of the book that is dedicated to all those who run around in the world searching for what they will never find—because they never lost it, and all their outside search will not help them to see the treasure they bear inside!

Now, how to access this inner realm, how to communicate with it? Is it at all possible to communicate it, or is religion bound to remain ultimately an intimate experience that cannot be shared?

I do not give an answer to this question here, and for good reason, as our little self-inquiry will result in an overall insight that *intuition bears its own veracity* that need not be corroborated by rational mental concept making. On the contrary, we are going to see that when we talk about religion, that is, contact with our inner source, such concept making is a fallacy as it leads to a highly distorted communication. As the terms and phrases used to describe religious experience are always bound to be personal, their sharing leads to an impasse, *when such sharing is verbal.* It may be shared through silence, sitting together in silence, yes, as in such a case the sharing is on a deeper, telepathic, ethereal or metaphorical level, on a level of shared beingness, on a level of one may call 'total communication.'

But what our big dominator religions always did is to encourage verbal sharing of religious experience, through scriptures, holy books, and *preaching*, that is, the verbal transmission of such content. And here is where the maze opens up because thought comes in and with it, mental concepts, which are in turn conditioned by previous experience and by beliefs of all kinds. I have questioned all belief, and making of belief in this text, as belief is another obstacle to the religious experience, as it distorts direct perception and may even stand in the way of it.

Eventually, as many religions distinguish between belief and faith, we may ask if faith is the trigger of the religious experience? But faith is but an inner attitude, it's a certain openness to the miraculous, and in that sense it may be conducive.

However, in most cases, when people say they have Christian faith, or Muslim faith or Buddhist faith, their faith is not just mere openness to experiencing the unknown, but conditioned by their particular religious belief system. In such a case, faith is not conducive to experiencing the unknown. Krishnamurti said it very lucidly in telling us that we always find what we are searching for. The Christian will encounter the Virgin Mary, the Muslim will experience the Prophet, the Buddhist will see the Buddha when they make such transcendental experiences. Hence, they do not meet the unknown; they encounter projections of their own mind when they are in that state of trance where we experience the content of our consciousness. This is not what the religious experience is about. And that is why I conclude that faith is not conclusive to that purpose either.

What really leads us there cannot be expressed verbally which is why I cannot answer the questions I am asking.

Answers anyway are temporary, while the questions, the basic and great questions of life, remain. So we need not bother about answers, and don't need to search for them. When we leave the questions open, subtle answers will come through all kinds of circumstances, *visions, intuitions, hunches, encounters, dreams, spontaneous insights or sudden realization of transcendental truth.* But as long as we search for answers, this whole process is blocked and cannot unfold.

It is intuition, pure intuition, that leads us there, by *not* leading us there. We cannot approach the divine, we cannot step out of blindness and into total enlightenment in a second. But the divine can do that, and approach us that way when we remain supple, open, and innocent in the right sense of the word. Hence, true *religio* is actually more of a state of innocence than anything else; it is pretty much the contrary of what religions do, it's more on the passive side of life, more on the contemplative side of life, and requires *very little or no ritual,* other than inner silence and a poised attitude that is nonviolent and non-demanding.

The Unique Self

Self-development is not a modern idea. Truly it is age-old, and was practiced by the sages of ancient times; it was an integral part of the Egyptian and later the Greek initiation rites, and it was taught by the Celtic seers and many other wistful peoples around the world.

This kind of work is really at the basis of shamanism, which is one of many pathways to human perfection. It is also to be found in our holy books around the world, as well as in Sufi literature and the books written by masters and gurus from the Far East, and last not least, the pamphlets of yogis and alchemists.

When there is an excessive thirst for novelty, as it's the sign of the times in our modern society, there is no consistent line of systematized wisdom about life and living, but trends, fashions, and interest groups that bombard and influence our national and international media.

What happens here is that simply an old vocabulary is being re-baptized and millenary teachings are sold under new names and fashionable slogans that fit the addiction of the day. What we need instead is to define the role of man in the cosmos on both the individual and the collective, transpersonal levels. What are the sources of knowledge that lead us there? The danger in such a situation is that we try to respond to our present problems with old recipes that we find on the flea market, or the new age bazaar, instead of finding answers from deep inside us.

This is what is called the 'vulgarization of knowledge,' which leads to not an evolution of culture, but rather to the decline of culture.

When one is unable to see the common roots behind the multiple problems, and behind the thousand and one manifestations of those problems, one is quickly caught by the number one ghost of our times, *boomeritis*. The temple merchants get those, mostly from our younger generations, who have lost their souls and navigate on the waves of one or the other 'spiritual' addiction, and they make huge profits with this kind of eye-wiping.

I do of course not talk about serious and respected authors in this context, who, before they propose their novel ideas, take explicit reference to appropriate perennial teachings or native wisdom. Unfortunately, in the big confusing new age bazaar, these authors are rather the exception that confirms the rule. It seems to me that books that deny the origin of their ideas are sold much better, while their appalling arrogance in allegedly producing 'striking novelty' is all-too-typical for our modern media culture.

To read about concepts, old or new, is nourishing our left brain, but it does not serve the synthetic thirst of our right brain hemisphere.

Hence, for developing *holistic thinking capability,* which is the way the unique self 'reasons', we need to establish a *harmonious syncing of our two brain hemispheres.* This is best done by listening to music and by relaxation, to enter a *receptive* state of mind.

In this particular state of mind that is known under the term of *alpha state*, we become creative and can begin to express our inner talents.

A guide then is readily at our disposition, the unique self. It directs not only our spiritual evolution but also our creative process. It doesn't obey to any guru for the unique self is itself the guru.

Any guru you find crossing your path, in whatever dimension this happens, is an incarnation of the unique self.

Before I come to the essence of my intuitive journey toward true *religio*, I would like to give you some practical advice how you can strengthen the bond with your unique self.

First Advice

Observe

Observe what is in your way, here and now, to reach a complete state of inner peace, a state of total happiness, of divine bliss! What is it you are lacking out on to get there?

Take a sheet of paper and list all the points that come to mind. This is a *negative list*. In this list, you note all the obstacles to your happiness, be it financial hurdles, but it personal issues, be it a historical or global situation you find is oppressing you. If you believe that because you are Jewish, you can't get what you deserve in this world, write on the paper: 'It is because I am Jewish that I cannot be rich, recognized and happy.' If you are a young girl and you can't find a lover, write: 'It is because I am too timid [stupid, fat …] that I do not find a man who desires me.'

Why should you do this? When you write down your negative thoughts, the negativity that is attached to those thoughts slowly vanishes off and disappears. Why?

It's because you focus your attention on what doesn't work in your life. What is the result? You are going to dissolve what doesn't work in your life. And why that?

Because all dissolves under the light of consciousness. Is that uncanny? Is that disturbing as an insight? Are you interested to know why this is so? The answer is that consciousness is fluid, and problems are static. This is an insight from bioenergetics. Speak of the devil, and the devil comes to you. Speak constantly of the devil, and you will build a shield against the devil.

Or, to express it in Buddhist terms: if you press too hard when you have a fish in your hand, the fish is going to escape your grasp. When you affirm that you are stupid, one moment later, you are going to be less stupid! And wait a moment, look at this. You are going to write down what you always thought and once of a sudden, this affirmation appears to be ridiculous to you. It is namely because it was not always that way, because you were not always negative. You will then see that some of those affirmations, once you have fixed them on paper and reread them, will appear to be so stupid that you will begin to question them. It is exactly in this moment of doubt that the truth can begin to operate in your psyche, and that you can begin to hear the voice of the unique self.

Once you have done this list, do another list, an even more important one. Do a *positive list!* This list will contain all your desires, material or immaterial, all you wish to have or to be. This intellectual work on preparing and programming your future, it's well with your left brain that you do it. Then another task is waiting for you, this time of a totally different nature.

Second Advice

Focus

All religion results from connecting with the unique self. Are you aligned with it? How to get there? In watching inside of you. Introspection is an age-old technique for getting in touch with your source, and that's why this kind of work is called religion.

For religion means *religio*, derived from the Latin verb *relinquere*, linking back. The term correctly connotes the meaning. However, and unfortunately so, the practice of so-called 'religious organizations' has perverted the original meaning of the term and has reversed it to its contrary. Natural religion namely proceeds from inside-out, through acquiring self-knowledge, while religious organizations work at the periphery of our being, and thus by using *indoctrination*.

The Secret and the Real

An inner approach to life, an exam of what it means to be religious, an introspection that is meant to lead to the discovery of the eternal mysteries, must it not be extremely rigorous?

You are going to ask me if this approach is mystical, or rather scientific? And my answer is that our soul is an infamous garden where there are the deepest abysses of our beingness but also the greatest resemblance with the divine, our inner god, our unique self. There is no difference between mystical and scientific reality. All inquisitiveness is gradual, all knowledge comes in junks and quanta; the distinction between mysticism and science stems from pure ignorance.

The more you know about the mysteries of life, the more you move from the *mythical-personal* to the *verifiable-transpersonal,* and as a result, the more you can share with others. If you see only the outside shell, if you remain at the periphery of your being, you will lose yourself in endless projections, in endless mental concepts, in endless rationalizations and superstitions.

It is by questioning that you gain knowledge, not by answering your questions. I am not giving answers here. I ask questions. If the question stays without an answer, it germs, it develops, it transforms itself and becomes creative. That's why it is better you stay with your questions than giving temporary answers to them. For you must see that all answers are temporary. Only the questions remain.

To begin with, how can we know what another person expresses? Do you know your own language?

Do you know to correctly use the words you put on things? Do you know how the way you see the world is accurately transcribed by the language you are using? I am not talking about musicians here, nor painters, but people who express themselves and their philosophical views primarily through verbal language.

Have you observed how you create a personal vocabulary over time, and how you change it, and how you recreate it from time to time? Have you observed to what point the language you are using is the result of your mental, social, cultural, emotional, psychic and sexual conditioning?

Everybody has their language, right? But language, is it not the final outcome of a long apprenticeship? Everyone has his or her personal language, using certain notions, words, phrases, which depend on their particular personal, cultural or religious conditioning in the sense of a cult, a ritual, an organized something.

For giving an example of this essential problem in all human relations, I will talk about a man that people use to call a saint. We go there and we listen to him. This man speaks of *reality*. He made certain spiritual experiences, people say. And he talks, almost constantly, of 'reality.'

And we don't know what to think of that term and wonder *which reality* he conveys?

What do we know about how this person perceives the 'reality' he is talking about? Is it at all something that can be communicated? How can you know the meaning of that word he uses, the word 'reality,' as you are different, and thus live in a different reality? Can you ever know exactly the meaning of that term he uses, given that his verbal description of that reality is but a transcription of his sensorial or extrasensorial perception of it, and given also that you did not share in his experience? But even if you had shared that experience, you would certainly have perceived things in a different way, because you are *other*, because you are the *summa summaris* of your own conditioning.

Everyone of us, it seems to me, is conditioned in a different way, even if we have gone through very similar life experiences. What essentially is different is not the stimulus but how we *react* to the stimulus, which means how we react to the conditioning influences. This reaction is always genuinely personal for it depends on the state of our body and our soul.

So after you see this, how can you imagine any possible communication between people about religious experience and thus about reality?

Body and Soul

We are distinct because our bodies and souls are distinct. There is desire. We find certain bodies beautiful, attractive, seductive, wonderful and sweet.

We love those bodies, and our own body, through our desire. We want to unify our body with theirs, through loving copulation. And it is desire that makes us grow when we are still in childhood. Desire gives us satisfaction, joy, ecstasy, and when we understand it intelligently, we develop our intrinsic beauty and grace.

Desire is at the origin of all life; it creates, procreates, constructs, transforms. Desire animates us and ensures the pulsation of the vital energy, so essential for our physical and psychic health and our longevity.

It is this same desire that lets us choose certain groups of people, or a specific person emotionally, as a matter of predilection, and as a result we feel that *this desire sexualizes somehow.* We feel that love is both, the emotional and the sexual attraction, and some higher form of attraction that is *neither emotional nor sexual,* nor related to pleasure. We feel that love is all of that and that we cannot reduce it to any part of that whole.

We may ask then, if there are different desires, emotional, sexual desires, or only one desire? In other words, the essential question is if we can just desire a body? When we desire to make love with a certain person, does that mean we desire only their body? This seems to be the prevailing view. But how is that possible, given that there is no body that is not animated by an incarnated soul? Only those who desire cadavers, which is a very rare perversion, desire only a body.

More generally put, we see now that we cannot *not* desire the whole of that person, that we cannot desire 'just their body;' it is logically not possible to be attracted only by the body of that person, and not by their soul and their whole being. For the soul expresses itself through the body, and forms the body, giving it its beauty, its vibrancy, its erotic flair, its charm, its aura.

A body, as a body only, can it possibly desire anything? If you follow the dualistic principle that postulates a distinction between body and soul, a Platonic and later Christian concept, body and soul can exist at different levels, so to speak. But a body without soul is dead! A body without soul is a cadaver for death is defined exactly by the fact that the soul leaves the body in a fluid subtle shell, that goes elsewhere, to another field of vibration.

The body as such can thus not desire anything. It's always the soul or, as psychologists say, the psyche that desires. Desire is thus located in the psyche, and it's only from there that it gets to be felt in the body and becomes visible through physiological reactions. And love, we have seen, is equally related to the soul.

Sexual desire and love, how can they be separate, as the dualistic concept assumes? How, when there is union with another through loving embrace, can there be separation at the same time? Does the body desire another body because it is not content with itself?

There is an ancient myth, recounted in Plato's *Banquet*, which explicates that desire comes from the fact that in olden times, we have been *androgynous and bisexual*, more complete thus, as we had both sexes within us. Then we somehow lost the other half, which is why we run after it. But desire, is it always desire for the other sex? *And homosexual desire, is it not desire?*

Psychoanalysis reveals that we are all bisexual on the psychic level. The Cabala, Tantra, Taoism and other ancient religions affirm this since times immemorial. In the Tarot, the arcana of the *Monde* (World) represents the end of the voyage of the Fool, the androgynous being, the superior, integrated form of human accomplishment. The archetype of complementarity, the completeness of being, they can only be conceived hermaphroditically. By the same token, the terms of *Naljorpa* in Tibetan language and *Yogi* in Sanskrit mean 'the person who has unified the male and females principles.'

This archetype is not at the root of desire, it is rather at the root of the sublimation of desire, in the form of self-contentment.

It is at the same time the beginning, the childhood, and the end of life, old age. Desire thus cannot be said to be per se projected upon the other sex. However, we can say this, desire is always projected upon a person, and it always, as we saw, embraces both the body and the soul of that person. It doesn't really matter in this context how we explain the origin of desire, if we recur to that old myth, or otherwise. What about staying with the question?

It is obvious that without desire, there is no life. Desire thus belongs to life. This simple observation, can it not suffice as an answer?

Desire and Morality

Morality, be it of religious or ideological origin, has arrogated itself the right to regulate desire, to regulate the choice of love objects, and the choice how desire may be satisfied, or not be satisfied.

It went as far as creating a concept called *chastity* which boils down to a metaphorical castration of desire, if not a condemnation of it, or a sacrifice of it for some vague notion of 'purity.' What is purity? We may ask where compulsive morality or moralism takes its legitimacy from? Is it based upon natural right? But how could nature grant a right that basically betrays and defeats nature itself, and its own survival mechanism? Moralities have made laws, first ecclesiastic laws, later state laws that regulate desire according to certain criteria such as sex or age of the partner, and the way the sexual embrace is carried through.

Morality gives answers. Life asks questions.

One of these questions is how love and desire have come to be separated, as they are, in fact, in our days?

What has morality done to love? Has it not profoundly sullied love, has it not dissected love into loves—parental love, self-love, sexual love, child love, charitable love, and so on and so forth? What remains of that body called love after it has been vivisected that way? Has it become a mental concept, or a commercial concept? Does it bear a label now 'Love such-and-such?' Has it become respectable? Or has it become a hypocrite lie that has not deserved the word *love?*

In all ancient religions as in Tantra, Taoism or the Cabala, sexuality, the embrace of a noble man with his young wife have been considered as an essential element of the Divine in man, the vital flow, the mystery of the deep unity of all life. Can we go from there, now at the beginning of the 21st century and recognize the goodness of *all desire*, in all its forms?

Would we thereby not embrace and honor the wholeness of life, and its vast space of freedom? Would we not honor humanity within that creation, given that human desire is *not an animal-like automatism or instinct,* but is living flow, emotional flow, which swings, like a lotos flower, in the wind of destiny?

Would we not be able to draw more happiness from our existence, and reach the peak of *wellbeing,* and at the same time the peak of transcendence?

Why has this wisdom been buried down so deep in the course of history, in the course of what we call civilization?

Why does moralism destroy life, pleasure, ecstasy, contentment, happiness? Why has it destroyed the primal continuum of childhood, to replace it with endless taboos, moral terror and shallowness?

Why have we come to crucify the person for expanding the collective, and collective guilt, by subduing the individual under pseudo-religious doctrines that only bring about violence? Why, under the pretext of progress, have we created murderous ideologies, by they capitalist, militarist, socialist, fascist, communist or other? Why crucifying natural life functions, why creating guild and shame for doing what is natural and feels good? Why regulating, condemning, vivisecting desire, love? Where does that *hubristic arrogance* originate from that pretends to know what kind of desire is 'natural' and what kind of desire is 'unnatural?' How did this life hate come about, this very denial of happiness, of pleasure?

And why have effectiveness, duty and utilitarian concepts become more important that love in our society?

Why have we allowed violent moralism to kill love, desire, life, in the first place?

Why do our highly industrialized postmodern cultures bring about decay? Why is their emotional flow locked? Why is there so much ice in human relations, and so much misery, so much suspicion and persecution?

It's the agony of a culture that is dying to its old skin, and all the *false values*, all the *pseudo values* it was based upon and that have brought about nothing of real value.

Fortunately, the signs of a global sociocultural transformation are visible to us today. But our regard should rather go inside and contemplate our inevitable inner cataclysms. Where we can act, where we have the power to act, inside of us, there is really a lot to do!

Approaching the Divine?

Can we approach the divine? Can you approach what is unknown, by forging a mental concept about it, an intellectual rationalization of it, or by calling it Gee Oh Dee or otherwise? Can you get there by belief?

What is belief? Is it not a mental concept as well? Is it not a construct of thought just as ideals are, as ideologies are, as religious or scientific theories are? Faith, is that the answer and the way to go? Can go go toward the divine at all? Or do you have to wait patiently until the divine approaches you? The divine in yourself, can you cultivate it? Can you become a religious person, free of all concepts, free of all conditioning, free of all belief?

Can you become a saint—and sain? Or are we chosen people in the sense that we are chosen by the divine, and cannot choose ourselves? Are we predestined to be vessels or vassals?

What is a religious life? Is it to follow a certain belief system, a sect, a religious or spiritual dogma? *Is to to believe anything at all?* Is it reasoning? Or is it to sense things on an intuitive level? Is it spiritual or esoteric knowledge to get there, or is it done by rigorous daily practice, yoga, asceticism, abnegation of self, chastisement of ego? Is it to follow the teaching of Christ, the Prophet or Buddha?

Is it discipline for carrying out certain rituals, or a particular cult? Is it sacrifice, mental torture or the appeasement of thought, the quest for inner silence? Is it to follow shamanic wisdom or Zen or a particular guru who rejects one thing by indoctrinating another? Is it all of this, or nothing of this?

Is it not rather a *personal path* that, in all freedom, leads to an abyss? Is it not living in abundant joy and love for all beings, a love so strong that it seems to tear apart our heart? Is it not to remain open and supple, to accept our oscillation, to accept change and constant transformation as a pattern of life? Is it not to live with all our senses, and sense all, not just ourselves, but all other beings, all other living things, and to embrace them sensually and lovingly?

It is not to see and hear what goes on around us, and in the world, instead of closing our eyes for 'not being hurt' by human suffering? Is it not to get out of our walls of silence, out of our prejudice, out of our mental concepts, and theories—and start to really communicate with others? Is it not to give up all self-serving security and to give oneself in the hand of destiny? Is it not to observe, to question, to be critical, while being humble, avoiding to become arrogant, cynical or cold? Is it not to develop true empathy for self and others, true patience with self and others, true latitude with self and others? Is it not embracing all-that-is, both joy, and suffering, desire and satisfaction, and the whole dualism of life, while being observant of the unity behind that apparent dualism? Is it not to accept life as it is, instead of striving for what should be? Is it not to remain childlike and joyful, creative and spontaneous? Is it not to observe all attachments without trying to brutally tear them off, but to understand their significance? Is it not to recognize that attachment is related to a certain form of consciousness, and that we can grow beyond it?

Is it not, first of all, to love and not flee it?

Chapter Six

Visions of an Integrative Worldview

Introduction

In the present chapter, I shall give an account of *intuitive insights* that came to me spontaneously after years of meditation and assiduous study of both *spiritual, shamanic and channeled literature* from sources around the world, including native cultures. These insights, as paradoxical as it appears, show that the ancient shamanic understanding of the universe, and reality, was basically scientific, not prelogical, nor mythical.

It was based upon observation of nature, while this observation was much more holistic than our today's 'scientific' worldview, in that the observer was not just a logical freak, but a full human who was absorbing reality on all levels, the rational, the emotional and the spiritual level.

I also contend that the science of shamanism was *methodological* in just the sense modern science is, in that observed phenomena were meticulously catalogued and systematized.

This is hardly known because the shamanic tradition is, as most ancient traditions, an oral tradition. It was possible only because at that time, scholars, be they shamans or alchemists within our own tradition, had to have huge memories; it was virtually in most cases only on memory that they could rely upon when, for example, concocting a healing tincture composed of a *mix of collateral plants* and where the composition had to be precise.

The overall impression I gained from these insights is that our human consciousness today is rather limited, and not worth the great human that was originally set in this world, as a unique and self-regulating creation. On a mass scale, geniuses excluded, what we have today is the 'small human,' an almost grotesque reduction of its original plan, a dwarf being spiritually, mentally, emotionally and even sexually. A dwarf being not rendered a dwarf but *having himself restricted to a dwarf universe,* by putting all kinds of limitations to its original, unbounded and very versatile and flexible structure.

Nature created us totally free and we have done all we could to do away with this freedom. Nature created us totally intelligent and self-reliant and we have done all we could to do away with raising children in truth and intelligence, molding them to our hundreds of concepts that are not worth the ink spent on writing them. Nature has been honest with us; we are not born clothed, and we are not holy enough to not being urged for toilet visits once in a while where we face and smell the not-so-nice nature of our bodily universe. We have done everything to pay nature her honesty back, by being largely and irresponsibly *dishonest*, hypocrite and abject over millennia, and in a manner that I can only call psychotic.

And the most dishonest creatures are paid, in our society, for being 'professionally dishonest,' our politicians and members of parliaments, and those scientists that are top of the list when it goes to justify the past or present abuses, and that are generously funded by the military. Nature has been humble with us, to cloth all its supreme wisdom and power in a human skin, and to embody in the human being the greatest of intelligence among all creatures on the globe. We have paid nature this humility back by having become the most *hubristic, fragmented, violent and devastating creature on the globe* and probably within our planetary system, the creature that has accumulated so many weapons of mass destruction that it can unleash the overkill of the planet *a few thousand times*, and that has brought about, through its acclaimed and highly intelligent science, the ecological ruin of the entire planet.

Nature has been taking care of us, to preserve our species, and we have paid nature this care back by ruthlessly eradicating thousands of species, and, worse, to reduce our own species drastically through large-scale murder, persecution and genocide, and this independently of time and space, in virtually all epochs, throughout human written history.

Instead of repeating or paraphrasing the insights given in this chapter, I encourage the reader to just re-read it over and over again, for something is likely to happen on the consciousness level when doing this. It is much less likely to happen by paraphrasing the originally received insights, as they were coming from not my intellect and not even my being, but from a source I qualify as 'intuition' and that others would qualify as 'channeled' or 'spiritual.'

The word is not the thing. What is important to retain after having read this last chapter, is that you and me are equal in that we can walk a path of self-criticism and freedom, unaffected by the cultural and social hypnosis, and look over the fence.

I have tried to do this with the present book, and I went even a step further, showing that tribal cultures, native peoples around the world, and their wisdom, can be a real guideline for the development of our own culture—which namely is no culture—just as shamanic science can for our own science.

Of course, to be so humble and recognize our need for change and for new learning needs courage, and persistence, and while only very few humans do that on a consistent basis, that doesn't mean it's impossible. It means that nature, despite all the perversion the human being has brought about, holds the backdoor open for those who do not agree with the lies and fairy tales that are served in our lukewarm media soup with every day to come, and who begin to think for themselves.

Our culture has never fostered an *integrative worldview,* while this was since times immemorial the natural, native point of view and regard upon life. Our own cultural tradition, by contrast, was one of dissection, separation, in an attempt to intellectually grasp the world, and put it in our mental drawers—where it died. We have arrived at an impasse and it is time for a change of our basic life paradigm, and develop an *integrative vision of all living* that is based, physiologically speaking, upon a *higher coordination* of our two brain hemispheres. And on the level of religion, law and world order, of course, the change is one from punishing life to embracing life, and one from preferring the 'possible human' over the 'impossible human.' We are all naturally neither good nor bad, as these terms are bringing confusion and strife to creation which is perfect in its imperfection, and imperfect in its perfection.

It simply *is*, existentially so, and moral values have no place when it's about comprehending creation. Instead of judging creation, we could then get ready to eventually start with *understanding creation*. And from there it's but a step to understanding ourselves and our role, as shamans or simple humans, with a truly scientific mind, which is a mind that is neither purely rational, or mechanical, nor merely artistic or poetic, but *visionary*. It's the visionary mindset that best defines the shamanic experience, and the visionary mindset is one that is both deductive-logical and integrative-emotional.

Or, put simply, and in the words of Baron d'Holbach, 'knowledge becomes comprehension when it swings together with emotion.'

On Consciousness

§1

Reality is wake reality plus dream reality. Dreaming is not only, as it is assumed by mainstream psychologists, a form of psychological digestion and integration of conscious events and experiences, but also a *direct reception of knowledge* and thus, a special form of perception.

>—See, for example, Sigmund Freud, The Interpretation of Dreams (1980) and Carl Gustav Jung, The Meaning and Significance of Dreams 1991. However, the prevailing view in shamanic cultures is that dreams do not need interpretation, as they are not mental productions only, but assume their own reality. Interestingly, this is paralleled with what has been received as information from extrasensorial dimensions through the practice of channeling

In dream, our perception shifts and runs on altered frequencies allowing us to perceive reality not in a logical and sequential manner, but in a *synchronistic way* that allows time to stretch and dissolve. In dreams we have access to past and future events without the limits set by the rational and time-bound mind.

In dream, we perceive reality in a way more akin to the right brain; as a result, the rationality of dreams is one of *associative logic*. In addition, dreams are a test forum for ideas, plans and projects. In dreams, we can create unlimited virtual realities in which we can act at will, take roles and act out our ideas on a virtual stage in order to see how they will affect others and the world.

Nowhere in nature the Darwinian theory of the surplus power of the stronger is to be found. It was through this fundamental error that dominator philosophies until today have been backed and justified. In nature the main organizing principles are harmony, not strife, order, not chaos, balance, not the psychotic power abuse that humanity developed as a secondary drive structure because of repression and denial.

§2

Freud said: 'Wherever I went, a poet was there before me.' Many poets are more scientific than scientists because they see more of what is essential in living. Scientists, in most cases, are defined *more by what they blind out* from the abundance of life's appearances than by what they understand about them.

§3

No outside circumstances have an impact on the state of the world; it is our own beliefs that create our reality and consequently it's by changing our beliefs that we are going to change this somewhat ungainly reality that we collectively created through a mindset of limitation, prejudice, the belief in scarcity, and spiritual ignorance.

§4

Every change in life comes about first on a psychic or etheric level and only thereafter on the level of physical or material density.

§5

Our emotions have a *direct bioenergetic impact* on other humans, animals and plants, the environment and even the weather. There is a direct link between emotions and cosmic bioenergetic events through the natural streaming of the cosmic energy field—recognized today in science as the 'unified field'—that penetrates all and animates all.

§6

Our life experiences are not 'falling from heaven' but are the direct consequence of our beliefs and convictions. In this sense, all in life is *synchronistic* as a part of an all-connected web of higher logic. Nothing in our universe is single and unconnected.

§7

Consciousness consists both of an *outer and an inner reality*. The inner reality is as important as the outer, and its main functioning mode is intuition. Intuition is the highest form of intelligence. When we follow our intuition instead of acting according to our beliefs or, worse, because of outside signals and commands, we always act right.

§8

Psychology and religion have to meet because they are complementary halves of one and the same science: the science of *total awareness*. It will not end war when we hate war and it will not end racism and discrimination when we hate racism and discrimination. We have to begin to switch our inner polarity from negative to positive.

Then our vital energies will be used much more economically and we will dispose of a higher bioenergetic potential. With this *higher energy potential* we will naturally strive to connect more with the positive than with the negative forces of the universe.

We cannot filter out of our consciousness undesired events, situations, perceptions, insights or generally any knowledge that will burden us. But what we can do is to see the *relativity of all information* and counterbalance burdening knowledge with positive, uplifting information.

The world always offers both sides of the spectrum, and we are limiting our powers when we focus only on the negative, or the positive side of life or of people.

§9

All beings are born innocently and there is no original sin. Empowerment is a consciousness-enhancing process that acknowledges the natural absence of any guilt or shame; all existing guilt and shame are a result of *negative childhood conditioning* and came about through hypnotic spells and abuse.

§10

The belief in illness and faultiness of nature or the human body is the result of *guilt*. A guilt-free worldview looks upon life and studies health, and not death and sickness.

§11

Health and longevity depend on the capacity to render beliefs conscious and to feed the mind with positive and integrative beliefs. The body is as conscious and as intelligent as the mind and works in sync with a mind that is feedbacking well with the body.

Nobody dies without having taken the decision to pass over to another dimension and move on with his or her spiritual development in the other, more subtle, dimensions. By the same token, all those who die by accidents or catastrophes get to know in advance about their anticipated destiny, and can change it if they wish to. Their involvement in the event was a choice they have done on a subconscious level.

§12

We live many lives simultaneously. Reincarnation is a misleading belief as it suggests that we lived lives sequentially. In reality, we live several lives at the same time, but on different consciousness levels and dimensions.

§13

Most diseases are the result of repressing our natural emotions, especially our hot and aggressive ones. When aggressiveness cannot be expressed in constructive ways, it acts like poison inside of us and, in the long run, blocks our *emotional flow* which in last instance means to destroy inner organs.

§14

Our dreams have a major task in self-healing. Our psyche and soma are both cleansed through healing dreams, many of which we are not conscious of because we forget them in the moment or before we wake up.

§15

The identification with either the body or the mind is unhealthy and brings about imbalances. Identification with the body leads to the wrong belief that life ends with death, while identification with the mind locks us out from our body and therefore in the long run destroys the body, which leads to premature death.

Only the healthy integration of mind and body enhances vitality and generally leads to longevity.

§16

Music balances the bioenergetic polarities in the mindbody; in addition, it stimulates and enhances our natural self-healing capacities. However, effective self-healing is blocked to a large extent when the person cherishes beliefs that belittle or deny nature's inherent self-healing potential.

§17

Consciousness and science are linked to each other in the process of *perception*. Perception proceeds through *sensation*.

Sensation is something like a window through which consciousness accesses nature. Through the gates of perception we realize the depth of knowledge that with quantitative science alone is not accessible. A holistic and *whole-brain process of perception* is needed for accurately conceiving and comprehending reality in a scientific manner.

On Love

§18

Love is part of living like breathing and drinking; love is self-expression. This means that it is inherent in love that it wants to express itself. It is difficult to live love naturally in a pornographic society.

§19

A society that is *pornographic* is a society that represses emotions and allows to express them only in a very limited range of so-called *sexual behavior*; however, emotions are universal and by far not limited to sexual expression.

§20

Sexual love within the family has often karmic reasons. Parents and children are often *complementary* in that they incarnate highly different or even opposing characteristics.

For similar reasons, a couple may get a psychotic child because they are too stiff while the child incarnates the spontaneity that is lacking in their lives.

§21

All sexuality is an 'emosexuality' in the sense that emotions cannot be excluded from sexual attraction, and also in the sense that sexual attraction follows emotional attraction, and *not vice versa*. Western society has throughout history suffered from a schizoid split of love into *erós* and *agapé*, while this split does not exist in nature.

§22

Most people follow sexual roles that are *cliché models* and not the natural expression of their soul desire; many have not enough self-knowledge to know what they really want. That is why the majority of people are unable to really live their love.

Naturally, our love and sex desires go together and are not to be split on different partners, one for love, and one for sex. Many men suffer from a schizoid split of love and sex projected upon different partners. This schizoid split of love and sex has brought about and brings about war, destruction, civil war and genocide on a worldwide scale. It is largely the result of moralism.

§23

Sexuality is by no means fixated and rather of a moving, changing nature. It brings about strife, unhappiness and neurosis when people are exclusive in their sexual attractions. All exclusivity in love and sex is a matter of rigid conditioning, of rigidity and neurosis, and not of intelligence and emotional, erotic and sexual sanity.

For the future of humanity, it is essential that our bisexual be acknowledged and socially recognized and validated.

§24

Children are from birth emotionally and sexually *conscious and awake*, but their sexuality has hardly anything to do with what most psychologists project on it. To condition children into early gender separation means to destroy their innate bisexuality.

§25

Both lesbian and homosexual tendencies are natural with children, as pedophile tendencies are with adolescents, and are not to be interfered with. However, because sexual matters are generally little understood in our society, when children and adolescents display lesbian, homosexual or pedophile attraction, such desires more often than not are feared and repressed.

One of the results is that natural heterosexuality is a rare exception within Western culture because it is regularly destroyed by fearful and ignorant parents and educators during the psychosexual growth period of the child.

That is how psychosexual imbalances such a homosexuality or pedophilia, and similar patterns are created as bioenergetic imprints early in childhood.

This is because natural psychosexual growth processes are interfered with by ignorance instead of letting nature its course. Homosexuality and pedophilia as *exclusive love options* are unnatural, but they are not perverse; the paradox is that they arise with *higher frequency* when early homosexual or pedophile experiences have been repressed and sexual feelings were thus sullied by guilt and shame. The only perversion in the human setup is violence, which is a conditioned response, not a natural human behavior.

§26

Most children are conditioned upon toys and pets in order to get away from *feeling* and *being with their own body;* this alienation and conditioning upon body replacements is the condition for international consumer culture to function, and shows *how destructive this society model is in truth.* An overwhelming part of children's natural love potential is thus wasted and vested into material possessions.

§27

Elders have the right to live their love life and sexuality without limits until old age. Sexuality is not limited to a period between birth and menopause but extends into old age without limits but those set by people's own minds, habits and beliefs.

The Bible and other scriptures abound of examples of couples having had late childbirth, up until in their eighties. Natural fertility depends but on the uninhibited flow of the bioenergy. The body even after menopause is able to regenerate completely so that something like a second puberty can naturally come about with people whose bioplasmatic streaming is intact and strong.

When both partners are in this lucky condition, childbirth even in high age is no miracle and brings about happiness for parents and child.

§28

All those who have achieved self-knowledge and are in dialogue with their inner selves have discovered their bisexual nature and have integrated their other sexual persona. This work is the starting point of true spirituality.

§29

With observing some basic rules of conduct, every human life can be lived without destructive somatic disease in the form of cancer, aids, heart disease, rheumatism, arthritis, leukemia and others of the same kind, and without mental or emotional diseases such as neurosis, psychosis, schizophrenia, epilepsy or Alzheimer.

§30

Psychoanalysis and most psychotherapeutic treatments are not natural and effective methods for healing emotional entanglement and early trauma, but conform with the cultural credo to reeducate, if not to brainwash people according to certain cultural beliefs. Effective trauma healing can only be done by *healing the luminous body* and by honest shamans and clairvoyants. A developmental course is open for modern medicine to integrate these practices and wistful traditions in the future.

§31

A new society will have to take responsibility for socially coding sexual love between adults, children and adolescents, without punishing those love relations when they are not harmful to the child. The social code is the rule of life for all. Uncoded behavior creates individual and social chaos and brings about conflictual and harmful behavior patterns, sexual crime, violence, as well as black markets. Coding behavior requires social acceptance and the courage of the policy makers to tackle controversial issues.

On Power

§32

For constructive living and a growing network of fruitful and mutually beneficial relationships, we need to develop our natural soul power, which is an acute awareness of our spiritual human potential and all its possible expressions. Soul power typically manifests as a deep and lasting trust in the goodness, intelligence and integratedness of cosmic life and love, as well as one's own unique potential and creativity.

Soul power is the ability to live *one's unique form of love,* whatever our loving energies are attracted to and wish to be close with. Soul power is developed mainly through the integration of our dream knowledge and wisdom. This source of knowledge is unlimited and depends only on our skill to read the language of dreams so that it is intelligible for us. Dreams also are a most genuine source of creativity.

§33

Self-affirmation as a source of strength and goes along with soul power. Self-affirmation starts from the premise that we all have a unique potential and mission and do not need to accept others that are disagreeable for us or impeding us from realizing our mission.

§34

Self-acceptance is a spiritual, psychic and biological necessity and the primary condition for success in life and love. We have a right to say *no*. To accept all in life without wavering can indicate a *lack of self-acceptance.* Nobody is supposed to accept worldviews, beliefs and ideologies that deny the value of the individual.

§35

Traditional patriarchal education is based upon *smashing the genuine soul power of the child,* raising disempowered emotional cripples that, once the emosexual castration called education is completed, are proudly called *citizens.*

Only by a revolution in education, which is a *psychological revolution,* can this sad state of affairs gradually be changed and consciousness be raised about the need and the necessity of an education that respects the child as a person in her own right, as a spiritual entity and unique soul that incarnates with a definite mission as a learning process for his or her lifetime.

On Science

§36

Science as unbiased observation of nature and comprehension of the cosmic laws and functionalities has been misunderstood and distorted throughout patriarchy in all dominator cultures of the world.

Still in Antiquity, when science was in the hands of philosophers who had a meta-cognitive view upon nature, science gradually developed into a quantitative concept, out for construing measuring devices and defining reality more and more along the lines of what could be measured with these devices, declaring nonsense or banning from perception what could not be measured.

Unfortunately, the unresolvable rest regarded as trash and blinded out from reality was the greater half of nature.

As a result, the true science and its effective and functional counterpart, natural healing, had to go underground in Western civilization and survive under the threat of widespread official denial, slander and persecution by the Christian Church.

This science was first called *philosophy* during Antiquity, then hermetic science or alchemy, and then magnetism, spiritism, and finally perennial science or new age science.

§37

True science is first of all energy science, the intelligent understanding and use of the life force or cosmic life energy that is called *ch'i* in China, *ki* in Japan, *mana* or *aka* with the Kahunas from Hawaii and with most aboriginal peoples, *prana* in India, *ka* in old Egypt and that in Western alternative science was called *vis vitalis* by Paracelsus, *spirit energy* by Swedenborg, *animal magnetism* by Mesmer, *Odic force* by Reichenbach, *élan vital* by Coué and with most hypnotists, *universion* by Lakhovsky and *orgone* by Reich.

A future society's science agenda should put the *research on the human energy field,* the intelligent study of the use and functionality of the bioenergy at the first place of its science agenda. Modern science has done a first step in the right direction with the abandonment of the rigid observer standpoint and the acknowledgment of *probabilities* and *uncertainty* in quantum physics.

The next step can only be the acknowledgment of the existence of the super-string field or unified field as the ultimate modern discovery of the creator force the ancients have known about.

On Health

§38

For effective healing and medical care, we need to look at what is *health,* and not at what is sickness, at what is *wholeness* and not what is fragmentation, at what is *sane* and not what is insane, at what is *life* and not what is death.

§39

Western science, since Aristotle, has looked at death to find out about life. Medical science was and is a *death science.* It has accumulated knowledge about decaying processes by vivisecting cadavers. It knows about the skeleton, tissues and blood vessels, but it has no idea what it is that distinguishes a living body from a dead body. To get to know that, it would have had to look at the life force, the *bioplasmatic energy* or human energy field contained in living organisms, and which vanishes from the dead and decaying body shortly after the moment of death.

§40

Traditional medical science has asked the wrong questions and therefore got the wrong answers. It is merely palliative and cures symptoms *without having the slightest idea about the true causes of illness,* be it somatic, be it psychic illness.

It knows nothing about the energetic equilibrium of a healthy organism, and as a result ignores that all illness simply is a state of affairs where the natural equilibrium between positive and negative energetic polarities, called *yang* and *yin,* is out of balance.

It is as if somebody, in order to see the sun, builds a telescope, points it at the moon, looks through it and affirms: 'The sun is a dry planet, without life, without heat, without energy, a simple mass of stone; it appears heavy, stupid and useless.'

This is how Western medical science looks at the human body and what it understands about it. In reality, the human body is a luminous sun-like energy egg that irradiates a powerful bioplasmatic energy and is synergistically connected to, and resonating with, all other beings that vibrate at about the same frequency range, including animals, plants, and inanimate matter.

§41

The complete human body contains *twenty-four disc-shaped energy nods called chakras,* seven of which are around the upper half of the human body and five of which are higher up, floating in the ether, and bioenergetically resonating with the human organism. These twelve basic chakras are mirrored by another twelve *aura chakras* that are contained in the luminous body and which have similar bioregulative functions.

All sickness is to be seen, long before it manifests in the physical body, in the aura, the etheric body or bodies that build something like an egg-shaped luminous shell around the physical body.

Illness typically manifests as a certain irregularity in the color spectrum of the aura; this was scientifically identified and corroborated as early as in the 1930s by a photographic technique invented by Dr. Walter J. Kirlian, a British physician of Russian origin. The technique is known as *Kirlian Photography*. In addition, Tibetan medicine is specialized in measuring the pulse with such accuracy that it equals aura reading; disease can be foretold by this highly sophisticated traditional method several years in advance of their first somatization.

§42

Already today, with the knowledge we possess about energy science, especially acupuncture, magnetic and cell resonance healing, aura treatment, homeopathy and orgone refreshment as well as macrobiotic diet, psychosomatic healing techniques and psychosynthesis, we can *establish a body of futurist medicine* that is effective, affordable, human, organic and sustainable.

§43

The only reason why this has not yet been done so far is the worldwide medical and pharmaceutical establishment with their strong mercantile power monopoly and their resistance against any progress in holistic medical science.

§44

Each and every human being can be healthy from birth to death, *without any use of chemical pharmaceuticals,* without any visits to a medical doctor or hospital, and without any operations. This is true for the regular case; for accidents, especially road, train and airplane accidents highly effective urgency aid is of course needed, and in so far modern Western medicine has proven high effectiveness, indeed.

§45

Childbirth is a sexual, orgasmic and first of all pleasurable experience for mother, father and child and should be enjoyed at home, in the familiar setting, as a celebration of life and as a welcome party for the new soul that incarnates in the physical shell. For this to happen, the old profession of the *sage femme* could be re-instituted. Childbirth has to be taken completely out of hospitals because it has nothing to do with sickness, and giving birth to a child is not the task of a medical doctor but of a specialized helper who by preference is a woman.

Why this profession disappeared is clearly the result of the Church's witch hunts over several centuries and the persecution, torture and murder of hundreds of thousands of natural obstetricians and sage-femmes all over Europe.

What is true for childbirth is true for contraception and abortion as well. As it is the responsibility of the mother to carry her baby to birth or to decide to stop pregnancy, or else to avoid pregnancy altogether, a large body of methods existed over time in different cultures that was in the hands of natural obstetricians.

Effective natural means for contraception were available for affordable prices that ensured parents or a single mother got their children only in case they really wanted them, and thus were able to take care of them. This knowledge has been scattered for the most part if it is not completely forgotten.

§46

The *condom* is one of the most decrepit, ineffective and body-hostile devices man ever came up with to regulate sexual intercourse, as this device almost nullifies sexual pleasure for the man as it desensitizes the gland, and in addition forces largely built men who have tiny built partners to use an unusual amount of force and pressure to realize orgasm—which puts unnecessary strain and in many cases also vaginal soreness and genital abrasions on the female partner, not to talk about the displeasing smell and handling of condoms that must put off any sensitive human from sex altogether.

It is likely that behind the invention of the condom a sex-denying Puritan *Weltanschauung* has built up enough imbecility about natural functions to make the thought forms that eventually resulted in the invention of that murky, ineffective and unaesthetic solution for 'safer' intercourse, while the truth is that *real safety* comes from healthy living, not from plastics and idiotic devices that are but money-making machines for the multinationals that market them worldwide.

§47

As long as international medical care is in the hands of physicians and pharmacy multinationals, human health, on a worldwide scale, will deteriorate with every year to come, while the costs for this gigantic gambling machine of white-coated nonsense will astronomically increase.

On Emotions

§48

Present society confuses *natural aggressiveness with violence* and brings about violence through repressing healthy aggressiveness. Rage and anger are *positive emotions* because they help us to become conscious of unhealthy codependent attachments and be grounded through our first chakra energy.

In aggressiveness contained is a high communication potential that cannot be used when aggressiveness is totally repressed. Aggressiveness is not violence in that it is outgoing and creative, and as such an *expression of our soul power*, while violence is coming about through *suicidal and disempowering feelings* and is an expression of our weakness. In this sense, natural sexuality is aggressive, but it is not violent.

§49

Our emotions are naturally complete and intelligent, and they are *kaleidoscopically linked to each other*. All emotions have a place in life and should be lived consciously and without controlling or repressing any of them.

When one emotion is blocked, the natural cycle of emotions which can be visualized as a kaleidoscope, is broken with the result that the natural bioenergetic balance of our organism becomes impaired.

§50

Knowledge about our *primary power* or *soul power* frees us of all our fears and also from rage and hate feelings.

Natural soul power *cannot be gained when we deny our natural goodness,* and the creativeness of our subconscious mind. Even small children have a natural soul power potential that is regularly destroyed in patriarchal education, bringing about fearful and perversely obedient children who do not question the status quo and go along with every kind of abuse without defending themselves.

§51

Sex laws should be abandoned and sexual experience be completely decriminalized and taken out of the hands of the state.

Personal intimacy has no place on police agendas and in newspaper columns; what this leads to is that love and intimacy are screwed up, defiled and degraded into sexual acts without meaning and without soul. So save human love from vulgarity and perversion, and for fighting sexual crime, there is only one way: *freedom.* Hence, a body of independent consultants that function as *public welfare agencies* should step in and provide emotional and sexual consultancy in accordance with special statutes and regulations that establish their function and usefulness within a responsible medical and psychic health care system.

§52

Children have to be raised in a peaceful, natural and comprehensive environment, where their whole person, including their bodies and emotions are truly understood and accepted. For this to happen, any form of educational violence called corporal or physical punishment has to be definitely, by law, prohibited and abandoned.

—See, for example, Dean M. Herman, A Statutory Proposal to Prohibit the Infliction of Violence upon Children, 19 FAMILY LAW QUARTERLY, 1986, 1-52.

No adult has the right to exert violence upon a child, and education is no exception from this rule. To justify educational violence and at the same time *wonder why violence is one of humanity's major problems* testifies of the shortsightedness and thwarted emotional intelligence of most humans raised under patriarchy. It is for this reason that changes in this important area are so slow to come and that so many, even educated people, continue beating their children as masters are beating their slaves. Children who are regularly beaten cannot integrate their bodies and emotions into a non-fragmented and peaceful mindset because this very process is impaired through the presence of strong fear, guilt and shame in the child's psyche.

This means that children raised in a violent manner are crippled and handicapped for life!

Educational violence therefore should be prohibited by law for both parents and persons who act in loco parentis, such as educators, tutors and other caretakers.

Ideally physical and sexual child abuse in the form of violence acted out upon a child should be treated in one and the same legal bill, and not, as it is now the case, in diverse and difficult-to-find separate statutes and legislations.

On Peace

§53

World peace can be attained only by changing our basic paradigms about emotions and sexuality for they condition our views upon violence and how we handle this major problem in its manifold manifestations as domestic violence, street violence, gang violence, in-group versus out-group violence, racial and ideological violence, official governmental, military or police violence and structural violence.

§54

All research done over the last decades on the roots of violence points to violence being a direct result of repressing our natural *pleasure function* and the establishment, within patriarchy, of rigid and compulsive behavior rules.

Pleasure, joy and sexual excitement are *essential for bringing about novelty* in individual and collective life patterns and the bioenergetic exchange between organisms. This is independent of sex and age and it is valid for people from all walks of life and belonging to all races and cultures.

§55

When natural body pleasure is thwarted and man thus deprived of tactile stimulation, a *secondary drive structure builds up* that is violent and destructive. This secondary drive structure that is fed by stuck and pent-up bioenergy rigidifies over time into a character armor that impedes man from feeling and thus inhibits important functions in the human character, namely empathy and compassion.

This is how humanity could become as violent as it is today, ruthlessly building in-group empires that shut out billions of people and dozens of nations and that expand on the price of genocide and public insanity.

§56

Man is not by nature violent and destructive. Those who believe that build their worldview upon myths and a manipulative history science that denies the fact that before patriarchy came up about five thousands years ago, most peoples of the world *lived in peace and fruitful exchanges,* while they maintained partnership economies instead of dominator economies.

These cultures, one of them being the Kahuna natives from Hawaii, do not know strict moralistic behavior rules; they simply comply with the golden rule to not do to another what one wishes not to suffer oneself.

Anthropological and cross-cultural research has shown that a residue of these cultures luckily survived until this day, one of them being the Trobriand culture in Papua New Guinea, another being the Muria tribe in India. And there are certainly others that I did not have the chance to study.

These cultures have in common that they do not interfere with the emotions and sexual behavior of their children and thus practice what today is called *permissive education.*

They also tend to raise their children not as a result of economic constraints but with great respect for natural biological growth cycles. Thus, for example, puberty is naturally the period where the child takes a leave from his or her parents, marries and engages in a professional career, as this was still the case in the Middle-Ages in Europe but afterwards was completely eroded by the extended educational cycles as part of mechanistic and alienating industrial culture.

§57

Today's postmodern international consumer culture or *Oedipal Culture,* with its worldwide exportation of traditional Western values, is an utterly perverse upside-down movement that replaces life by a form of *collective psychosis* and rampant violence and that is based on denial and ignorance: denial of the most part of our natural and important pleasure function and ignorance about the most fundamental scientific and spiritual patterns of living.

For the peace agenda of a future society the following essential points have inter alia to be considered:

- Emosexual freedom for children and adolescents;

- Emosexual freedom for the elder;

- Respect and recognition of our natural bisexuality;

- Recognition of the cosmic energy field;

- A unified field theory for the cosmic energy field;

- Expert advice for contraception and abortion;

- Respect of nations' territorial and political integrity;

- Worldwide training of cross-cultural communication;

- Worldwide free-of-charge student exchanges;

- Scientific study of life-after-death and cosmic life cycles.

Chapter Seven
The Warrior-Scientist

The Shaman's Roles

The shaman is a catalyzer of the numinous experience, not a magician. The phenomena he invokes are not his own, and he has but limited control over them.

—Please allow me to use the masculine preposition 'he' here and in the following, while I am aware of the fact that in the oldest and most powerful shamanic traditions, the shaman was not a male but a female. My intention here is motivated by aesthetic reasons, simply to avoid rendering the script unnecessarily disrupted by the endless repetition of 'he or she.'

Eliade sees the shaman as a manipulator of the sacred, almost as a technocrat of ecstasy, as the prime religious experience. But he's not for that matter the originator of that experience, he's not even the trigger of it. In my view, the shaman is but a communicator between the realms of true morality and true humanity.

When I say 'true morality' I do not mean *moralism* in the sense that moralism stands for enforced and compulsive morality. I am speaking of *natural or cosmic morality,* which rules human conduct that deliberately avoids to attract a negative karmic response.

Here, the shaman differs from the Priest, the Imam, and the Buddhist monk in that he doesn't *moralize.* He doesn't tell people that what they do ought to be 'right' or 'wrong,' from a fixated morality scale. What he does is asking the spirits who then will render their verdict, through his mouth. The verdict may be surprising, as it may not comply at all with human moralistic rules and laws.

A good shaman, for this purpose, needs to be immoral, or rather *amoral,* for if he complies with a fixated concept of morality, he won't be able to *objectively communicate* the verdict of the spirits. And the morality of spirits is certainly not the one human patriarchy has brought about, with all its senseless compulsion, and all the violence that flows out from it.

So, the *first* role of the shaman is clearly to be a *communicator,* an intermediary between the eternal world of the spirits, gods and demons, and the perhaps rather *temporary* world of human beings. The *second* role, for the purpose also of the first, is to be a *traveler,* which includes to be a *time traveler.*

The shaman travels for three distinct purposes. He travels for receiving information from certain spirits he knows might have the answer he is looking for. He also travels to certain sacred places or energy vortexes for meeting spirits, or for receiving information through telepathic channels;

he also travels for collecting medical remedies for healing a particular disease of a client.

In addition to these feats, powerful shamans can time-travel as well, which means they can travel way back into the past or forward into the future to test a certain outcome, or receive a karmic feedback in advance of its actual realization. To give an example, if a man intends to marry a certain woman, and asks a shaman for guidance if it will be a good union, the shaman can travel both in the past, to connect with that woman's energy vortex, inquiring about her karma, and in the future, to see how the marriage is going to turn out.

This brings me to the shaman's third and major role, the role of the *healer*. What does that imply? It does *not* imply, first of all, to administrate medication from a known reservoir of remedies as the mainstream doctor does, or even the modern homeopathic healer. It means to administrate no medication at all. *The shaman doesn't heal the client at all.* What he does is to take over the sickness of the client in his own organism, and then heals himself, thereby healing both his own cloned sickness and its original version in the client.

This is obviously a sophisticated approach to healing, and not to compare with the mechanistic 'medical' healing approach practiced by major civilizations. In fact, it's not a healing approach at all, because the very concept of illness is *different* in shamanic cultures and in non-shamanic cultures, such as ours. In shamanic cultures, all illness is attributed to a violation of an eternal *morality code* imposed by the spirit world, not as a purely organismic deregulation. This morality code varies a little from one shamanic culture to another, but when you look closely at it, the differences are minor. It's more or less *always the same kind of interference* in healthy evolution and constructive human relations, through either the fact of committing incest, or murder, or both, or violating secondary rules, such as procreating a child with the wrong woman, or procreating it through rape, or by hunting the wrong animal, or the right animal at the wrong time, thereby risking to attract misfortunes to the clan by the animal spirit world, or else to violate the quietude of ancestors through lacking out on reverence for the ancestor cult rituals that are ongoing ceremonies and that require a considerable investment of time and effort in every single shamanic culture.

While some of these rules of conduct have been taken as the result of 'magical thinking,' it may well be that those who put up such a judgment are simply lacking out on the knowledge that would justify each and every of those rules in their cultural context.

It may not surprise to see such judgments coming from a culture that denies the existence of the spirit world because it denied, until recently, the existence of the human energy field and cosmic energy fields that interact with it, or are superimposed upon it.

Holger Kalweit, a German ethnologist who is specialized on shamanic healing, describes the shaman's role in rational terms, explaining each and every of his tasks as *functional* and *comprehensive* within the particular set and setting of a tribal culture. In his book *Shamans, Healers and Medicine Men (2000)*, Kalweit writes:

> Shamanic therapy means the healing of an entire life rather than just healing failing functions and disruptive pains. For shamans, healing involves philosophy, a view of life. In this regard, giving careful account of ways of healing is only one aspect of our task.

> The other is to depict the shamanic manipulation of energies of a higher dimension that for us are invisible and even unthinkable. (Id., 3)

Energy healing or *vibrational healing* as a sophisticated technique of manipulating cosmic energies, and the human energy field, is something that only very recently was being recognized within the Western scientific context.

—See Peter Fritz Walter, The Vibrant Nature of Life: A Science-Based Pathway for a Better, Richer, and More Abundant Life (2017).

While it has roots that reach back to antiquity and to Europe, Persia, Egypt, India, China and Japan, to name only these traditions, and can be considered as an integral part of perennial science, it was first forbidden as *heresy* by the Christian Church and then was discarded out as a 'vitalistic theory' by Cartesian science, from about the 17th century. It was only from about the second half of the 20th century that this age-old effective healing technique was being introduced into modern Western science, within the framework of so-called 'holistic science.'

At the same time, systems research corroborated it because all living systems were found to be information fields, where energy, consciousness and information are blended into functional units that can be understood not by focusing upon its parts, but upon the *relationships* between those parts, that is, *energy patterns*.

However, while cutting-edge science now can effectively embrace and explain *vibrational healing,* our culture is far from accepting such a reality; this knowledge, then, is reserved to a tiny minority of systems theorists and otherwise, to energy healers, vibrotherapists, Reiki practitioners, phytotherapists, homeopathic healers and those who practice *orgonomy,* the energy science that Dr. Wilhelm Reich created and that is founded on the same principles.

Kalweit considers our culture and tradition lacking in understanding of the principles that shamanic healing, and the functional use of higher energies are based upon. It has to be seen also that the notion of *initiation,* which is fundamental to the path of the healer in all shamanic cultures, has never been considered in our culture without a negative connotation, approaching it to realms of danger and abysmal sorcery.

Our culture's approach, in this respect, is such that it *suffocates natural spirituality,* while it is strangely open toward the artificial, merely ornamental and dogmatic organization of the religious experience. Kalweit writes:

> The path of initiation is branded in the West as degenerate; by contrast, in tribal society the initiation of the shaman is accepted, even encouraged and supported by everyone; and the teacher helps the student to decipher his experiences by means of cultural symbols. But in our culture the symbols of transformation are negative: they include hospitalization, schizophrenia, brain-wave tests, stupefying psychotropic drugs, and ostracism from society. How many unrecognized shamans, mediums, and saints fill the madhouses of rationalism? How many powers have been mangled and cut off during the long history of psychiatry? How many people has psychology reduced to mindless robots through its abasement of the psyche? The spiritual climate in our society shuts down shamanic experience in its incipient stages, distorts it and desacralizes it as neurosis and psychotic deception. But psychic transformation cannot be extirpated by societal taboos. Spiritual experience is a transhistorical, transcultural phenomenon and can break through in individuals at any time. (Id., 54)

Accordingly, Kalweit sees the role of the shaman primarily as a functional, effective, pragmatic manipulator of higher energy fields, with the intention to bring about a transformation of consciousness, and thereby, a form of total healing. Healing, in this connotation, must embrace the entire human, as it is a *transformative process,* not just the curing of some or the other symptoms or ailments.

The research Kalweit appears to have done on this complex question is admirable, and has delivered detailed knowledge of how the various tribal cultures around the world understand and describe the cosmic energy fields their shamans have witnessed.

I must admit that despite my own twenty years of research on the *energy nature* of human emotions and sexuality, I came across some of these specific notions of the *cosmic energy matrix* only through Kalweit's book. He writes:

> All tribal cultures live in unity with nature, in unity with the universal laws. Their sense of the world is a symbiosis of God, world, and ego. Thus, they have a worldview for which our 'high culture' is not yet ready. If the symbiotic, synchronistic, synergistic is the acme of the natural-mystical worldview of shamanism, another high point in the natural philosophy of natural societies is their belief that a power permeates all being. Each tribe has its own concept of this universal energy. Pacific peoples call it *mana;* the Crow speak of *maxpé,* the Dakota of *wakan,* the Hidatsa of *xupa,* the Algonquian of *manitou,* he Hurons of *oki,* the Tierra del Fuegans of *waiyuwen,* the African Sotho of *moya,* the Masai of *ngai,* the Bantu of *nzmbi,* the Pygmies of *megbe,* the Australians of *joja,* the Dajak of Indonesia of *petara,* the Batak of Sumatra of *tondi,* the Malagasy of *hasina.* The same is meant by the *ch'i* or the *ch'i gong* of the Chinese, the *ki* of the Japanese, the Hebrew *ruach,* and the *prana* or *akasha*

of the Indians—*akasha*, the matrix of the universe, the *mysterium magnum*, the primordial ocean. (Id., 228-229)

As I already mentioned, the astonishing difference between the way shamans cure and Western doctors cure is that the shaman takes the medicine, while in Western medicine it's the patient. The shaman, through the trance, *enters the vibrational field of the patient*, and can thus detect the real problem of their illness, by screening their luminous body. This is all the secret, or the most part of it.

No medicine is needed when you can alter vibrations within the aura, an insight that today has been made useful for medicine, and that is at the basis of what we call *vibrational medicine*.

—See, for example, Richard Gerber, A Practical Guide to Vibrational Medicine (2002).

Mircea Eliade observes in his classic, *Shamanism (1964)*:

> The morphology of shamanic cure is the same almost throughout South America. It includes fumigations with tobacco, songs, massage of the affected area of the body, identification of the cause of the illness by the aid of the helping spirits (at this point comes the shaman's trance, during which the audience sometimes ask him questions not directly connected with the illness), and, finally, extraction of the pathogenic object by suction. (Id., 329)

A particularity almost unknown in Western culture, that however can be found in many tribal nations is that illness is often attributed to the *interference of the spirit world*. While Western consciousness evolved from a merely palliative and mechanistic medical paradigm to one where the patient is seriously asked how he or she may have contributed to bring about their disease, the spiritogenic etiology, method used by shamanic cultures would by most doctors probably be qualified as schizophrenic.

Not so in tribal cultures. Rule and exception can be seen as reversed in the sense that in most native cultures, illness is primarily seen as a form of *superimposition* of malignant spirit power, and only in second instance as a possible result of an individual's condition, weakness, or fragility, or corruption to have let it happen. Eliade describes a healing ritual:

> Throughout Melanesia treatment of a disorder begins with sacrifices and prayers addressed to the dead person responsible, so that he will remove the sickness.

> But if this approach, which is made my members of the family, fails, a mane kisu, 'doctor,' is summoned.

> By magical means the latter discovers the particular dead man responsible for the sickness and begs him to remove the cause of the trouble. (Id., 364)

Shaman, Healer, Sage

Dr. Alberto Villoldo, a Western shaman and highly acclaimed expert on shamanism, teaches in his workshops techniques for *self-healing and awareness-building* that he himself needed almost twenty years to acquire during an apprenticeship with Laika shamans high up in the Andes.

Villoldo has written captivating and bestselling books on the matter that I have reviewed, considering them as prime literature for any intellectual who wants to know why our Western culture failed to bring about integrated humans, and how we can heal our collective inner split and become whole again, and *holy*.

> —See Annex for book reviews of Alberto Villoldo's major books.

While another who went that far would perhaps stayed with those who loved him enough to share their most ancient secrets about life, healing and peaceful living, Villoldo came back with the intention to share what he had learnt, and organized a series of ongoing workshops that are held at various destinations all over the United States. In studying and reviewing four of Villoldo's major books and his DVD *Healing the Luminous Body (2004)*, I was intrigued enough to include his insights in my own ongoing research on energy science and vibrational healing. To take up the thread of thought from the last sub-chapter, I would like to quote Villoldo on the main cultural difference between the shamanic and the modern-day perspective because Villoldo expresses it particularly well. He writes in *Shaman, Healer, Sage (2000)*:

> In the West we identify with the side of matter, which is by nature finite. The shaman identifies with the side of energy, which is by nature infinite. (Id., 9)

One of the novel insights that Villoldo gained on psychosomatic medicine was that the age-old dichotomy between body and mind eventually turned out to be a gigantic misunderstanding of the functional unit that the human body represents.

Here, modern science eventually meets the oldest of traditions that always affirmed there is no such split, except a culture brings it about through putting the mind 'over the body,' thereby separating the mind from the body.

It was through the new science of psychoneuroimmunology that Western scientists could eventually grasp the notion of an *'intelligent energy field'* that is upheld through *flow*, and the enormous liquidity of the human body, which consists of 98% of water. Villoldo writes:

> In the last few decades the field of psychoneuroimmunology (PNI), which studies how our moods, thoughts, and emotions influence our health, has matured. PNI investigators discovered that the mind is not localized in the brain but rather is generalized throughout the body. Dr. Candace Pert found that neuropeptides, which are molecules that continually wash through our bloodstream, flooding the spaces in between each cell, respond almost instantaneously to / every feeling and mood, effectively turning the entire body into vibrant, pulsing 'mind'. Our body as a whole experiences every emotion we have. (Id., 13-14)

Villoldo makes a complex field of research easier to understand by associating the realm of spirits and the vibrational field that is at the origin of life, as *infinity*. He explains to the reader that infinity in this sense doesn't mean eternity as eternity implies the notion of time, while infinity is outside of time, a realm of existence that knows no beginning and no end. In fact, our *higher self* belongs to this infinite realm of pure beingness. Villoldo explains that the powers the shaman receives during his psychedelic travels are coming from the fact that he encounters infinity.

For all of us, Villoldo explains, meeting with infinity is a transformative and rejuvenating experience because we realize that we are not defined by our history, by our past, by our accumulated karmic experience:

> We realize that we are not our stories. And the experience of infinity shatters the illusion of death, disease, and old age. This is a not a psychological or spiritual process only; every cell in our body is informed and renewed by it. Our immune system is unbridled, and / physical and emotional healing happen at an accelerated rate. Miracles become ordinary, and spontaneous remissions, those mysterious and baffling cures that confound medicine, become commonplace.
>
> And a spiritual liberation or illumination takes place. In the presence of infinity we are able to experience what we were before we were born and who we will be after we die. (Id., 22-23)

I mentioned already that the main reason I wrote this book was the idea that, contrary to what traditional anthropology asserted, the shaman is essential a scientist, a discoverer, and only randomly a magician or, as it was believed, or a trickster.

It was found out already by the late Terence McKenna that when shamans speak about 'spirits,' they mean *energy fields* or energy patterns that in one way or the other become *superimposed* upon our own human energy field, thereby triggering various kinds of responses.

These responses range from simple psychedelic visions, over various pathological states to highly dangerous paranoid delusions that can lead to sudden and dramatic suicide, as affirmed by Michael Harner in his revealing book *Ways of the Shaman (1980/1982)*.

Sorcery, the malevolent malignant kind of work done by shamans can be understood, under this scientific perspective, as an application of energy principles for deliberately triggering pathological conditions in the body of the person that the sorcerer intends to harm. The methodology of both doing harm and good is the same, a deliberate logical approach to manipulate energy fields in the *luminous body* of the person that the shaman is focused upon.

Villoldo explains what the luminous energy field is:

> We all possess a Luminous Energy Field that surrounds our physical body and informs our body in the same way that the energy fields of a magnet organize iron

filings on a piece of glass. Our Luminous Energy Field
has existed since before the beginning of time. It was one
with the unmanifest light of Creation, and it will endure
/ throughout infinity. It dwells outside of time but
manifests in time by creating new physical bodies
lifetime after lifetime. (Id., 42-43)

This has thus very little to do with tricking somebody
out, with creating illusions or with doing 'magic' in an
attempt to manipulate reality without knowing what the
factors are that are really in play for doing so. In this sense,
therefore, the shaman is *not a magician* for he knows what
he is doing and why he is doing it; he knows what those
factors are that are at the basis of reality creation.

He also knows that 'reality' is *not a fixated universal
condition* but a state of mind that is upheld through
consciousness, and influenced by energy fields. Logically
then, it is by manipulating these energy fields in the
luminous body of the client that the shaman changes the
reality of that person, through having that person
consciously experience *infinity*.

Now, the knowledge about the human energy field is
not a dubious vague matter, but a *body of detailed knowledge*
that was not understood by Western official science for the
simple reason that it was secret knowledge, not revealed to
the world until first the Toltec and then the Laika broke the
long silence. Dr. Villoldo explains:

The Luminous Energy Field is shaped like a doughnut
(known in geometry as a torus) with a narrow axis or

tunnel, less than a molecule thick, in the center. In the Inka language it is known as the *popo*, or luminous bubble. Persons who have had near-death experiences report traveling through this tunnel in their return voyage to the light. The human energy field is a mirror of the Earth's magnetic field, which streams out of the North Pole and circumnavigates the planet to reenter again through the South Pole.

Similarly, the flux lines or *cekes* of the Luminous Energy Field travel out the top of the head and / stream around the luminous body, forming a great oval the width of our outstretched arms. Our energy fields penetrate the Earth about twelves inches, then reenter the body through the feet. (Id., 48-49)

It is important to realize that wherever in the universe, there is consciousness, there is energy, and where there is energy, there is consciousness. But also, where there are consciousness and energy, there is *memory*.

Memory, thus, is a function of energy fields or energy patterns, and not just of 'chemical structures in the brain.' The chemical structures that were detected by neuroscience are real, but they are created by *energy streamings in the luminous energy field,* which are the true beholders of the memory interface. Villoldo explains:

The Luminous Energy Field contains an archive of all of our personal and ancestral memories, of all early-life trauma, and even of painful wounds from former lifetimes. These records or imprints are stored in full color and intensity of emotions.

Imprints are like dormant computer programs that when activated compel us toward behaviors, relationships, accidents, and illnesses that parody the initial wounding. (Id., 46)

—

Studying the once secret energy science of native cultures, such as the Laika, but also the Kahunas in Hawaii, first discovered for the West by Erika Nau and Max Long, we realize that all true knowledge about life and death, and about health and sickness, begins with the conscious perception and manipulation of energy fields. And interestingly so, this science, just as Wilhelm Reich's orgonomy and the old Chinese science of *Feng Shui*, make a clear distinction between the human energy field and other, planetary and cosmic energy fields.

—See Erika Nau, Self-Awareness through Huna (1981), Max Long, The Secret Science at Work (1958/1995) and Growing into Light (1955) as well as Wilhelm Reich, Cosmic Superimposition (1949/1972), Ola Raknes, Wilhelm Reich and Orgonomy (1970), Ong Hean Tatt, Amazing Scientific Basis of Feng Shui (1997), and Valerie Hunt, Infinite Mind (2000)

If shamanic energy science was, as still many mechanistic scientists assume, but a 'vitalistic' belief system combined with delusions produced by a 'psychotic delirium' that is believed to be a 'suggestive healing' ceremony, and effective only because of *belief*, it couldn't be learnt by a Western doctor and applied with clients who *do not harbor the cultural beliefs* that it was originally based upon. Dr. Villoldo writes in *Shaman, Healer, Sage (2000)*:

> Over the years I developed the ability to perceive the streams of light that flow through the luminous body, and read the imprints of health and disease. I believe that this is an innate ability that we all possess but either do not develop or lose after the age of seven or eight because we are taught to believe that the material world is the only 'real' world. Shamans throughout the Americas rely on their ability to perceive the energetic realm. (Id., 50)

I personally consider a witness report originating from a rather ignorant outsider *higher* than such report written by a member of that wistful culture itself.

This is so because *we are all biased,* if we want it or not, and, while this sounds queer, the danger to distort reality is *higher* when we judge *our own cultural reality* than when we try to learn and comprehend a *different* cultural reality.

It is exactly the strangeness and queerness of the experience that straightens and reinforces our awareness level; when we deal with everyday life, we tend to be more shallow and unaware. When we enter novelty, we are fully in the present!

This is one of several reasons why Castaneda's and Villoldo's accounts of shamanic reality are primed sources of knowledge because the cross-cultural researcher intends to *strip research of its cultural bias and of its innumerable projections.*

When we penetrate into shamanic energy science, we gain detailed knowledge about the human body's energy system and its rotating chakra wheels that are primordial energy vortexes, managing each a certain *clearly definable frequency range* of the total energy rainbow that is the base layer of all life in the cosmos—for *life is light*. This knowledge is not reserved to tribal cultures only, but has a long tradition in our own culture through *clairvoyance*.

—See, for example, the revealing study by Shafica Karagulla and Dora van Gelder, The Chakras (1989)

Alberto Villoldo explains the chakras as follows:

The chakras are the organs of the Luminous Energy Field. They are swirling disks with wide mouths that spin a few inches outside the body; through which they drink in the radiant fuel stores in the luminous body to nurture us spiritually, emotionally, and creatively. The narrow, funnel-shaped tip hooks directly into the spine.

The chakras transmit information of past trauma and pain, contained in imprints in the Luminous Energy Field, into the nervous system. The chakras inform our neurophysiology, affecting our moods and influencing our emotional and physical well-being.

The chakras also connect to endocrine glands that regulate all of human behavior. (Id., 53)

Now, this is the entry point for understanding how shamanic healing works, how the shaman really effects the total healing of the organism, through a *deliberate interference with the luminous energy field* of the client. Alberto Villoldo explains:

> The blueprint that shaped and molded us since we were inside our mother's womb contains the memories of all of our former lifetimes—the way we suffered, the way we loved, how we were ill, and the way we died. In the East these imprints are known as karma, forces that sweep through our life like a giant tide that we cannot swim free of. These imprints contain instructions that predispose us to *repeating certain events from the past.* We want to learn where these energy imprints are located in the Luminous Energy Field and how to erase them so that the body, mind, and spirit can return to health. (Id., 56)

The science of *vibrational healing* is too complex to grasp by quacks and charlatans who are, according to common Western media culture, the only participants in the ecstasy of the participatory healing experience that is defined by the fact that the healer is but a catalyzer of cosmic energies that are *already present* in the client's human energy field— but that are locked by the particular disease that is at stake.

This being said, it may well be that energy healing is not a transmission of vital energy from the healer to the patient, but *activation of the patient's own energy resources* that are stalled or in a state of stagnation that is the result of neurosis—which in turn may be the consequence of abuse suffered in early childhood. Villoldo explains comprehensively how distortions in the luminous energy field impact negatively upon our emotions:

Imprints etched into the emotional-mental layer of the Luminous Energy Field predispose us to live in particular ways and to become attracted to certain people and relationships. These imprints dictate the course of our emotional lives. It is very difficult to change our lifestyle without clearing the imprints in this layer.

Imprints stored in the etheric or soul layer inform and organize our physical reality. Imprints in the causal or spiritual layer choreograph our journey through life, including the kind of spiritual peace and fulfillment that we will attain. (Id.)

In my own long-term research on human emotions that goes back to the 1970s, I came to the same result, namely that *emotional memory* is not stored in the brain but in the aura or luminous energy field.

The language of computers consists of magnetically charged zeros and ones. / The Luminous Energy Field is similarly coded. Childhood abuse is not recorded as an image of a child being battered. Likewise, a cancer does not appear like a blob in the energy template. They both appear like pools of dark, stagnant energy to those who can see. (Id., 56-57)

Imprints are formed when the negative emotions that accompany trauma are not healed. (...) Crises or emotional stress would trigger the script contained within the imprint, which would begin to play itself out again. (Id., 57)

> Psychologists believe that the subconscious motifs and behaviors we inherit from our parents might be encoded into the circuitry of our brain, and that the only way we can reprogram these circuits is through psychotherapy. I'm convinced that these energy patterns and habits are encoded in the Luminous Energy Field as well and that the Illumination Process can accomplish in one session what can often take years to heal through psychotherapy. (Id., 61)

Our medical and mental health industries and professionals probably have an interest in that psychotherapy remains long and costly, while there is a trend to make for a shift toward shorter and lesser costly therapies, such as *hypnotherapy* and other, recently developed therapies.

Our mainstream scientific and medical authorities are *still far from recognizing a therapy approach that directly works with repatterning the luminous energy field,* thereby tackling the primary memory surface of the human mindbody unit.

Another aspect to healing in general is to see it as a learning experience. Our traditional medical science has this 'bullet approach' to it, that lets us see disease as an enemy that has to be attacked and killed, while in native cultures there is a lesser judgmental tone regarding the fact that humans turn ill and well again.

This has been seen already back in the 1970s by the Simontons as a major handicap in our understanding of health, and as a factor to keep people from healing, because they themselves, and the whole medical establishment behind them, is completely focused on disease.

—See Otto Carl Simonton et. al., Getting Well Again (1978).

It's a fact of life, and a feature of human consciousness that we reinforce what we direct our attention upon; so if it's not health but disease which is the main focal point of our attention, we *reinforce disease,* and when we do that on a group level, then we as a society will have a hard stand on 'fighting disease.' In fact, then we as a group or nation will be preoccupied with nothing but disease and as a result, our health statistics will worsen with every year. And this is exactly what's going on and what the Simontons have already found thirty years ago.

Another factor may be our primarily intellectual understanding of life and living, in our Western scientific tradition, while the approach of most native cultures is holistic, intuitive and kinesthetic. This in turn has of course an impact upon our readiness for change, our else *our rigidity to avoid change.* Villoldo writes:

> Change happens first at a core energetic level, and then the intellect gets it. In contrast, in the West we insist that understanding must precede healing. We first rehash and rationalize how our mother or father was not emotionally available for us before we embark on change. In luminous healing, the mind can have its insight after the energy field and body change, but true

transformation *can never be preceded by the intellect. (Id., 113)*

It may well be that in so far phylogenetic factors come into play, especially when we consider the recent cutting-edge research on *morphogenetic fields,* by Dr. Rupert Sheldrake and others.

—See, for example, Rupert Sheldrake, A New Science of Life (1995).

If a mouse in New York City learns to get out of a maze because a mouse in Los Angeles was able to do so, while the two mice are connected with each other through nothing but a general *'morphic' resonance pattern,* then humans certainly, and even more likely than mice learn their basic abilities not only through individual development, but also through the *memory surface of the entire species* or large groups within the species, such as tribes, races, nations.

And here we have the phenomenon that the Inka have the ability to see the vital energy streamings, as we know it from cobra snakes and other animals, but most humans on this planet, including the author of this book, have not developed this ability. We know it well from singular exemplars within our own culture that often are taken for charlatans, who well possess this ability. I am speaking of mediums, paranormally gifted individuals, and clairvoyants. Also, what might stand against developing these abilities is our left-brainism, our group fantasy of 'total reason' which disconnects us from our bodies, our hypertrophy of *deductive logic* to the detriment of *associative logic,* and our almost political focus on 'yang' values in education and the general social code. It is our *moralism* that stands in the way, our judgmental attitudes, our constant obsession with 'good' and 'bad' judgments that pervade our media world, our religions, and our talk shows.

It seems that in tribal cultures, this is very different, if not completely absent. Villoldo writes:

> In the Inka shamanic traditions there are no 'bad' energies. There are only energies that are 'light,' and so support life, and energies that are 'heavy,' which cannot be digested. (Id., 157)

This is what Wilhelm Reich termed the 'functional regard' upon nature, well aware that at that time, more than half a century ago, there were very few scientists ready to see that this *holistic view* was going to be the leading paradigm of future science, and not what we know today was 'mechanistic science.'

We can only hope that the energy view of life will soon be part of our own science, and will after a while even become the mainstream of it. There are many road signs to be made out already now that show that this is indeed what's most likely going to happen, in a few decades from now.

Postface

The Role of Intention in the Shamanic Experience

Looking over the fence of social and cultural conditioning, and expanding conscious awareness is what the shamanic quest is about; it is a quest of our days.

Developing awareness about the limitations of perception is one of the reasons why the mind-opening journey has much significance today for intellectuals and seekers of truth from all walks of life.

Entheogens have not deserved the label 'psychedelics' as their purpose is authentic and religious. They are not set in the world for distorting perception and render us 'high' or to alter consciousness, nor do they serve entertainment purposes. What they do is not really altering consciousness; they actually *sharpen* it; instead of distorting perception, they in a way *purify* it and render it more immediate, *more direct*, and less conditioned by culture and language.

Native peoples around the world understand this sacred purpose of entheogens, which is why they have created that term in the first place, which means that these plants are 'awakeners of the god within.' It is unthinkable for most natives to use entheogens for entertainment, as there is a belief among them that doing so desacralizes the plants and offends their protective spirits. In modern society this view is not shared, at least not on the government level, with the result that entheogens are indiscriminately put on the index of forbidden drugs, with the idea in mind that, if allowed, they would be used, and abused, for mere entertainment, pleasurable indulgence and debauchery.

The idea is not as far-fetched as it sounds; if this view is the dominant one in a society, the government probably just acts on the line of the general opinion. In addition, if behavior results in harm suffered by citizens, it is correct that responsible government prohibits that behavior. That harm can be done to self and others with strongly active compounds is a fact that even pro-psychedelic researchers and activists such as Terence McKenna have openly admitted. The solution here, then, cannot be short-term, and it cannot just target at proving our governments wrong when they only act upon a belief that is shared by the meta group. The solution is to change that very belief of entheogens being 'leisure drugs,' and to give the right information, and also *transmit the ethical values*, their sacred purpose, their correct use, and proper education given for their ingestion. This cannot be done short-term but takes a real educational effort from the side of science and government working jointly and with the correct vision and motivation.

Entheogenic plant substances *do not render addictive* but in the contrary tend to undo addictive behavior, which is why in some countries, they are used in the therapies targeting at healing heroine or cocaine addictions. It is equally important to know that experienced shamans do exert a guidance for the proper use of entheogens. Not many researchers write about the details, which is why my personal experience was important for me in this context for understanding how the shaman can direct the experience of the client by using his intention.

I have for that matter presented several anomalies occurring within the course of my experience that cannot be explained in any other way than by saying that what really happened was that *the shaman triggered and directed the trance by his own intention and psychic energy,* using the psychoactive compounds as a transmitter matrix.

In other words, the 'biochemical' etiology of trance inducement is mechanistic, which my experience shows with quite some evidence. Some intricate details of my experience namely make only sense when we see shamanic voyages as not directed by plant chemicals, but by *human intention* that uses the plant matrix as an information amplifier and transmitter.

This may represent a scientific novelty in our culture; however for natives it is clear that it's the shaman, not a plant chemical, who controls the consciousness-opening voyage. In addition, natives consider the manifesting spirits, called *plant teachers* as real beings, not just chemicals or molecules, or photon emission—but living beings on another, namely higher, vibrational level. It would never enter the mind of a native to say that plant teachers are just chemicals that flood the consciousness interface of those who ingest them, thereby bringing about 'hallucinogenic visions.'

My hypothesis focuses on the *real function* of the shaman and the interaction that is taking place, in authentic shamanic voyage, between the shaman's consciousness, the consciousness of the client, and the consciousnesses of the spirits who are somehow involved, through the mystery of the psychoactive compounds contained in the entheogenic plants. It is namely this *interaction between various conscious forms of living* that brings about the amplifying effect, the opening of consciousness, the sharpening of perception, the pristine intelligent awareness of reality that is typically the unique gift one carries away from such experiences.

After all, looking at the details of my experience as a single case among many cases to be studied and evaluated, we can safely conclude that the mechanistic 'chemical' explanation of consciousness-opening shamanic experiences is a reductionist concept that cannot truly and objectively explain what really happens in such kind of experiences. By contrast, my hypothesis forwards an epistemological approach to these experiences that is systemic and complex enough to explain the uncanny details of such voyages, and that understands that all about consciousness, after all, is *intention*. It has been seen in other fields of research, such as quantum physics as well that intention really is the greatest influential agent in the universe, to a point that scientists now even argue that the big bang, the very starting point of creation, was already a result, and not the cause. The cause, as it appears, was a form of *cosmic intention*.

What I learned through the psychedelic experience is that reality is not the semantic mantel that we are wrapping around our life experiences, that language, to say it with Zen, is merely like the finger that points to the moon, but is not the moon. In other words, language is the map, not the terrain. Hence, to conclude from this insight, we can say that we cannot perceive reality through language, as language itself is conditioned and related to the thought interface, which can only operate *within the known*, shying away from experiencing the unknown. Hence, when we want to experience the unknown, we need to let go of language.

—See also J. Krishnamurti 'Freedom from the Known' (1969-2010).

Thus there is no split in the *cognitive assessment of natural healing* practiced within shamanism and by shamans when looked at through the eyes not of mainstream science, but using the millenary cognitive tools of *alternative science*, and particularly our insights into the functioning of hypnosis.

Entheogens are plants that contain psychoactive compounds, such as DMT, and others, and that, when taken at appropriate doses, produce a consciousness-altering effect upon our psyche and perception. While there are methods to alter consciousness without plants, modern researchers agree that from a point of view of *effectiveness* there is a large gap between those latter techniques, on one hand and the use of entheogens, on the other, as entheogens are several hundreds of percent more effective than non-plant based methods.

Some researchers have seriously tackled the question why this is so, and one of the most persisting on this specific point was the late Terence McKenna. In his book *The Archaic Revival (1992)*, McKenna affirms that entheogenic plants contain the very essential genetic code, the basic information about the evolution of life on earth, and that for this reason the ingestion of their plant essence leads to an *immediate expansion of consciousness*. In fact, McKenna's visionary and illuminating books would probably not have had such a powerful impact if the entheogenic journey was but a form of entertainment.

Anthropologists and shamanism researchers who don't understand the unique phenomenon of shamanism tend to reduce the entheogenic experience to a mere social game, a distraction or a search for some kind of nirvana; they are of course misled. It is therefore not surprising that most anthropologists, and especially those of them who really do not understand shamanic cultures, tend to employ expressions such as *hallucinogens, narcotic drugs, narcotics* or *psychedelics.* Apart from the fact that these plants are *not narcotics,* because a narcotic drug, such as for example *opium,* renders somnolent but does not alter consciousness, the important thing to know is that entheogens are not understood, in shamanic cultures, as leisure drugs. They really are considered as assets of the religious and numinous experience.

That is why the only expression that comes close to the shamanic mindset is the term 'entheogens,' facilitators for getting in touch with the god within. And as such they form part of the religious ritual, and not of party time. This is generally little understood in our culture where so-called 'drugs' are usually associated with leisure, distraction, party time and sex. Yet in native cultures the very idea to for example relate an entheogenic voyage with sex would offend every shaman if told about it.

It has been equally affirmed that entheogens, apart from their helping us to reach the inner mind, also dissolve nasty and somehow destructive habits such as alcoholism or heroin addiction, and generally help in a process of social deconditioning. Entheogens help us to see behind the veil of the normative behavior code in any given society as they show us options of positive, yet *different* behavior.

What we can thus learn from taking these plants as a sort of *social medicine* is to recognize the pattern of normative behavior we are caught in and that obstructs our creativity and self-realization.

People who are socially oppressed, racial, ethnic, religious or sexual minorities, may want to inquire into the possible dissolution of rigid behavior rules and oppressive normative standards in society. They may thus look for the ultimately most intelligent catalyzer that exists to see all the options reality offers and as a result may want to experience the thrill of a consciousness-opening voyage.

The human soul expresses its originality in paradoxes and sometimes in extreme behavior and the very attempt to 'classify' human behavior into rigid *standards for all* is in itself an ideology. The more a given society puts up general standards, the more it is alienated from life and its creative roots and the more it is subject to decay. Shamanism is an effective guidepost for reentering the realm of nature's wisdom and true connectedness to *all–that–is*.

The entheogenic quest is an inner quest, not necessarily a defeatist approach on a social level, but certainly an important add-on to any social activism for any possible social or humanitarian cause. The shaman is not a theorist, not a scientist and not a theologian. He is a pragmatist, a solution-finder and his first rule is effectiveness. He is something like a highly effective Zen manager in his universe of natural laws, and he is a communicator. He communicates with the spirit world, the world of the ancestors and the world of the animal and plant spirits.

A shaman receives his basic education from the entheogenic plant teachers, and only at a minor degree from another, elder, shaman tutor. Shamans around the world, asked how they got to know this or that secret about healing, answer they learnt it directly from the plant spirits. They tend to affirm that they know little and that they just humbly ask plant spirits every time they can't solve a problem or do not find a remedy for a certain illness. And the effectiveness of a shaman, then, is exactly to maximize the response-ability he has for all possible problems he is asked to solve.

This involves curing sickness, doing counter-magic, finding the right timing for hunting or harvest and even the task to solve political questions in inter-tribal relations.

The shaman does that by maximizing his unique communication with the invisible world, the world of the spirits. By the same token, shamans around the world, when asked about *reality* tend to affirm that visible reality is a rather insignificant part of reality and that the *real* reality is the hidden one, the one that is unveiled during the entheogenic visionary experience.

If we refuse this bias of a *more or less* in terms of reality assessment, we can still enrich our mindset with the option that there might be *parallel realities* and that all realities, visible or invisible, or visible only through facilitating drugs or other consciousness-altering devices, are equally valid and equally important.

My hypothesis is that the consciousness-transforming cognitive experience subsequent to ingesting the ritual *Ayahuasca* brew is not, as often suggested, the direct result of plant chemistry, but of the shaman's conscious intention reaching the experiencer's consciousness through the medium of plant chemistry as a thought and energy transmitter. This view is not to be understood in a reductionist sense. I do not say that all is to be *reduced* to one single root cause, but propose to consider *one more option* in our scientific investigation of paranormal phenomena. To corroborate my hypothesis I shall report a mind-opening experience with *Ayahuasca* during a visit to a Shuar native shaman in Ecuador, back in 2004.

My hypothesis provides a *non-linear* explanation of the psychedelic experience; it does not deny the existence of the chloride and its possible effects on the human psyche. But I contend that the mind-opening effects noticed by the novice after ingesting the brew are a result of the shaman's consciousness impacting upon a *passive perception matrix* that is part of the plant realm and that the shaman uses as a transmitter platform. My point is not to invalidate any of the current hypotheses about psychedelic plant substances, but to *help finding a valid theory* that shows what it is that effectively opens, modifies or expands human consciousness during the Ayahuasca experience.

—See, for example, Mircea Eliade, Shamanism (1972), Piers Vitebsky, Shamanism (2001), Ralph Metzner (Ed.) Ayahuasca (1999), Michael Harner, Ways of the Shaman (1990), Jeremy Narby, The Cosmic Serpent (1999), Richard Evans Schultes et al, Plants of the Gods (2002), Terence McKenna, The Invisible Landscape (1994), True Hallucinations (1998), The Archaic Revival (1992), Food of the Gods (1993), Robert Forte (Ed.), Entheogens and the Future of Religion (2000), Luis Eduardo Luna & Pablo Amaringo, Ayahuasca Visions (1999), Adam Gottlieb, Peyote and Other Psychoactive Cacti (1997), Rick Strassman, DMT (2001).

Most of the researchers seem to defend a rather *mechanistic causation theory* that sees the source of all paranormal phenomena in the chemical plant substances, or else in biophoton emission. For example Terence McKenna, under the spell of his large knowledge on ethnopharmacology, and his brother Dennis McKenna, an ethnobotanist, never left a doubt in all their writings on the subject of psychedelics that the causation of altered states of consciousness is due to psychoactive compounds in plants called *entheogens*. The question what exactly the role is that the shaman plays in opening greater pathways of consciousness is left open or subject to speculation.

Jeremy Narby, in his book *The Cosmic Serpent (2003)*, puts up the daring hypothesis that causation is due to biophoton emission, not plant chemistry.

> Researchers working in this new field mainly consider biophoton emission as a cellular language or a form of nonsubstantial biocommunication between cells and organisms. Over the last fifteen years, they have conducted enough reproducible experiments to believe that cells use these waves to direct their own internal reactions as well as to communicate among themselves and even between organisms. For instance, photon emission provides a communication mechanism that

could explain how billions of individual plankton organisms cooperate in swarms, behaving like super organisms. (Id., 127-128)

Now, succinctly speaking, what Narby wants to show is that what the shamans perceive as *spirits* are in reality biophotons emitted by the cells of the human body:

> What if these spirits were none other than the biophotons emitted by all the cells of the world and were picked up, amplified, and transmitted by shamans' quartz crystals, Gurvich's quartz screens, and the quartz containers of biophoton researchers? This would mean that spirits are beings of pure light—as has always been claimed. (Id., 129)

In fact, Narby's theory does not exclude that causation might also be due to plant chemistry, but he surely concludes that what is seen, what is perceived, is not parallel reality but the reality contained in our own DNA and the *superconscious memory surface* that is connected to it. A perhaps more convincing evidence of causation being an effect of the shaman's own superconscious powers, and not of plant chemistry, is brought forward, or at least hypothesized by the American medical anthropologist, shaman and psychologist Alberto Villoldo.

In his book *Shaman, Healer, Sage (2000)*, Dr. Villoldo introduces the third chapter entitled *The Luminous Energy Field* with an entry from his journals. Don Eduardo was one of the powerful Inca shamans Villoldo studied with for many years:

> I've found that the San Pedro potion does nothing other than make me sick. (…) I'm convinced that the altered state I'm in is created by Don Eduardo's singing. And then there is the energy that he claims enters the ceremonial space when he summons the spirits of serpent, jaguar, hummingbird, and condor. (…) What I can't explain is the fact that I'm seeing energy. It only happens when I sit next to Don Eduardo. When I go more than a few feet away from him I sense nothing. It's like he is surrounded by an electric space, where the air actually tingles. When I'm inside his space I see everything he sees. (Id., 41)

The perhaps most convincing corroboration of my research comes from theosophy and the pulpit of Charles W. Leadbeater. If clairvoyant research is or is not considered as valid scientific research under the present science paradigm is not *my* problem. From the point of view of *real* science as the methodically sound, holistic, mentally sane and intelligently communicated observation of nature, clairvoyance *is* science.

As a little excursion, let me quote what a clairvoyant herself has to say about this extraordinary faculty of perception that is clairvoyance. Dora van Gelder writes in her book *The Real World of Fairies (1999)* that she attributes the faculty of clairvoyance to the pituitary gland, which may somehow be more highly developed in clairvoyants than in ordinary people:

The fact is that there is a real physical basis for clairvoyance, and the faculty is not especially mysterious. The power centers in that tiny organ in the brain called the *pituitary gland*. The kind of vibrations involved are so subtle that no physical opening in the skin is needed to convey them to the pituitary body, but there is a special spot of sensitiveness just between the eyes above the root of the nose which acts as the external opening for the gland within. (Id., 4)

In his book, *The Astral Plane (1894)*, Leadbeater stresses the fact that the spirits natives communicate with have certain well-defined characteristics and they are quite distinct of human beings.

We might almost look upon the nature-spirits as a kind of astral humanity, but for the fact that none of them— not even the highest—possess a permanent reincarnating individuality. Apparently therefore, one point in which their line of evolution differs from ours is that a much greater proportion of intelligence is developed before permanent individualization takes place; but of the stages through which they have passed, and those through which they have yet to pass, we can know little. The life-periods of the different subdivisions vary greatly, some being quite short, others much longer than our human lifetime. We stand so entirely outside such a life as theirs that it is impossible for us to understand much about its conditions; but it appears on the whole to be a simple, joyous, irresponsible kind of existence, much such as a party of happy children might lead among exceptionally favourable physical surroundings. Though tricky and mischievous, they are

rarely malicious unless provoked by some
unwarrantable intrusion or annoyance; but as a body
they also partake to some extent of the universal feeling
of distrust for man, and they generally seem inclined to
resent somewhat the first appearances of a neophyte on
the astral plane, so that he usually makes their freaks,
they soon accept him as a necessary evil and take no
further notice of him, while some among them may even
after a time become friendly and manifest pleasure on
meeting him. (Id., 61)

This means that through thought and intent, and
mental focus, we actually create *elementals*, which are
thought forms that are somehow embodied and
individualized.

Now, what I conclude from this insight, extrapolating
the research of clairvoyant Charles W. Leadbeater to
shamanism, is that the shaman, when concocting the
psychedelic brew, and when focusing on it, actually builds
elementals by his strong intent and the thought forms
resulting from this focus. These elementals then are
absorbed by the plant matrix, or the psychoactive
compounds in entheogenic plants, and are transmitted to
the adept who desires to be initiated by the shaman, by
ingesting the brew.

If our intent projected upon time and space creates
what Leadbeater and others call *elementals* or if it creates
thought–forms or if it creates a collapsing of the wave
function, to use an expression of quantum physics, really
does not matter. We might as well call it magic thought

power or telepathy. What imports is that we see that there is no magic other than the impact of spirit upon visible and tangible reality.

When I extrapolate this research that is amply documented in the meantime, I must conclude that shamanic power is more than the mechanistic ingestion of plant chemistry 'to make things happen.' Then I will see that it's the preparation of the concoction much more than its chemical ingredients that make for the outcome of the experience, and that's ultimately *intent projected into the subtle matrix of plant consciousness* that is the trigger here.

In my discussions with the shaman and his assistant, it appeared clear that they themselves rejected the linear and single-causative theory of the kind stating 'it's the DMT that makes for all that Ayahuasca does,' explaining that all the art was in the traditional procedure of preparing the cure and the consciousness focus that forms part of it.

The cognitive experience with Ayahuasca is probably not a simple direct consequence of the plant-containing DMT, as this has been suggested, for example, by Terence McKenna and his brother, the ethnobotanist Dennis McKenna in their book *The Invisible Landscape (1994).*

In the particularities I have brought forward and commented upon, there appears to be a certain weight of the evidence for a causation of the cognitive experience by shamanic consciousness acting as a hypnotic agent on the plant matrix that serves as a *resilient transmitter and amplifier of thought energy*. The specific cognitive elucidation and the insights experienced after ingestion of the brew seem to have been brought about through a *multi-causative impact* with the shamans consciousness acting upon my own through the catalyzing agent of the plant compound.

It all points to the fact that this impact was brought about through the strong focus of the shaman's thought energy on my perception matrix and reception frequency both during the preparation of the brew and at the onset of the intake ritual. Concentration of thought and attention is known from both psychic research and clairvoyant experience, and from medical hypnosis to bring about an energy imprint in form of a *consciousness overlay* on the perception interface of the receiver.

I am talking about a multi-causative effect here because the evidence at stake does not allow to exclude any *proprietary additional impact* of the plant consciousness in the process of triggering the consciousness overlay. In fact, there are details in my report that indicate such an additional impact directly from the side of the plant realm, as a *genuine plant-proprietary consciousness* reaching out into my human consciousness.

The most striking detail in this context was that I had myself the clear intuition of being in touch with a proprietary *plant consciousness* or even an unspecific *universal consciousness* that I was in an ongoing telepathic exchange with as long as the trance lasted.

The most important detail in this context is well the fact that there is a *plant-specific matrix* involved in this process, and not just a shaman focusing thought energy on myself as his client. This is the specific contextual link with plant consciousness acting as a *matrix receiver* for *intent*, similar as this has been reported for water, by the elucidating research of the Japanese researcher Masaru Emoto.

As Emoto's water research suggests, it is possible to leave imprints in the memory surface of water by positive or negative affirmations, for example in the form of text labels glued on the water bottles for some time, that produce or not in the water specific crystals. Typically so, the aesthetically appealing crystals are formed by positive and uplifting intent and correlated affirmations rather than by negative and defeating intent and affirmations.

My argument here is on the same lines of reasoning. My idea is that the consciousness interface of plants, at least of plants that are qualified as *entheogens* or as plants containing mind-altering compounds, serves as a *transmitting and amplifying interface* for the thought imprint given to it by the shaman's consciousness and thought energy.

In how much the plant here participates with its own consciousness-altering compounds, such as DMT, cannot be evaluated from this experience with Ayahuasca, but needs additional, tightly curtailed research. It is namely possible that the plant chemistry, instead of being a unilateral agent of altering human consciousness, serves as a receiver, transmitter and amplifier interface for human intent and thought energy, as this has been reported by Masaru Emoto and others for the *hado*, the specific energy-interface of water.

But even Masaru Emoto has not found, and not even tried to explain the ultimate reason why human intent can have an energetic impact on water, and other substances. The explanation, or one possible explanation is given by Charles Webster Leadbeater in his 1894 booklet *Astral Plane* where he describes the function of elementals in the communication between humans and all realms of nature.

As I have shown, Leadbeater explains that thought is an energetic phenomenon: thoughts are *vibrations*, and as such they bring about thought forms or *elementals*. These elementals, he says further, gain permanence over time and depending on how much *emotional energy* we invest in those thoughts. And here we encounter the philosophy of the natives who speak about *spirits* when asked about the communicating agents between humans and plants. The solution of the riddle is to view the natives' explanation and the theosophical or clairvoyant view together.

The technique consists thus in imprinting intent in the plant matrix by gestating, through the power of thought energy, elementals that function as communicating agents between the human and the plant realm. These elementals are created during the process of collecting the Ayahuasca liana and carefully preparing the brew, and it is these elementals impacting on the plants' psychoactive substances which are becoming active and *communicative* as it were in the initiate's consciousness.

Book Reviews

Alberto Villoldo, A Western Shaman

Books and Media Reviewed
Healing States (1984)
Shaman, Healer, Sage (2000)
The Luminous Body, DVD (2004)
The Four Insights (2006)

Alberto Villoldo, Ph.D., a psychologist and medical anthropologist, has studied the healing practices of the Amazon and Inka shamans for more than 25 years. While at San Francisco State University, he founded the *Biological*

Self-Regulation Laboratory to study how the mind creates psychosomatic health and disease.

Villoldo directs the *Four Winds Society,* where he trains individuals throughout the world in the practice of energy medicine and soul retrieval. He has training centers in New England, California, the UK, Holland, and Park City, Utah. The author of the best-seller *Shaman, Healer, Sage,* Villoldo now draws on his vast knowledge to bring us a practical and revolutionary way to discover the source of an original wound that may have occurred during childhood or in a former lifetime, and that derailed our destiny. He then shows us how to track forward along our time lines to find our best and highest future.

—From: Inlay of *Mending the Past and Healing the Future with Soul Retrieval.*

—Website: www.thefourwinds.com

I should mention that I was attracted to these books through the beautiful DVD entitled *Healing the Luminous Body* that was produced by *Sacred Mysteries,* and which I am going to review further down. Dr. Villoldo, besides the phenomenal cultural gap that his teaching closes and the amazing perspectives for soul retrieval in the future, stands out by his remarkable pedagogical talent; in fact he is able to convey the complex matter in relatively simple words and with many examples and excerpts from his personal journal.

He writes a poetic style, and irradiates warmth, compassion and empathic understanding of human suffering; he also stands out by his sometimes childlike inquisitiveness that led him win the sympathy and support of people and peoples who are, for reasons that we all know, rather hostile toward our culture.

His popularity is growing presently. A documentary has been released as his web presence informs and many interviews with him can be found on Youtube. Besides, his 'shamanic healing' seminars are popular throughout the United States.

I am not surprised about his success given the void in our culture in the domain of genuine and personal spirituality, and the need for non-mechanistic healing. Villoldo's books are among the most important books I have ever read in my life.

Healing States

With Stanley Krippner
A Journey into the World of Spiritual Healing and Shamanism
New York: Simon & Schuster (Fireside), 1984

Healing States is a research volume that Alberto Villoldo co-authored
with Stanley Krippner, and it's a glorious onset of his own career in
spiritual healing. The research presented in this book is highly
thought-provoking if not mind-boggling, and it's well presented.

The point of departure of the author's scientific journey
was his research on *psychosomatic medicine*. He was
interested what exactly makes the soma follow the psyche,
or why the spirit imprints itself on the soma, thus causing
either health or disease. The authors write:

> A growing number of allopathic physicians believe that
> as much as 80 percent of all illness may contain a
> psychosomatic component. Allopathic medical science,
> which does not publicly acknowledge the psychic realm,
> is still at a loss to explain the origin and treatment of

many of these psychosomatic disorders, often merely referring to 'unconscious conflicts' that can trigger disease./19

The phenomenon of contact with spirits is highly uncanny and unusual for the modern mind. The authors, well aware of this cultural bias or denial, have found that in fact, it may be a question of terminology as psychotherapists talk about 'complexes' and 'subpersonalities' when they refer to the same causal agents as for example a medium refers to. In fact, in my own research on what transactional analysis calls our *inner selves*, I have found that here we encounter just another of those hidden key formulas that open windows to other, wider, and deeper realms of insight.

My research on Huna, the ancient religion of the Kahuna natives in Hawaii, brought to daylight and gave me evidence for the assumption that inner selves are not just psychic modalities but inner spirits, real entities that are part of our *multidimensional psyche*. And in my practice of the inner dialogue and spontaneous art, I had at least in once instance, a real encounter with a spirit, and I became acutely aware of the fact that many of our thoughts and ideas are not entirely our own but that we can, consciously or involuntarily, benefit from the ideas sent to us by guiding spirits. Yet for the authors, the idea of encountering spirits seemed novel and daring and they write:

But as we prepared to leave São Paolo we were struck with the thought that communications from the spirit world could be happening all the time, and that we might simply not be aware of them. Is it possible that many of our intuitions and creative thoughts come from outside ourselves? Although most scientists believe that contacts with spirits are fantasies of the unconscious mind, a small but growing number of investigators believe that the human brain may behave like a complex transmitting and receiving apparatus, which under certain conditions can pick up thoughts from other minds, and even across space and time./18

The first landmark research described in the book regards *The Spiritual Psychiatry of Dr. Mendes*, a Brazilian spiritual healer located in the suburbs of São Paolo and specialized on healing epilepsy, schizophrenia and multiple personality disorder.

The interviews with this phenomenal natural healer revealed that it's by following the natural principle of *self-regulation* that healing states are realized. The authors summarize their interviews with Dr. Mendes as follows, fully quoting his reply to their questions:

> You could say that we encourage the full expression of madness and of epilepsy. We then give them bioenergetic and psychic exercises that correct their improper use of altered awareness. After many years of observation, we have come to the conclusion that epilepsy, schizophrenia, and multiple-personality disorders can all result from inappropriate states of consciousness. Therapeutic exercises help to organize

the guest/patients' psychic energies and teach them to manage their highly developed yet poorly trained mediumship and trance abilities./41

On the same line of reasoning, the healing state is triggered not by exerting control over the sickly condition, but by giving the psychosomatic unity of the organism the opportunity to regulate its own healing, which in Dr. Mendes' experience always leads to the original wounding. It is by allowing this regression to take place that full healing of the condition is achieved.

> When we asked if learning to control the seizures constituted the basis of the treatment, Mendes explained that control is not the issue—as the basis of his therapy is hypnotic regression. This regression can take the patient back to childhood, or to a prenatal state when the person was still inside the womb, or even to former lifetimes. Mendes believes that, to cure themselves, most epileptics must discover and resolve the highly charged emotional events that contribute to their illnesses. But, unlike conventional psychotherapists, he feels that these traumatic events may have happened in another lifetime./43

> The healing would be accomplished by having one of the clinic's mediums incorporate the former personality and help her psychologically integrate and discharge that experience, just as if it had happened in this lifetime./44

Alberto Villoldo, long before he was famous as an alternative spiritual healer, already had grasped the importance of bringing self-regulation into healing; it was namely before he had departed to the Andes that he was directing the *Biological Self-Regulation Laboratory* at San Francisco State University. One of the motivational triggers for this doctor's extraordinary journey was his research experience with Dr. Mendes.

Stanley Krippner reported that he was especially struck, in the discussions with Dr. Mendes, by 'the likelihood that the treatment *encourages a type of self-regulation.'* He explains:

> All the various types of epilepsy involve dramatic alterations of consciousness, some of them quite spectacular. An epileptic may see auras before a seizure, may have a sense of déjà vu, or may have sensory

alterations which indicate that a seizure is about to occur. Through biofeedback, some epileptics have been able to exert some type of control over the episode, thus minimizing its symptoms. Perhaps Mendes' successful clients are doing something similar by shifting their epileptic episode into a mediumistic experience./53

In *The Shaman's Journey*, the authors come to an important conclusion about shamanism, which points to the important fact that shamanism, at its very core, is basically non-judgmental and does not steer toward any fixated position in terms of morality. It's thus free of the all-pervasive moralism that is part of the cultural bias inherent in all monotheistic religions and their respective cultural incarnations (such as, mainly, Judaism, Christianity and Islam).

The authors conclude:

> If we were to become polarized toward either the light or the dark we would become trapped by that aspect of reality and our spiritual development would be crippled./89

Shaman, Healer, Sage

How to Heal Yourself and Others with the Energy Medicine of the Americas
New York: Harmony Books, 2000

Shaman, Healer, Sage is perhaps Villoldo's best book. It was anyway the book that made him famous, a real bestseller. It has given me an ultimate peak of reading enjoyment and illumination, and it has also emotionally touched me.

The author comes over in this book as a really honest, competent, emotionally mature, wistful and empathetic person who went through a personal transformation that only few people in these times can say to have accomplished. This book is not only highly recommended lecture; it can perhaps be considered as one of the best books so far in the century on the issues of shamanic healing and the challenging task to render an outlandish practice of Inka shamans comprehensive to the modern mind!

The literary abilities of the author, besides his expertise, are out of question, and the book is an easy read despite the complex and unusual subject. This might be due to the author's penetration of the subject and his sense for vivifying theoretical content by practical and often uncanny experiences, and because of his highly developed sense for poetic language and expression.

This being said, I would like to start the discussion of this book with the term *infinity*. Dr. Villoldo explains that infinity is not eternity and that it is not a stretching of time but as it were a realm of 'no time', a sort of transliteration of another vibrational dimension, that is reigned by laws more majestic and more complex than our own, and of which our space-time reality forms only a tiny part. One of the intentions of the author in this book was to render comprehensive the fact that being in touch with shamanic healing means to be in touch with infinity. This appears to be the key to understanding the miraculous effectiveness of shamanic cures.

> And the experience of infinity shatters the illusion of death, disease, and old age. This is a not a psychological or spiritual process only; every cell in our body is informed and renewed by it. Our immune system is unbridled, and / physical and emotional healing happen at an accelerated rate. Miracles become ordinary, and spontaneous remissions, those mysterious and baffling cures that confound medicine, become commonplace. And a spiritual liberation or illumination takes place. In the presence of infinity we are able to experience what

we were before we were born and who we will be after we die./22-23

And as he went through traditional medical training in the United States at first, Dr. Villoldo then was going to look at that medical science tradition he was coming from, and that he had left when departing to the Andes in order to learn with the Inka shamans. And he concludes:

> Many years later I understood that Western medicine, in an effort to change the physical body, was merely moving the iron filings around the glass. Surgery and medication often brought about violent, traumatic change on the body. This approach struck me as crude and invasive, like scattering the iron filings with my hand, rather than moving them by shifting/45

The other main purpose of the book is to explain to the interested reader what the *Luminous Energy Field* represents, what it does in natural healing and how the shaman can access it for altering its energetic vibration in certain areas that contain so-called *imprints*. The author explains:

> We all possess a Luminous Energy Field that surrounds our physical body and informs our body in the same way that the energy fields of a magnet organize iron filings on a piece of glass. Our Luminous Energy Field has existed since before the beginning of time. It was one with the unmanifest light of Creation, and it will endure / throughout infinity. It dwells outside of time but

manifests in time by creating new physical bodies
lifetime after lifetime./42-43

This reservoir of vital force is a sea of living energy as
indispensable to our health as the oxygen and nutrients
carried by the bloodstream. They are the energies of the
Luminous Energy Field, the purest and most precious
fuel for life./43

Indian or Tibetan mystics who documented the existence
of the Luminous Energy Field thousands of years ago
described it as an aura or halo around the physical body.
At first it seemed odd to find the same concept of a
human energy field among the jungle and mountain
shamans in the Americas. Once I grasped the
universality of the human energy field, however, I
understood that every culture must have discovered it.
In the East, mandalas depict the Buddha enveloped by
blue and gold bands of fire. In the West, Christ and the
apostles are shown with luminous halos around them. In
the mystical literature, the Apostle Thomas is said to
have glowed with the same radiance as Christ. Native
American legends speak of persons who shimmered in
the night as if lit by an inner fire. The Andean
storytellers recall the ruler Pachacutek, considered to be
a Child of the Sun, who sparkled with the light of the
dawn./43

In view of our cutting-edge science revelations over the
last two decades, and the insights we gained from
quantum physics about the quality of light, and of
universal memory, the teaching Dr. Villoldo received from

the Laika shamans becomes comprehensive in a larger context, and is actually corroborated by newest scientific insights. The author writes:

> Every living thing on Earth is composed of light. Plants absorb light directly from the sun and turn it into life, and animals eat green plants that feed on light, so that light is the fundamental building block of life. We are light bound into living matter. / 43

In the light of Integral Theories of Everything, and especially the revealing book by *Ervin Laszlo, Science and the Akashic Field (2005)*, what the author reports about the Akashic memory does not sound so esoteric after all:

> The Luminous Energy Field contains an archive of all of our personal and ancestral memories, of all early-life trauma, and even of painful wounds from former lifetimes. These records or imprints are stored in full color and intensity of emotions. Imprints are like dormant computer programs that when activated compel us toward behaviors, relationships, accidents, and illnesses that parody the initial wounding. / 46

What Dr. Villoldo writes about the earth's magnetic field, and how the luminous energy field connects us to the luminous matrix of the entire universe, reminds the extraordinary research by Dr. Wilhelm Reich on what he called the *orgone*, which he described equally both as a bioplasmatic energy and as *cosmic orgone*, being responsible, inter alia, for the changes in weather.

> —See also my reviews of Reich's books in The New Paradigm in Science and Systems Theory (2004). It must be seen that Reich was one of the first systems researchers in modern history, at a time when this kind of knowledge was not yet embraced by science, which is why Reich had to suffer a lot of hardship throughout his career as a medical doctor, psychoanalyst and bioenergetic healer.

It is a well-known fact that Reich, on the basis of these discoveries, was able to bring about rain in desert regions and under conditions of severe drought. Dr. Villoldo writes:

> Although the strength of the Earth's magnetic field drops off very rapidly the farther it travels from the planet, it never actually reaches zero. It extends for hundreds of miles into space before diminishing in strength, and travels at the speed of light, at about 186.000 miles per second, to the edge of the Universe. The human energy field appears to extend only a few feet beyond the body since, like the magnetic field of the Earth, it diminishes in strength very rapidly. Yet it also travels at the speed of light, connecting us to the luminous matrix of the entire Universe, known to the Inka as the texemuyo or all-pervading web./49

> Over the years I developed the ability to perceive the streams of light that flow through the luminous body, and read the imprints of health and disease. I believe that this is an innate ability that we all possess but either do not develop or lose after the age of seven or eight because we are taught to believe that the material world is the only 'real' world. Shamans throughout the Americas rely on their ability to perceive the energetic realm. / 50

Now, what happens when for example we have been suffering trauma in early childhood? Dr. Villoldo explains that in such a case an imprint is formed in the luminous energy field.

> Unresolved psychological and spiritual traumas become engraved like scratch marks in our luminous fields. Positive experiences do not leave a mark in our luminous body. / 55

> The blueprint that shaped and molded us since we were inside our mother's womb contains the memories of all of our former lifetimes—the way we suffered, the way we loved, how we were ill, and the way we died. In the East these imprints are known as karma, forces that sweep through our life like a giant tide that we cannot swim free of. These imprints contain instructions that predispose us to repeating certain events from the past. We want to learn where these energy imprints are located in the Luminous Energy Field and how to erase them so that the body, mind, and spirit can return to health. / 56

Healing the Luminous Body

How to Heal Yourself and Others with the Energy Medicine of the
Americas
New York: Harmony Books, 2000

Healing the Luminous Body was my first access to Dr. Villoldo's unique
healing methods that he exposes in more detail in his books. This DVD
is very well done, a calm and peaceful introduction into the philosophy,
the development and the effectiveness of healing the luminous body..

Dr. Villoldo expresses himself fluently, and he is able to
inform about the unusual subject in a competent and
poised manner. It becomes clear that he speaks of
experience, not of theory. The video also retraces his
professional way, how he got to the knowledge that today
benefits so many people in the West, and how, at the start,
he was really a pioneer. In this sense, despite enlightening
new openings presented to a greater public in the film
'What the Bleep Do We Know!?,' people like Alberto Villoldo
swim against the stream. For the enlightenment, as in all
times of turmoil and change, does not seem to reach the
small oligarchy that handle the levers and push the

buttons, and that use red telephones and secret services. I say this to prevent you from falling in an unreal new age enthusiasm that deprives so many people today of their feet and lets them float in the pure air of meditation, spirituality and angels. Villoldo is not one of those lofty spirits! His teaching is grounded, and therefore helps us connect with the not so luminous forces in us, our inner shadow, or all the shadows that are the results of the imprints in our luminous body, which are for the most part the consequences of early abuse suffered as children, or that go back to former lifetimes.

Villoldo is not only a fabulous author, who is able to wrap his teaching in a beautiful and wistful poetic style, but he's also a great orator, and his way of talking triggered in me pure hope, love, and enthusiasm. I am thankful for this wonderful DVD as it helps to introduce in his teaching which is not as easy to apply as it seems on first sight. After all, it is taken from a culture almost opposite to ours, a culture that is psychologically and spiritually much higher evolved than ours.

> In this fascinating and informative video, Alberto Villoldo, Ph.D., introduces viewers to the luminous energy field that surrounds and informs our physical body like a blueprint of life. Unveiling the secret of ancient shaman-healers, he teaches us that many of our physical and psychological problems stem from imprints within our luminous body. Dr. Villoldo reveals the nature of this luminous field, how it acts as a blueprint for our physical body and how by understanding its nature, we can actually heal ourselves and each other. Once the luminous body is cleared, Dr. Villoldo explains, physical and emotional healing can begin.

> Trained as a Medical Anthropologist, Dr. Villoldo left the academic world behind twenty years ago to study among the Inka shamans. It was in the Andes Mountains of South America that he discovered the wisdom of the luminous body from the indigenous shamans. This ancient knowledge reveals the secret of true health and happiness.

> To aid Dr. Villoldo explaining the luminous energy field, the paintings of visionary artist Alex Grey are presented. No other artist has depicted the luminous energy form in all of its intricacies as clearly as Alex Grey. Dr. Villoldo's presentation, together with Alex Grey's images

help all of us understand the nature of our spiritual and physical being.

Many of our illnesses, physical disorders, addictions and failed relationships can be traced to faulty imprints in our luminous body. In this video, Dr. Villoldo unveils how to heal and recover from these destructive imprints and regain our physical, mental and spiritual well-being. Join us as we travel to the Andes Mountains to learn the secret of the ancient shamans, a secret that can lead all of us to health, happiness and beauty.
—From: DVD Back Cover

The Four Insights

How to Heal Yourself and Others with the Energy Medicine of the
Americas
New York: Harmony Books, 2000

The Four Insights chronologically is the last of the three books by Dr.
Villoldo that I review here, as it was the most recent at the time I drafted
these reviews.

The book is structured very differently from the
preceding ones, in that it condenses the teaching into *Four
Insights*.

Part One: Understanding the Energy of Perception
The Four Levels of Perception
Your Energetic Anatomy

Part Two: The Four Insights

Insight One – The Way of the Hero
The Practice of Nonjudgment
The Practice of Nonsuffering

The Practice of Nonattachment

The Practice of Beauty

Insight Two – The Way of the Luminous Warrior

The Practice of Fearlessness

The Practice of Nondoing

The Practice of Certainty

The Practice of Nonengagement

Insight Three – The Way of the Seer

The Practice of Beginner's Mind

The Practice of Living Consequently

The Practice of Transparency

The Practice of Integrity

Insight Four – The Way of the Sage

The Practice of Mastering Time

The Practice of Owning Your Projections

The Practice of No-mind

The Practice of Indigenous Alchemy

In a way, and perhaps logically so, this book is much more condensed than any of the former books by the author. Every sentence, and every word counts, and is full of meaning, and you are not going to read this in the same speed as, for example, *Shaman, Healer, Sage*. This indicates perhaps that this book is more conceptual than the earlier books, and that the author has in the meantime created a concise framework for his teaching. To give an example of this density that reminds the highly focused content of theosophical writings, the author writes in the Introduction:

> The Earthkeepers teach that all of creation—the earth, humans, whales, rocks, and even the stars—is made of vibration and light. /x

> Thanks to the discoveries of quantum physics, we've come to understand that all matter is densely packed light. But the Laika have known about the luminous nature of reality for millennia - they know that vibration and light can organize themselves into a thousand shapes and forms. /xiii

There is another elucidation forwarded by the author about his teaching that I consider extremely important—and that he should perhaps have provided in earlier publications. It's the fact that the Laika tradition he was initiated in is not to be confounded with mainstream Inka tradition.

All those who know about the Inka tradition are aware of the fact that it was a Sun God cult, what Joseph Campbell came to call a 'solar culture' that practiced ruthless slavery, the oppression of the female, violent warfare, torture of prisoners of war, and human sacrifice. The author explains:

> As fortune or destiny would have it, I ended up meeting my mentor, don Antonio. He was one of the last of the living Laika, and he took me under his wing and trained me for nearly 25 years. He was a man of many lives—

during the day, he was a university / professor; in the evenings, a master medicine man. He was born in a high mountain village and worked with the tools and practices of the 15th century, yet he was conversant in the way of the 21st. Although he was a descendant of the Inka, he would tell me that the Laika are much older than the Inka, whose culture was masculine and militaristic. The Laika's teachings were from that earlier time, when the feminine aspect of the divine was recognized. / xi-xii

Over millennia, the Laika learned to access the biological blueprint of light and assist Spirit in the unfolding of creation. They also learned how to heal disease and create extraordinary states of health, as well as to craft and shape their personal destinies, by changing the LEF [Luminous Energy Field]. / xiii

The powerful message of this teaching is that we can overcome our negative individual and collective karma by rejoining the original pattern, through overcoming and healing what the Kahunas call *complexes*, and what Dr. Villoldo calls *imprints* in the Luminous Energy Field (LEF).

We can think of the LEF as the software that gives instructions to DNA, which is the hardware that manufactures the body. Mastery of the insights lets us access the latest version of the software and allows each of us to create a new body that ages, heals, and dies differently. Without the ability to reprogram the LEF, we're trapped in the stories we inherited; that is, we age, heal, live, and die the way our parents and grandparents did, reliving their physical ills and emotional ailments.

The four insights contained in these pages allow us to break free of the tyranny of our familial curses, the stories that haunted our ancestors. / xiv

In becoming Homo luminous, we'll give up the ways of the conquistador and discard the masculine theology that values command, control, and dominion over nature, a theology that justifies the exploitation of the earth's rivers and forests because they're seen merely as resources for human consumption. Instead, we'll embrace an older mythology that has become lost to most humans, a feminine theology of cooperation and sustainability. / xiv

It is a daring perspective, and I can only admire the courage of the author to forward his wonderful mission in a time of change that perhaps really contains a vortex, an opening for the new to emerge from the old.

The book contains much more than the little window that I opened here in my book review, and perhaps contrary to my other reviews, I restrain myself here. And for good reason. It's a symbolic act. Discover for yourself, and see what more you can learn from this extraordinary book! I feel unable to convey it.

Bibliography

Contextual Bibliography

Abrams, Jeremiah (Ed.)

Reclaiming the Inner Child
New York: Tarcher/Putnam, 1990

Anderson, Victor

Etheric Anatomy
The Three Selves and Astral Travel
With Cora Anderson
New York: Penguin Arkana, 1993
Albany, CA: Acorn Guild Press, 2004

Arntz, William & Chasse, Betsy

What the Bleep Do We Know
20th Century Fox, 2005 (DVD)

Down The Rabbit Hole Quantum Edition
20th Century Fox, 2006 (3 DVD Set)

Bachofen, Johann Jakob

Gesammelte Werke, Band II
Das Mutterrecht
Basel: Benno Schwabe & Co., 1948
Erstveröffentlichung im Jahre 1861

Bateson, Gregory

Steps to an Ecology of Mind
Chicago: University of Chicago Press, 2000
Originally published in 1972

Beaulieu, John

Music and Sound in the Healing Arts
London: Barrytown/Station Hill Press, 1995

Besant, Annie

An Autobiography
New Delhi: Penguin Books, 2005
Originally published in 1893

Blavatsky, Helena Petrovna

The Secret Doctrine
New York: Tarcher, 2009
Originally published in 1888

Bohm, David

Wholeness and the Implicate Order
London: Routledge, 2002

Thought as a System
London: Routledge, 1994

Quantum Theory
London: Dover Publications, 1989

Brennan, Barbara Ann

Hands of Light
A Guide to Healing Through the Human Energy Field
New York: Bantam Books, 1988

Burwick, Frederick

The Damnation of Newton
Goethe's Color Theory and Romantic Perception
New York: Walter de Gruyter, 1986

Campbell, Herbert James

The Pleasure Areas
London: Eyre Methuen Ltd., 1973

Campbell, Joseph

The Hero With A Thousand Faces
Princeton: Princeton University Press, 1973 (Bollingen Series XVII)
London: Orion Books, 1999
Occidental Mythology
Princeton: Princeton University Press, 1973
(Bollingen Series XVII)
New York: Penguin Arkana, 1991

The Masks of God
Oriental Mythology
New York: Penguin Arkana, 1992
Originally published in 1962

The Power of Myth
With Bill Moyers
ed. by Sue Flowers
New York: Anchor Books, 1988

Capra, Fritjof

The Tao of Physics
An Exploration of the Parallels Between Modern
Physics and Eastern Mysticism
New York: Shambhala Publications, 2000
(New Edition) Originally published in 1975

The Turning Point
Science, Society And The Rising Culture
New York: Simon & Schuster, 1987 (Author Copyright 1982)

Green Politics
With Charlene Spretnak
Rochester, VT: Inner Traditions, 1986

The Web of Life
A New Scientific Understanding of Living Systems
New York: Doubleday, 1997
Author Copyright 1996

The Hidden Connections
Integrating The Biological, Cognitive And Social
Dimensions Of Life Into A Science Of Sustainability
New York: Doubleday, 2002

Steering Business Toward Sustainability
New York: United Nations University Press, 1995

Uncommon Wisdom
Conversations with Remarkable People
New York: Bantam, 1989

The Science of Leonardo
Inside the Mind of the Great Genius of the Renaissance
New York: Anchor Books, 2008
New York: Bantam Doubleday, 2007 (First Publishing)

Learning from Leonardo
Decoding the Notebooks of a Genius
San Francisco: Berrett-Koehler, 2013

Castaneda, Carlos

The Teachings of Don Juan
A Yaqui Way of Knowledge
Washington: Square Press, 1985

Journey to Ixtlan
Washington: Square Press: 1991

Tales of Power
Washington: Square Press, 1991

The Second Ring of Power
Washington: Square Press, 1991

Chaplin, Charles

My Autobiography
New York: Plume, 1992
Originally published in 1964

Cho, Susanne

Kindheit und Sexualität im Wandel der Kulturgeschichte
Eine Studie zur Bedeutung der kindlichen Sexualität unter besonderer
Berücksichtigung des 17. und 20. Jahrhunderts
Zürich, 1983 (Doctoral thesis)

Chomsky, Noam

Manufacturing Consent
The Political Economy of the Mass Media
New York: Pantheon Books, 2002

Profit Over People
Neoliberalism & Global Order
With Robert W. McChesney
New York: Seven Stories Press, 2011

Chopra, Deepak

Creating Affluence
The A-to-Z Steps to a Richer Life
New York: Amber-Allen Publishing (2003)

Life After Death
The Book of Answers
London: Rider, 2006

Synchrodestiny
Discover the Power of Meaningful Coincidence to Manifest Abundance
Audio Book / CD
Niles, IL: Nightingale-Conant, 2006

The Seven Spiritual Laws of Success
A Practical Guide to the Fulfillment of Your Dreams
Audio Book / CD
New York: Amber-Allen Publishing (2002)

The Spontaneous Fulfillment of Desire
Harnessing the Infinite Power of Coincidence
New York: Random House Audio, 2003

Clarke, Ronald

Einstein: The Life and Times
New York: Avon Books, 1970

Constantine, Larry L.

Children & Sex
New Findings, New Perspectives
Larry L. Constantine & Floyd M. Martinson (Eds.)
Boston: Little, Brown & Company, 1981

Treasures of the Island
Children in Alternative Lifestyles
Beverly Hills: Sage Publications, 1976

Where are the Kids?
in: Libby & Whitehurst (ed.)
Marriage and Alternatives
Glenview: Scott Foresman, 1977

Currier, Richard L.

Juvenile Sexuality in Global Perspective
in : Children & Sex, New Findings, New Perspectives
Larry L. Constantine & Floyd M. Martinson (Eds.)
Boston: Little, Brown & Company, 1981

De Bono, Edward

The Use of Lateral Thinking
New York: Penguin, 1967

The Mechanism of Mind
New York: Penguin, 1969

Sur/Petition
London: HarperCollins, 1993

Tactics
London: HarperCollins, 1993
First published in 1985

Serious Creativity
Using the Power of Lateral Thinking to Create New Ideas
London: HarperCollins, 1996

DeMause, Lloyd

The History of Childhood
New York, 1974

Foundations of Psychohistory
New York: Creative Roots, 1982

DiCarlo, Russell E. (Ed.)

Towards A New World View
Conversations at the Leading Edge
Erie, PA: Epic Publishing, 1996

Dolto, Françoise

La Cause des Enfants
Paris: Laffont, 1985

Psychanalyse et Pédiatrie
Paris: Seuil, 1971

Séminaire de Psychanalyse d'Enfants, 1
Paris: Seuil, 1982

Séminaire de Psychanalyse d'Enfants, 2
Paris: Seuil, 1985

Séminaire de Psychanalyse d'Enfants, 3
Paris: Seuil, 1988

Dossey, Larry
Recovering the Soul
A Scientific and Spiritual Approach
New York: Bantam Books, 1989

Dürckheim, Karlfried Graf
Hara: The Vital Center of Man
Rochester: Inner Traditions, 2004

Zen and Us
New York: Penguin Arkana 1991

The Call for the Master
New York: Penguin Books, 1993

Absolute Living
The Otherworldly in the World and the Path to Maturity
New York: Penguin Arkana, 1992

The Way of Transformation
Daily Life as a Spiritual Exercise
London: Allen & Unwin, 1988

The Japanese Cult of Tranquility
London: Rider, 1960

Eden, Donna & Feinstein, David
Energy Medicine
New York: Tarcher/Putnam, 1998

The Energy Medicine Kit
Simple Effective Techniques to Help You Boost Your Vitality
Boulder, Co.: Sounds True Editions, 2004

The Promise of Energy Psychology
With David Feinstein and Gary Craig
Revolutionary Tools for Dramatic Personal Change
New York: Jeremy P. Tarcher/Penguin, 2005

Einstein, Albert

The World As I See It
New York: Citadel Press, 1993

Out of My Later Years
New York: Outlet, 1993

Ideas and Opinions
New York: Bonanza Books, 1988

Albert Einstein Notebook
London: Dover Publications, 1989

Eisler, Riane

The Chalice and the Blade
Our history, Our future
San Francisco: Harper & Row, 1995

Sacred Pleasure: Sex, Myth and the Politics of the Body
New Paths to Power and Love
San Francisco: Harper & Row, 1996

The Partnership Way
New Tools for Living and Learning
With David Loye
Brandon, VT: Holistic Education Press, 1998

The Real Wealth of Nations
Creating a Caring Economics
San Francisco: Berrett-Koehler Publishers, 2008

Eliade, Mircea

Shamanism
Archaic Techniques of Ecstasy
New York: Pantheon Books, 1964

Elwin, V.

The Muria and their Ghotul
Bombay: Oxford University Press, 1947

Emerson, Ralph Waldo

The Essays of Ralph Waldo Emerson
Cambridge, Mass.: Harvard University Press, 1987

Emoto, Masaru

The Hidden Messages in Water
New York: Atria Books, 2004

The Secret Life of Water
New York: Atria Books, 2005

Erickson, Milton H.

My Voice Will Go With You
The Teaching Tales of Milton H. Erickson
by Sidney Rosen (Ed.)
New York: Norton & Co., 1991

Complete Works 1.0, CD-ROM
New York: Milton H. Erickson Foundation, 2001

Erikson, Erik H.

Childhood and Society
New York: Norton, 1993
First published in 1950

Evans-Wentz, Walter Yeeling

The Fairy Faith in Celtic Countries
London: Frowde, 1911
Republished by Dover Publications
(Minneola, New York), 2002

Fericla, Josep M.

Al trasluz de la Ayahuasca
Antropología cognitiva, oniromancia y consciencias alternativas
Barcelona: La Liebre de Marzo, 2002

Forte, Robert (Ed.)

Entheogens and the Future of Religion
Council on Spiritual Practices, 2nd ed., 2000

Freud, Sigmund

Totem and Taboo
New York: Routledge, 1999
Originally published in 1913

Geldard, Richard

Remembering Heraclitus
New York: Lindisfarne Books, 2000

Gerber, Richard

A Practical Guide to Vibrational Medicine
Energy Healing and Spiritual Transformation
New York: Harper & Collins, 2001

Goethe, Johann Wolfgang von

The Theory of Colors
New York: MIT Press, 1970
First published in 1810

Goldenstein, Joyce

Einstein: Physicist and Genius
(Great Minds of Science)
New York: Enslow Publishers, 1995

Goldman, Jonathan & Goldman, Andi

Tantra of Sound
Frequencies of Healing
Charlottesville: Hampton Roads, 2005

Healing Sounds
The Power of Harmonies
Rochester: Healing Arts Press, 2002

Healing Sounds
Principles of Sound Healing
DVD, 90 min.
Sacred Mysteries, 2004

Gordon Wasson, R.

The Road to Eleusis
Unveiling the Secret of the Mysteries
With Albert Hofmann, Huston Smith, Carl Ruck and Peter Webster
Berkeley, CA: North Atlantic Books, 2008

Goswami, Amit

The Self-Aware Universe
How Consciousness Creates the Material World
New York: Tarcher/Putnam, 1995

Gottlieb, Adam

Peyote and Other Psychoactive Cacti
Ronin Publishing, 2nd edition, 1997
Baltimore, London: Williams & Wilkins, 1980

Grof, Stanislav

Ancient Wisdom and Modern Science
New York: State University of New York Press, 1984

Beyond the Brain
Birth, Death and Transcendence in Psychotherapy
New York: State University of New York, 1985

LSD: Doorway to the Numinous
The Groundbreaking Psychedelic Research into Realms of the Human
Unconscious
Rochester: Park Street Press, 2009

Realms of the Human Unconscious
Observations from LSD Research
New York: E.P. Dutton, 1976

The Cosmic Game
Explorations of the Frontiers of Human Consciousness
New York: State University of New York Press, 1998

The Holotropic Mind
The Three Levels of Human Consciousness
With Hal Zina Bennett
New York: HarperCollins, 1993

When the Impossible Happens
Adventures in Non-Ordinary Reality
Louisville, CO: Sounds True, 2005

Hall, Manly P.

The Secret Teachings of All Ages
Reader's Edition
New York: Tarcher/Penguin, 2003
Originally published in 1928

Hargous, Sabine

Les appeleurs d'âmes
L'univers chamanique des Indiens des Andes
Paris: Albin Michel, 1985

Harner, Michael

Ways of the Shaman
New York: Bantam, 1982
Originally published in 1980

Hofmann, Albert

LSD, My Problem Child
Reflections on Sacred Drugs, Mysticism and Science
Santa Cruz, CA: Multidisciplinary Association for Psychedelic Studies,
2009 (Originally published in 1980)

Holmes, Ernest

The Science of Mind
A Philosophy, A Faith, A Way of Life
New York: Jeremy P. Tarcher/Putnam, 1998
First Published in 1938

Hunt, Valerie

Infinite Mind
Science of the Human Vibrations of Consciousness
Malibu, CA: Malibu Publishing, 2000

Huxley, Aldous

The Doors of Perception and Heaven and Hell
London: HarperCollins (Flamingo), 1994
(originally published in 1954)

The Perennial Philosophy
San Francisco: Harper & Row, 1970

Jung, Carl Gustav

Archetypes of the Collective Unconscious
in: The Basic Writings of C.G. Jung
New York: The Modern Library, 1959, 358-407

Collected Works
New York, 1959

On the Nature of the Psyche
in: The Basic Writings of C.G. Jung
New York: The Modern Library, 1959, 47-133

Psychological Types
Collected Writings, Vol. 6
Princeton: Princeton University Press, 1971

Psychology and Religion
in: The Basic Writings of C.G. Jung
New York: The Modern Library, 1959, 582-655

Religious and Psychological Problems of Alchemy
in: The Basic Writings of C.G. Jung
New York: The Modern Library, 1959, 537-581

The Basic Writings of C.G. Jung
New York: The Modern Library, 1959

The Development of Personality
Collected Writings, Vol. 17
Princeton: Princeton University Press, 1954
The Meaning and Significance of Dreams
Boston: Sigo Press, 1991

The Myth of the Divine Child
in: Essays on A Science of Mythology
Princeton, N.J.: Princeton University Press Bollingen
Series XXII, 1969. (With Karl Kerenyi)

Two Essays on Analytical Psychology
Collected Writings, Vol. 7
Princeton: Princeton University Press, 1972
First published by Routledge & Kegan Paul, Ltd., 1953

Kalweit, Holger
Shamans, Healers and Medicine Men
Boston and London: Shambhala, 1992

Karagulla, Shafica
The Chakras
Correlations between Medical Science and Clairvoyant Observation
With Dora van Gelder Kunz
Wheaton: Quest Books, 1989

Krishnamurti, J.

Freedom From The Known
San Francisco: Harper & Row, 1969

The First and Last Freedom
San Francisco: Harper & Row, 1975

Education and the Significance of Life
London: Victor Gollancz, 1978

Commentaries on Living
First Series
London: Victor Gollancz, 1985

Commentaries on Living
Second Series
London: Victor Gollancz, 1986

Krishnamurti's Journal
London: Victor Gollancz, 1987

Krishnamurti's Notebook
London: Victor Gollancz, 1986

Beyond Violence
London: Victor Gollancz, 1985

Beginnings of Learning
New York: Penguin, 1986

The Penguin Krishnamurti Reader
New York: Penguin, 1987

On God
San Francisco: Harper & Row, 1992

On Fear
San Francisco: Harper & Row, 1995

The Essential Krishnamurti
San Francisco: Harper & Row, 1996

The Ending of Time
With Dr. David Bohm
San Francisco: Harper & Row, 1985

LaBerge, Stephen

Exploring the World of Lucid Dreaming
With Howard Rheingold
New York: Ballantine Books, 1991

Lakhovsky, Georges

Secret of Life
New York: Kessinger Publishing, 2003

Laszlo, Ervin

Science and the Akashic Field
An Integral Theory of Everything
Rochester: Inner Traditions, 2004

Quantum Shift to the Global Brain
How the New Scientific Reality Can Change Us and Our World
Rochester: Inner Traditions, 2008

Science and the Reenchantment of the Cosmos
The Rise of the Integral Vision of Reality
Rochester: Inner Traditions, 2006

The Akashic Experience
Science and the Cosmic Memory Field
Rochester: Inner Traditions, 2009

The Chaos Point
The World at the Crossroads
Newburyport, MA: Hampton Roads Publishing, 2006

Leadbeater, Charles Webster

Astral Plane
Its Scenery, Inhabitants and Phenomena
Kessinger Publishing Reprint Edition, 1997

Dreams
What they Are and How they are Caused
London: Theosophical Publishing Society, 1903
Kessinger Publishing Reprint Edition, 1998

The Inner Life
Chicago: The Rajput Press, 1911
Kessinger Publishing

Leary Timothy

Your Brain is God
Berkeley, CA: Ronin Publishing, 2001

Leboyer, Frederick

Birth Without Violence
New York, 1975

Inner Beauty, Inner Light
New York: Newmarket Press, 1997

Loving Hands
The Traditional Art of Baby Massage
New York: Newmarket Press, 1977

The Art of Breathing
New York: Newmarket Press, 1991

Liedloff, Jean

Continuum Concept
In Search of Happiness Lost
New York: Perseus Books, 1986
First published in 1977

Long, Max *Freedom*

The Secret Science at Work
The Huna Method as a Way of Life
Marina del Rey: De Vorss Publications, 1995
Originally published in 1953

Growing Into Light
A Personal Guide to Practicing the Huna Method,
Marina del Rey: De Vorss Publications, 1955

Lowen, Alexander

Bioenergetics
New York: Coward, McGoegham 1975

Depression and the Body
The Biological Basis of Faith and Reality
New York: Penguin, 1992

Fear of Life
New York: Bioenergetic Press, 2003

Honoring the Body
The Autobiography of Alexander Lowen
New York: Bioenergetic Press, 2004

Joy
The Surrender to the Body and to Life
New York: Penguin, 1995

Love and Orgasm
New York: Macmillan, 1965

Love, Sex and Your Heart
New York: Bioenergetics Press, 2004

Narcissism: Denial of the True Self
New York: Macmillan, Collier Books, 1983

Pleasure: A Creative Approach to Life
New York: Bioenergetics Press, 2004
First published in 1970

The Language of the Body
Physical Dynamics of Character Structure
New York: Bioenergetics Press, 2006
First published in 1958

Luna, Luis Eduardo & Amaringo, Pablo

Ayahuasca Visions
North Atlantic Books, 1999

Maharshi, Ramana

The Collected Works of Ramana Maharshi
New York: Sri Ramanasramam, 2002

The Essential Teachings of Ramana Maharshi
A Visual Journey
New York: Inner Directions Publishing, 2002
by Matthew Greenblad

Malinowski, Bronislaw

Crime und Custom in Savage Society
London: Kegan, 1926

Sex and Repression in Savage Society
London: Kegan, 1927

The Sexual Life of Savages in North West Melanesia
New York: Halcyon House, 1929

Martinson, Floyd M.

Sexual Knowledge
Values and Behavior Patterns
St. Peter: Minn.: Gustavus Adolphus College, 1966

Infant and Child Sexuality
St. Peter: Minn.: Gustavus Adolphus College, 1973

The Quality of Adolescent Experiences
St. Peter: Minn.: Gustavus Adolphus College, 1974

The Child and the Family
Calgary, Alberta: The University of Calgary, 1980

The Sex Education of Young Children
in: Lorna Brown (Ed.), *Sex Education in the Eighties*
New York, London: Plenum Press, 1981, pp. 51 ff.

The Sexual Life of Children
New York: Bergin & Garvey, 1994

Children and Sex, Part II: Childhood Sexuality
in: Bullough & Bullough, Human Sexuality (1994)
Pp. 111-116

McKenna, Terence

The Archaic Revival
San Francisco: Harper & Row, 1992

Food of The Gods
A Radical History of Plants, Drugs and Human Evolution
London: Rider, 1992

The Invisible Landscape
Mind Hallucinogens and the I Ching
New York: HarperCollins, 1993
(With Dennis McKenna)

True Hallucinations
Being the Account of the Author's Extraordinary
Adventures in the Devil's Paradise
New York: Fine Communications, 1998

McTaggart, Lynne

The Field
The Quest for the Secret Force of the Universe
New York: Harper & Collins, 2002

Mead, Margaret

Sex and Temperament in Three Primitive Societies
New York, 1935

Metzner, Ralph (Ed.)

Ayahuasca, Human Consciousness and the Spirits of Nature
ed. by Ralph Metzner, Ph.D
New York: Thunder's Mouth Press, 1999

The Psychedelic Experience
A Manual Based on the Tibetan Book of the Dead
With Timothy Leary and Richard Alpert
New York: Citadel, 1995

Miller, Alice

Four Your Own Good
Hidden Cruelty in Child-Rearing and the Roots of Violence
New York: Farrar, Straus & Giroux, 1983

Pictures of a Childhood
New York: Farrar, Straus & Giroux, 1986

The Drama of the Gifted Child
In Search for the True Self
translated by Ruth Ward
New York: Basic Books, 1996

Thou Shalt Not Be Aware
Society's Betrayal of the Child
New York: Noonday, 1998

Monsaingeon, Bruno

Svjatoslav Richter
Notebooks and Conversations
Princeton: Princeton University Press, 2002

Richter The Enigma / L'Insoumis / Der Unbeugsame
NVC Arts 1998 (DVD)

Montagu, Ashley

Touching
The Human Significance of the Skin
New York: Harper & Row, 1978

Moore, Thomas

Care of the Soul
A Guide for Cultivating Depth and Sacredness in Everyday Life
New York: Harper & Collins, 1994

Murphy, Joseph

The Power of Your Subconscious Mind
West Nyack, N.Y.: Parker, 1981, N.Y.: Bantam, 1982
Originally published in 1962

The Miracle of Mind Dynamics
New York: Prentice Hall, 1964

Miracle Power for Infinite Riches
West Nyack, N.Y.: Parker, 1972

The Amazing Laws of Cosmic Mind Power
West Nyack, N.Y.: Parker, 1973

Secrets of the I Ching
West Nyack, N.Y.: Parker, 1970

Think Yourself Rich
Use the Power of Your Subconscious Mind to Find True Wealth
Revised by Ian D. McMahan, Ph.D.
Paramus, NJ: Reward Books, 2001

Murphy, Michael

The Future of the Body
Explorations into the Further Evolution of Human Nature
New York: Jeremy P. Tarcher/Putnam, 1992

Myss, Caroline

The Creation of Health
The Emotional, Psychological, and Spiritual Responses
that Promote Health and Healing
With C. Norman Shealy, M.D.
New York: Harmony Books, 1998

Narby, Jeremy
The Cosmic Serpent
DNA and the Origins of Knowledge
New York: J. P. Tarcher, 1999

Nau, Erika
Self-Awareness Through Huna
Virginia Beach: Donning, 1981

Neill, Alexander Sutherland
Neill! Neill! Orange-Peel!
New York: Hart Publishing Co., 1972

Summerhill
A Radical Approach to Child Rearing
New York: Hart Publishing, Reprint 1984
Originally published 1960

Summerhill School
A New View of Childhood
New York: St. Martin's Press
Reprint 1995

Newton, Michael
Life Between Lives
Hypnotherapy for Spiritual Regression
Woodbury, Minn.: Llewellyn Publications, 2006

Nichols, Sallie
Jung and Tarot: An Archetypal Journey
New York: Red Wheel/Weiser, 1986

Odent, Michel
Birth Reborn
What Childbirth Should Be
London: Souvenir Press, 1994

The Scientification of Love
London: Free Association Books, 1999

Primal Health
Understanding the Critical Period Between Conception and the First
Birthday

London: Clairview Books, 2002
First Published in 1986 with Century Hutchinson in London

La Santé Primale
Paris: Payot, 1986

The Functions of the Orgasms
The Highway to Transcendence
London: Pinter & Martin, 2009

Ong, Hean-Tatt

Amazing Scientific Basis of Feng-Shui
Kuala Lumpur: Eastern Dragon Press, 1997

Ostrander, Sheila & Schroeder, Lynn

Superlearning 2000
New York: Delacorte Press, 1994

Supermemory
New York: Carroll & Graf, 1991

Pert, Candace B.

Molecules of Emotion
The Science Behind Mind-Body Medicine
New York: Scribner, 2003

Ponder, Catherine

The Healing Secrets of the Ages
Marine del Rey: DeVorss, 1985

Prescott, James W.

Affectional Bonding for the Prevention of Violent Behaviors
Neurobiological, Psychological and Religious/Spiritual Determinants
in: Hertzberg, L.J., Ostrum, G.F. and Field, J.R., (Eds.)

Violent Behavior
Vol. 1, Assessment & Intervention, Chapter Six
New York: PMA Publishing, 1990

Alienation of Affection
Psychology Today, December 1979

Body Pleasure and the Origins of Violence
Bulletin of the Atomic Scientists, 10-20 (1975)

Deprivation of Physical Affection as a Primary Process in the Development of Physical Violence
A Comparative and Cross-Cultural Perspective,
in: David G. Gil, ed., *Child Abuse and Violence*
New York: Ams Press, 1979

Early somatosensory deprivation as an ontogenetic process in the abnormal development of the brain and behavior,
in: Medical Primatology, ed. by I.E. Goldsmith and J. Moor-Jankowski,
New York: S. Karger, 1971

Phylogenetic and ontogenetic aspects of human affectional development, in: Progress in Sexology, Proceedings of the 1976 International Congress of Sexology, ed. by R. Gemme & C.C. Wheeler
New York: Plenum Press, 1977

Prevention or Therapy and the Politics of Trust
Inspiring a New Human Agenda
in: *Psychotherapy and Politics International*
Volume 3(3), pp. 194-211
London: John Wiley, 2005

Somatosensory affectional deprivation (SAD) theory of drug and alcohol use,
in: Theories on Drug Abuse: Selected Contemporary Perspectives,
ed. by Dan J. Lettieri, Mollie Sayers and Helen Wallenstien Pearson,
NIDA Research Monograph 30, March 1980
Rockville, MD: National Institute on Drug Abuse, Department of Health and Human
Services, 1980

The Origins of Human Love and Violence
Pre- and Perinatal Psychology Journal
Volume 10, Number 3:
Spring 1996, pp. 143-188The Origins of Love and Violence
Sensory Deprivation and the Developing Brain
Research and Prevention (DVD)

Radin, Dean
The Conscious Universe
The Scientific Truth of Psychic Phenomena
San Francisco: Harper & Row, 1997

Entangled Minds
Extrasensory Experiences in a Quantum Reality
New York: Paraview Pocket Books, 2006

Raknes, Ola

Wilhelm Reich and Orgonomy
Oslo: Universitetsforlaget, 1970

Reich, Wilhelm

Children of the Future
On the Prevention of Sexual Pathology
New York: Farrar, Straus & Giroux, 1983
First published in 1950

CORE (Cosmic Orgone Engineering)
Part I, Space Ships, DOR and DROUGHT
©1984, Orgone Institute Press
XEROX Copy from the Wilhelm Reich Museum

Early Writings 1
New York: Farrar, Straus & Giroux, 1975

Ether, God & Devil & Cosmic Superimposition
New York: Farrar, Straus & Giroux, 1972
Originally published in 1949

Genitality in the Theory and Therapy of Neurosis
©1980 by Mary Boyd Higgins as Director of the Wilhelm Reich Infant
Trust

People in Trouble
©1974 by Mary Boyd Higgins as Director of the Wilhelm Reich Infant
Trust

Record of a Friendship
The Correspondence of Wilhelm Reich and A. S. Neill
New York, Farrar, Straus & Giroux, 1981

Selected Writings
An Introduction to Orgonomy
New York: Farrar, Straus & Giroux, 1973

The Bioelectrical Investigation of Sexuality and Anxiety
New York: Farrar, Straus & Giroux, 1983
Originally published in 1935

The Bion Experiments
reprinted in *Selected Writings*
New York: Farrar, Straus & Giroux, 1973

The Cancer Biopathy (The Orgone, Vol. 2)
New York: Farrar, Straus & Giroux, 1973

The Function of the Orgasm (The Orgone, Vol. 1)
Orgone Institute Press, New York, 1942

The Invasion of Compulsory Sex Morality
New York: Farrar, Straus & Giroux, 1971
Originally published in 1932

The Leukemia Problem: Approach
©1951, Orgone Institute Press
Copyright Renewed 1979
XEROX Copy from the Wilhelm Reich Museum

The Mass Psychology of Fascism
New York: Farrar, Straus & Giroux, 1970
Originally published in 1933

The Orgone Energy Accumulator
Its Scientific and Medical Use
©1951, 1979, Orgone Institute Press
XEROX Copy from the Wilhelm Reich Museum

The Schizophrenic Split
©1945, 1949, 1972 by Mary Boyd Higgins as Director of the
Wilhelm Reich Infant Trust
XEROX Copy from the Wilhelm Reich Museum

The Sexual Revolution
©1945, 1962 by Mary Boyd Higgins as Director of the Wilhelm Reich
Infant Trust

Roberts, Jane
The Nature of Personal Reality
New York: Amber-Allen Publishing, 1994
First published in 1974

The Nature of the Psyche
Its Human Expression
New York, Amber-Allen Publishing, 1996
First published in 1979

Roman, Sanaya

Opening to Channel
How To Connect With Your Guide
New York: H.J. Kramer, 1987

Rush, Florence

The Best Kept Secret
Sexual Abuse of Children
New Jersey: Prentice-Hall, 1980

Satinover, Jeffrey

Homosexuality and the Politics of Truth
New York: Baker Books, 1996

The Quantum Brain
New York: Wiley & Sons, 2001

Schlipp, Paul A. (Ed.)

Albert Einstein
Philosopher-Scientist
New York: Open Court Publishing, 1988

Schultes, Richard Evans, et al.

Plants of the Gods
Their Sacred, Healing, and Hallucinogenic Powers
New York: Healing Arts Press
2nd edition, 2002

Sheldrake, Rupert

A New Science of Life
The Hypothesis of Morphic Resonance
Rochester: Park Street Press, 1995

Simonton, Otto Carl et al.

Getting Well Again
Los Angeles: Tarcher, 1978

Small, Jacquelyn

The Sacred Purpose of Being Human
A Journey Through the 12 Principles of Wholeness
New York: HCI, 2005

Smith, C. Michael
Jung and Shamanism in Dialogue
London: Trafford Publishing, 2007

Stiene, Bronwen & Frans
The Reiki Sourcebook
New York: O Books, 2003

The Japanese Art of Reiki
A Practical Guide to Self-Healing
New York: O Books, 2005

Stone, Hal & Stone, Sidra
Embracing Our Selves
The Voice Dialogue Manual
San Rafael, CA: New World Library, 1989

Strassman, Rick
DMT: The Spirit Molecule
A doctor's revolutionary research into the biology of near-death
and mystical experiences
Rochester: Park Street Press, 2001

Talbot, Michael
The Holographic Universe
New York: HarperCollins, 1992

Tiller, William A.
Conscious Acts of Creation
The Emergence of a New Physics
Associated Producers, 2004 (DVD)

Psychoenergetic Science
New York: Pavior, 2007

Conscious Acts of Creation
New York: Pavior, 2001

Van Gelder, Dora
The Real World of Fairies
A First-Person Account
Wheaton: Quest Books, 1999
First published in 1977

Villoldo, Alberto

Healing States
A Journey Into the World of Spiritual Healing and Shamanism
With Stanley Krippner
New York: Simon & Schuster (Fireside), 1987

Dance of the Four Winds
Secrets of the Inca Medicine Wheel
With Eric Jendresen
Rochester: Destiny Books, 1995

Shaman, Healer, Sage
How to Heal Yourself and Others with the Energy Medicine of the
Americas
New York: Harmony, 2000

Healing the Luminous Body
The Way of the Shaman with Dr. Alberto Villoldo
DVD, Sacred Mysteries Productions, 2004

Mending The Past And Healing The Future with Soul Retrieval
New York: Hay House, 2005

Vitebsky, Piers

The Shaman
Voyages of the Soul, Trance, Ecstasy and Healing from Siberia to the
Amazon
New York: Duncan Baird Publishers, 2001
Originally published in 1995

Znamenski, Andrei A.

Shamanism
Critical Concepts in Sociology
New York: Routledge, 2004

Zukav, Gary

The Dancing Wu Li Masters
An Overview of the New Physics
New York: HarperOne, 2001

Personal Notes